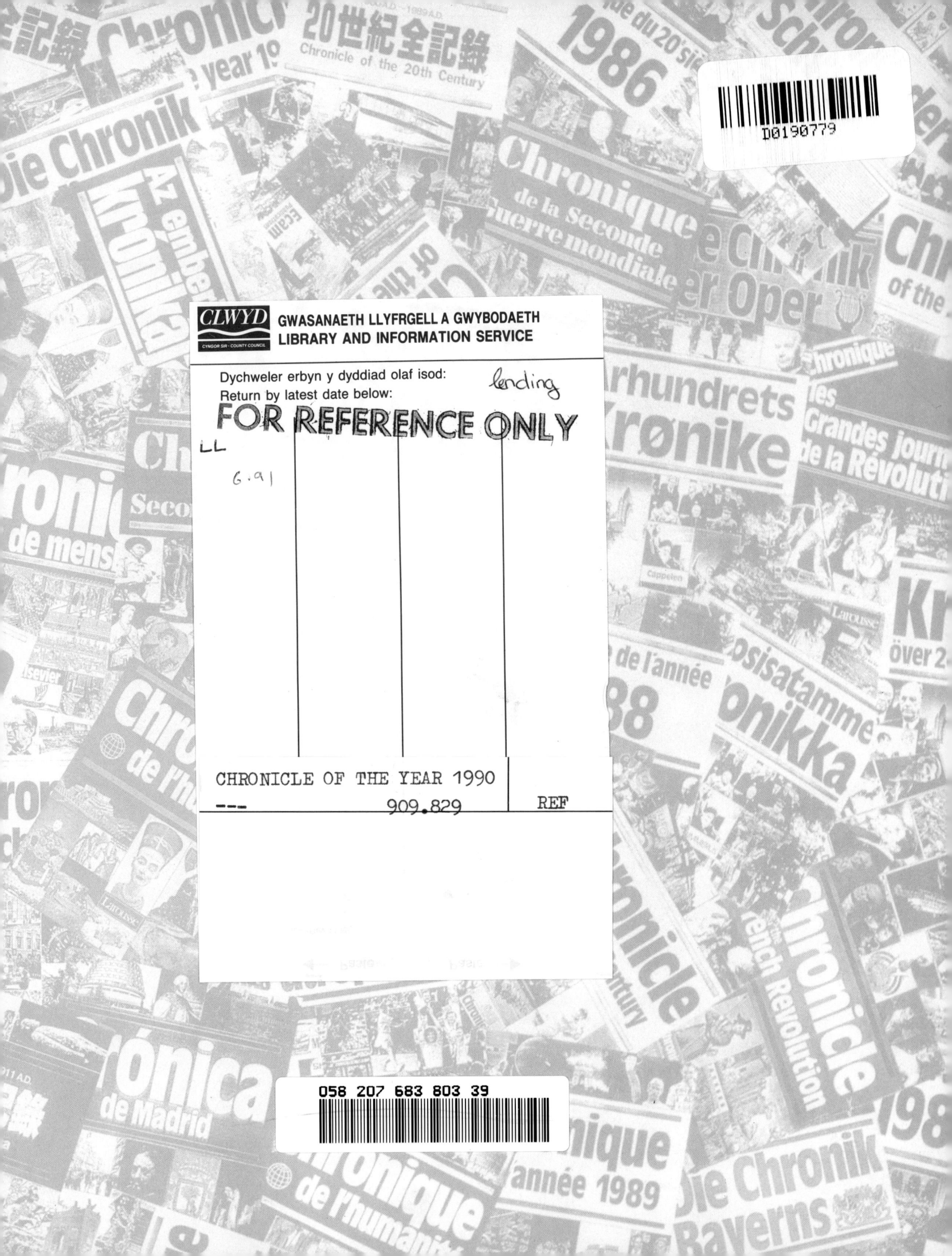

D0190779

Chronicle
of the year 1990

Chronicle of the Year 1990

has been conceived and co-ordinated by Jacques Legrand

Contents

Contributors

Editors	**David Gould, Henrietta Heald**
Picture Editors	Ruth Darby, Susanna Harrison
Associate Editor	John Ross
Art Editor	Christopher Jackson
Writers	Elizabeth Abbott, Bruce Arnold, Hazel Bedford, Peter Bently, Robert Carvel, Chris Dobson, Godfrey Hodgson, Charles Langley, Peter Lewis, Nicholas Mason, John Miller, Curtiss Pierson, Charles Phillips, Denis Pitts, Jason du Sautoy
Production Director	Catherine Balouet
Production	Nathalie Palomba (manager), Chris Allman, Martine Colliot, Laura Hicks, Barbara Levinson, Bronwen Lewis, Joan Thomas

Editor-in-chief: Derrik Mercer

How to use this book

Chronicle of the Year 1990 follows the formula of what is in may ways its parent volume – *Chronicle of the 20th Century*. By reporting the events of the year as though they had just happened, it makes it easy to understand how the dramatic developments of 1990 unfolded and how they were interpreted at the time. At the same time, it captures the mood and flavour of the year in words and photographs.

To help readers follow events, there is not only an index but also a system of cross-references which links news reports and the weekly summaries. The cross-references, which appear as arrows pointing to the next link in a chain of events, point only forward in time and work like this:

• If a cross-referenced event occurs in the same month, only the day of that month will appear after the arrow – for example: (→ 15).

• If the next linked event occurs in another month, then the month will also appear – for example: (→ 15/3).

• The arrow can lead to either an entry in the weekly summary or one of the fuller reports.

• An arrow by itself (→) after a weekly summary entry means that the event and its consequences are covered in the adjoining pages.

The reports of the year's news, recalled here as it happened, are supplemented by essays on world and national politics, extra reports on the year in the arts and the year in sport, and a photographic essay on some of the personalities who made 1990 the extraordinary year it was.

© Jacques Legrand s.a., International Publishing, Paris, for World English rights

© Chronicle of the Year 1990, Chronicle Communications Ltd., London

Chronicle System, 1986, Harenberg Kommunikation, Dortmund

First published in 1990 by Chronicle Communications Ltd, ISBN 0582 076838 in UK & Ireland and ISBN 1-87-2031-102 in Canada.
Published in Australia and New Zealand by Chronicle Australasia Pty Ltd, ISBN 1-87 2031-84-6.

Typesetting: Imprimerie Louis Jean, Gap
Colour processing: Christian Bocquez, Saga Compoprint
Printing and Binding: Brepols, Turnhout

Distributors:
UK & Ireland: Longman Group UK Ltd.,
Longman House,
Burnt Mill,
Harlow,
Essex CM20 2JE

Australia: Penguin Books Australia Ltd.,
487 Maroondah Highway,
Raingwood,
Victoria 3134

New Zealand: Penguin Books (N.Z.) Ltd.,
182-190 Wairau Road,
Auckland 10

Canada: Raincoast Books Ltd.,
112 East 3rd Avenue
Vancouver,
British Columbia V5T 1C8

Chronicle
of the year 1990

CHRONICLE
Communications Ltd

January
1990

Su	Mo	Tu	We	Th	Fr	Sa
	1	2	3	4	5	6
7	8	9	10	11	12	13
14	15	16	17	18	19	20
21	22	23	24	25	26	27
28	29	30	31			

1. UK: Glasgow begins a year as the Cultural Capital of Europe (→ 2/3).

1. Cuba: Cuba rejoins the UN Security Council after a 30-year break.

1. Morocco: Efforts are under way to clear up a 100-square-mile oil slick from an Iranian tanker.

2. E Germany: President Manfred Gerlach says that the Berlin Wall will one day be completely dismantled (→ 4).

2. UK: The inland revenue publishes its revaluation of commercial property in England and Wales.

2. Ireland: Charles Haughey, the Irish prime minister, starts a six-month presidency of the European Council of Ministers.

2. Belfast: An IRA bomb kills a loyalist taxi-driver (→ 7).

3. US: General Motors says that it has developed a practical electric car.

3. UK: Lord Young, the former trade secretary, refuses to give evidence to the public accounts committee on the sale of Rover to British Aerospace.

4. USSR: Mikhail Gorbachev tells Lithuanian communists that he will not interfere with their decision to split from the Soviet Communist Party (→ 12).

4. UK: Ambulance crews seek the support of everyone in Britain for a 15-minute strike on 30 January (→ 13).

4. E Germany: The former leader Erich Honecker is freed from house arrest (→ 15).

5. USSR: A local Communist Party leader resigns in Azerbaijan as large-scale protests continue in the republic (→ 12).

5. Sudan: At least 600 people are reported killed in clashes between Moslem tribesmen and non-Moslem southerners.

6. Iraq: In a parade of strength, the army displays upgraded surface-to-surface missiles with a 400-mile (640-kilometre) range (→ 11/4).

DEATH

6. Ian Charleson, British actor (*11/8/49).→

Special KGB units sent into Azerbaijan

Azerbaijani protesters give vent to their frustrations at the Iranian border.

Jan 3. The southern Soviet republic of Azerbaijan was in turmoil today, as thousands of protesters went on the rampage and attempted to force open the border with Iran. Special KGB units have been rushed to the area to restore order and patrol the 500-mile (800-kilometre) frontier.

The troop deployment follows four days of riots in Nakhichevan, an Azeri enclave in neighbouring Armenia. The trouble – believed to have been inspired by a fast-growing nationalist movement, the Azerbaijani Popular Front – has spread to several other regions and to the Caspian port of Lenkoran.

The KGB took the decision to draft reserve troops with armoured cars into the frontier region after attacks by demonstrators on several checkpoints and the destruction of guard observation towers and electronic alarm equipment. The Azerbaijani Popular Front has been calling for unrestricted association with the Azeris living in Iran and for an open border.

The Kremlin has confirmed the rioting. Gennady Gerasimov, a Soviet foreign ministry spokesman, said: "There are extremists who think that a border with Iran is not necessary." Damage totalling some five million roubles was said to have been done to the checkpoints, and one person was killed in clashes with border guards (→ 5).

Bulgarian cities paralysed by ethnic strife

Jan 5. Strikes and mass protests by Bulgarians opposed to religious freedom for ethnic Turks paralysed towns and cities across the country today. The unrest follows a demonstration in Sofia yesterday by about 10,000 Bulgarians demanding the resignation of the government. The new communist leadership last week restored to the country's 1.5 million Moslem Turks the civil rights denied to them under the former leader, Todor Zhivkov. Under Zhivkov – ousted last November after 35 years in power – the Turks were forced to assume Bulgarian names and banned from practising their religion. About 300,000 Turks fled the country last year to escape persecution (→ 15).

Bulgarian nationalists in Sofia call for the resignation of the government.

McCartney returns to stage in style

Jan 2. Crowds of excited fans packed the National Exhibition Centre in Birmingham tonight to welcome Paul McCartney back to the British stage for the first time for 13 years. McCartney, who has sold more records since the Beatles split up than he did when they were still going, was framed by the flashiest of technology – laser displays and vaults of articulated lights – but still managed to put himself over as, at heart, the chummy Scouse lad. The music did not disappoint, with old favourites like "The Fool on the Hill" and "Sergeant Pepper" alongside new songs such as "We Got Married" and "My Brave Face".

McCartney: still pulling the crowds.

Judge jails mother and baby daughter

Jan 2. The controversial judge James Pickles caused an outcry today by jailing a nineteen-year-old supermarket cashier and her ten-week-old baby.

Tracey Scott, from Huddersfield, who became pregnant after being charged, admitted helping shoplifters. She was given a six-month sentence, although she had no criminal record. Judge Pickles said that he had to let women know that they could not avoid custody just by becoming pregnant.

The sentence has been condemned by MPs and the pressure group Women in Prison, which called the judge a "vain self-publicist" (→ 16).

Romania abolishes hated secret police

Jan 1. Just one week after the dictator Nicolae Ceaucescu and his wife, Elena, were executed by firing squad, Romania has abolished the death penalty. The announcement was made in a New Year speech by the interim president, Ion Iliescu. Perhaps more significant for the Romanians, he also announced the abolition of the Securitate, the secret police who fought so bitterly to maintain the Ceaucescus in power and who many believe have gone underground with their weapons to prepare a counter-revolution. Mr Iliescu sought to allay these fears by promising democracy. "We are not slaves of ideology," he said (→ 18).

No snow for skiers

Jan 6. Would-be skiers are playing tennis or sunbathing on the slopes, as European ski resorts suffer a potentially disastrous lack of their indispensable commodity: snow. After poor early-season falls, there was almost no snow left by mid-December and, for the third consecutive year, many resorts are struggling to operate at all in January. Snow-making machinery is working overtime in parts of the Alps, but there are concerns about the environmental effects of artificial snow. Pessimists blame the climatic changes on global warming.

Noriega flown to Miami

Noriega aboard the US plane that flew him from Panama City to Miami.

Jan 4. Panama's fallen strong-man, Manuel Noriega, stood impassive and mute in a Miami courtroom today charged with trafficking in drugs. Noriega was arrested when he left the Vatican embassy in Panama City, where he took sanctuary on 24 December following the US invasion of Panama. His lawyers claimed that as a "political prisoner" the general was not subject to US jurisdiction.

After a "siege" in which US troops used low-flying helicopters and heavy-metal rock music to unnerve Noriega, the papal nuncio gave him notice to quit. The FBI was waiting. The captive was flown to an air base near Miami, where he was met by a 300-strong crowd with banners bearing slogans such as "Goodbye, Pineapple Face".

The US insists that no deals were made with the Vatican. President Bush has assured the pope that the general will get a fair trial. If found guilty, Noriega faces a jail term of up to 145 years and £900,000 in fines on today's charges. More criminal charges are likely.

Noriega's close links with the CIA are sure to figure in his defence and may prove embarrassing to President Bush, a former director of the agency – as may what some see as excessive US force, including the use of the top-secret Stealth bomber, during the invasion.

At least 225 die in Pakistan rail crash

Jan 4. At least 225 people were killed and 400 injured in southern Pakistan early this morning when a passenger train bound for Karachi collided with freight carriages in thick fog. Just after midnight, a signalling failure at Sangi allowed the express to plough into a stationary goods train at some 65mph. The victims, who included whole families, were mainly poorer travellers crowded into second-class compartments. A shattered bridegroom emerged from the wreckage as the sole survivor of a marriage party of nine. The train driver is alive only because he flung himself from the engine.

Actor dies of Aids

Ben Cross (Harold Abrahams) and Charleson (r) in "Chariots of Fire".

Jan 6. Ian Charleson, the actor who won fame in 1981 for his portrayal of Eric Liddell in *Chariots of Fire*, died this evening from septicaemia brought on by the Aids virus. The 40-year-old Scot, a printer's son, came late to acting after taking a fine arts degree in his native Edinburgh. His first film part came in 1977, in Derek Jarman's *Jubilee*. After his leading athletic role in David Puttnam's Oscar-winning *Chariots*, he went on to appear in Richard Attenborough's *Gandhi* as a pastor embroiled in the Indian struggle for independence. He gave several strong performances on TV and the stage. Until nine weeks ago he was playing the lead in *Hamlet* at the National theatre (→ 11).

Fowler resigns from cabinet to devote more time to his family

Jan 3. Norman Fowler shook the already punch-drunk Tory Party by resigning from the cabinet today. He told Mrs Thatcher: "Government is a very hard taskmaster. I have a young family and I should like to devote more time to them." Mr Fowler stressed that he has quit as employment secretary for this reason only and not because of a policy rift; the prime minister confirmed this by announcing a knighthood for him. Mr Fowler is not wealthy; he is expected to take a job as a company director. Coming so soon after Nigel Lawson's resignation as chancellor, his departure leaves anxious Tories asking: "Will there be more to go?" Labour talked cruelly about a sinking ship.

The former employment secretary flanked by his wife and two daughters.

January
1990

Su	Mo	Tu	We	Th	Fr	Sa
	1	2	3	4	5	6
7	8	9	10	11	12	13
14	15	16	17	18	19	20
21	22	23	24	25	26	27
28	29	30	31			

7. USSR: Soviet troops are deployed in a remote Caucasus region to quell clashes between Georgians and Ossetians.→

7. N Ireland: A Catholic taxi-driver is found murdered.

8. S Africa: Winnie Mandela, the wife of the jailed ANC leader Nelson Mandela, says that she expects her husband to be freed within weeks (→ 2/2).

8. UK: Five football managers are found guilty of bringing the game into disrepute.

8. London: The Brompton hospital intensive care unit is shut after five babies' deaths from a pneumonia-like illness.

9. Bulgaria: Eastern European nations propose the adoption of a more market-orientated approach to trade.

9. Hong Kong: A draft bill of rights is rejected as inadequate to protect freedoms under Chinese rule after 1997.→

10. Ireland: Patrick Ryan, wanted in Britain on terrorist charges, is fired from his order of the Catholic priesthood.

10. Belfast: Fire destroys the operations room of the team investigating alleged loyalist collusion with security forces.

10. Belfast: Danny Morrison, the vice-president of Sinn Fein, is charged with conspiracy to murder.

11. UK: Health department figures show that 1,612 people had died from Aids in Britain by the end of 1989 (→ 13/2).

12. Space: The US space shuttle *Columbia* successfully captures a malfunctioning bus-sized satellite.

12. London: Dawn Griffiths appeals for the return of her newborn baby, abducted from St Thomas's hospital (→ 27).

13. USSR: At least 25 people are killed in a riot in Baku, the capital of Azerbaijan (→ 15).

DEATHS

7. Lord (Gerald) Gardiner, former British lord chancellor (*30/5/00).

8. Thomas Terry Stevens (Terry-Thomas), British actor (*4/7/11).

Martial law lifted in China as Hong Kong governor arrives for talks with Li Peng

Jan 10. Sir David Wilson, the governor of Hong Kong, arrived in Beijing today for talks with Li Peng, the Chinese premier, on the return of Hong Kong to China in 1997. Sir David strongly rejected rumours of a "sell-out", but refused to reveal what he hoped to achieve by the visit. He is expected to argue that Britain's plan to offer passports to 225,000 key Hong Kong citizens is vital to help restore the confidence shattered by China's suppression of its pro-democracy movement.

Li Peng marked Sir David's arrival by lifting martial law in Beijing and withdrawing the troops from Tiananmen Square, which they have occupied ever since opening fire on that bloody night in June 1989. Praising the troops, Li Peng insisted that they had saved China from "the abyss of misery" by crushing the state of anarchy. "For this," he said, "the people will never forget them."

His action has lifted spirits slightly in Hong Kong, but most people there remain deeply suspicious of China's intentions for 1997, and Sir David's visit is doing little to allay those suspicions (→ 15).

Soldiers kill three in Belfast shooting

Jan 13. An army undercover unit shot dead three men robbing a betting shop in West Belfast this morning. Two of the raiders, who were hooded and carried replica guns, went into the shop while the third waited in their getaway car.

It appears that the army patrol stumbled on the robbery and opened fire when it saw that the masked men were carrying what appeared to be real guns. The shootings have predictably provoked an outcry among republicans, who want to know why the men were not arrested instead of being killed.

Thousands march in London in support of ambulance workers

Jan 13. The heart of London was packed today as 50,000 people demonstrated in support of Britain's ambulance workers, whose pay dispute began last September. Roger Poole, the chief union negotiator, told the rally that the public backed crews' demands for more than the 6.5 per cent rise on offer from the NHS. There is speculation that health service managers, doctors and dentists may soon win double-figure rises; this will only fuel the crews' anger, which has already led some – in defiance of their unions – to declare an all-out strike. In West Sussex, where workers are on strike, a man died today after a 50-minute wait for an ambulance (→ 30).

Crowds pack Trafalgar Square to demand a better deal for ambulance crews.

The all-woman crew of the British yacht "Maiden", which won her class in the second and third legs of the Whitbread Round the World Race. On 9 January her skipper, Tracy Edwards, was named Yachtsman of the Year.

Destitute teenagers take to the streets

Jan 8. Increasing numbers of teenagers are sleeping rough on British streets, says a report out today. The survey, by the Family Policy Studies Centre, calls for a urgent strategy to close the gap in the welfare "safety net". Charities for the homeless agree that the problem results largely from recent social security changes. Since autumn 1988 many 16 and 17 year olds have lost their rights to unemployment benefits, while their parents cannot claim for them as dependants. A lot of those on the streets have a background of council care, without any family support.

Soviet republics face growing unrest

Jan 12. Ethnic turmoil continues to rock the Soviet empire. In the Baltic republic of Lithuania yesterday Mikhail Gorbachev put forward a law to cover the mechanism for secession. Meanwhile, around the country's southern rim of Transcaucasia, there has been more unrest, involving murder and sabotage; protests have intensified in Azerbaijan and Nakhichevan, the Azerbaijani enclave in Armenia.

President Gorbachev is visiting Vilnius, the Lithuanian capital, to persuade nationalist leaders of the rebellious republic to drop plans for outright independence. Lithuania and the two other Baltic states of Latvia and Estonia were annexed by the Soviet Union in a secret 1939 deal between Hitler and Stalin.

In direct encounters with Lithuanians, the Soviet leader tackled head-on the touchy issue of independence. He warned that a break with Moscow could lead to tragedy and that nationalists should "not hurry", adding that his personal fate depended on the success of his reform policies in the republics.

Gorbachev's concession to calls for independence emerged as a law offering a detailed procedure for secession by any of the country's 15 constituent republics. It will be put before the Soviet parliament later this year. But Lithuania's leaders today dismissed the draft law as a "cheap lie for naive people in the West", which was intended to make secession impossible (→ 13).

Azeris in Nakhichevan shout to relatives in Iran across the river Araks.

Mikhail Gorbachev puts his point to Lithuanians on the streets of Vilnius.

MP found guilty of criminal damage

Jan 9. The Labour MP Ron Brown left court today celebrating a "moral victory", despite being found guilty of criminal damage after smashing up the Sussex flat of his ex-mistress, Nonna Longdon. The MP for Edinburgh Leith was fined £1,000 and ordered to pay £628 compensation to Ms Longdon, but was found not guilty of the more serious charge of theft – it had been alleged that he stole her knickers. His wife, May, said she was not surprised at her husband's behaviour "knowing men and having lived with one for 27 years".

"Mad cow disease" threatens farmers

Jan 9. The government today gave an extra £2.2 million for research into bovine spongiform encephalopathy (BSE) – known as "mad cow disease" – after a report recommended a thorough study of the transmission and diagnosis of the disease. About 600 new cases of BSE are now being identified each month, and British farmers face major losses in beef exports to Europe as well as losses from the slaughter of sick animals. Labour said it was clear that BSE was entering the food chain, but an agriculture ministry spokesman insisted: "There is absolutely no evidence whatsoever of a risk to human health" (→ 10/5).

Mikhail Gorbachev's turbulent empire

The Baltic states of **Estonia**, **Latvia** and **Lithuania** – victims of the Nazi-Soviet pact of 1939 – are the most fiercely separatist of the Soviet Union's 15 republics. Lithuanian communists led the Baltic revolt in December when they voted for a multi-party system and independence.

Moldavia, annexed from Romania in 1940, seeks closer links with a neighbour whose history, language and culture it shares.

In Transcaucasia, Moslem **Azerbaijan** and Christian **Armenia** remain locked in conflict, while nationalism – resurgent in **Georgia** – gathers pace in Azerbaijan (capital: Baku).

Moscow fears a rise in Islamic fundamentalism and ethnic tensions in the fast-growing Moslem republics of **Kazakhstan**, **Kirgizia**, **Tajikistan**, **Turkmenistan** and **Uzbekistan**.

Fledgling separatism in the **Ukraine** and **Byelorussia** presents a relatively minor threat to Soviet cohesion, but there has been a nationalist surge in the vast republic of **Russia** itself. The formation of the Popular Front of the Russian Federation may herald a Russian backlash.

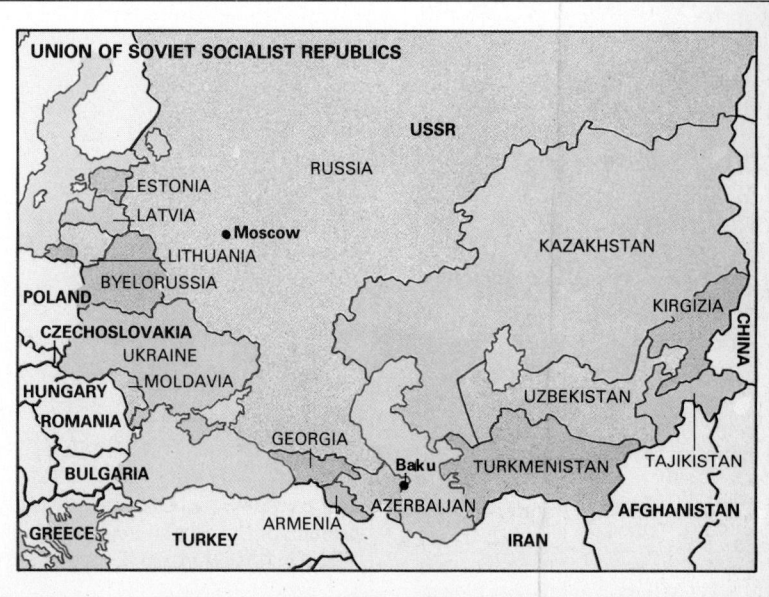

UNION OF SOVIET SOCIALIST REPUBLICS

USSR

RUSSIA

ESTONIA
LATVIA
LITHUANIA
BYELORUSSIA
POLAND
CZECHOSLOVAKIA
UKRAINE
MOLDAVIA
HUNGARY
ROMANIA
BULGARIA
GREECE
TURKEY

• Moscow

KAZAKHSTAN

KIRGIZIA

CHINA

UZBEKISTAN

TURKMENISTAN

TAJIKISTAN

AFGHANISTAN

GEORGIA
ARMENIA
AZERBAIJAN
Baku
IRAN

January
1990

Su	Mo	Tu	We	Th	Fr	Sa
	1	2	3	4	5	6
7	8	9	10	11	12	13
14	15	16	17	18	19	20
21	22	23	24	25	26	27
28	29	30	31			

14. Spain: A fire at a Saragossa discotheque kills 43.

14. UK: Nina Temple is elected the first woman general secretary of the Communist Party of Great Britain.

15. USSR: A state of emergency is declared in and around Nagorny Karabakh.→

15. Bulgaria: Two key sections of the constitution enshrining the Communist Party's leading role are abolished (→1/2).

15. Mongolia: Five thousand pro-reform agitators march in the capital, Ulan Bator.

16. UK: Tracey Scott, the young mother jailed with her baby, is freed after serving two weeks of a six-month term.

17. UK: Mrs Thatcher is said in a leak to be "fizzing with fury" over the clearing banks' decision to pull out of a scheme for student loans.

17. UK: A top Scottish judge, Lord Dervaird, is reported to have resigned over allegations of homosexual behaviour.

18. The Tory majority in the Commons is cut to 36 in a vote on the poll tax (→28/2).

18. Romania: Planned referendums on the death penalty and the status of the Communist Party are cancelled (→26).

19. UK: Sir Anthony Meyer, who last year stood for the Tory leadership, is deselected as MP for Clwyd North West.

19. El Salvador: Nine army men are charged with the murder last year of six priests.

20. Haiti: Prosper Avril, the military ruler, declares a state of siege and arrests dozens of opposition politicians (→10/3).

DEATHS

14. Gordon Jackson, British actor (*19/12/23).→

16. Ruskin Spear, British painter (*30/6/11).

19. Bhagwan Shree Rajneesh, Indian guru (*1931).→

19. Alberto Semprini, British radio music-show presenter (*23/3/08).

19. Mel Appleby, British pop singer (*1967).→

Hong Kong visit spurs democracy hopes

Jan 15. Shrugging off a noisy protest by Vietnamese boat people, the British foreign secretary ended his fact-finding visit to Hong Kong in buoyant mood today. Douglas Hurd denied that he had met cynicism about British policies and said he had found much more hope for the future than expected. He insisted that the British government was keen not just to keep the colony ticking over until the Chinese takeover in 1997, but wished to maintain democratic progress. Although his words may boost confidence in the short term, they may not quell Hong Kong's profound fears about life under Chinese rule (→16/2).

Hurd promises democratic progress.

Security police HQ wrecked in Berlin

Jan 15. Years of resentment boiled over into fury today when thousands of East Germans rampaged through the headquarters of the hated Staatssicherheitspolizei, or Stasi – the state security police. The premier, Hans Modrow, rushed to the Stasi's vast East Berlin office block to appeal for calm after a huge rally by the opposition New Forum backfired. New Forum officials sealed off the complex and asked people to calm down. No one was hurt in the incident, but many offices were wrecked and slogans were daubed on the walls (→21).

England rebel cricket tour protest brutally smashed by police

Jan 19. England's rebel cricketers flew into South Africa today as club-wielding police used tear-gas and unleashed dogs to disperse a crowd of 150 protesters at Johannesburg airport. More than a dozen demonstrators suffered dog bites. Others were beaten and temporarily blinded by tear-gas sprayed from aerosol cans at close range. The anti-apartheid National Sports Congress had expected a trouble-free protest. The violence started when people with banners reading "Gatting go Home" and "To Hell with Rebels – We Want Land" were stopped 50 yards from the airport's arrivals entrance. Mike Gatting, the captain of the England rebels, said that he continued to back peaceful demonstration (→26).

An angry demonstrator protesting against the rebel tour in Johannesburg.

The world of entertainment lost two popular stars this week: veteran actor Gordon Jackson, who made a splash in "Upstairs, Downstairs", and singer Mel Appleby (l) of the duo Mel and Kim, who died of cancer, aged 22.

Boxer accused of shooting manager

Jan 18. Terry Marsh, the former world light-welterweight boxing champion, was today charged with the attempted murder of his ex-manager, Frank Warren. Warren was shot at point-blank range as he arrived for a boxing promotion at the Broadway theatre, Barking, last November. He made a quick recovery after emergency surgery and left hospital two weeks later. Managed by Warren during the 1980s, Marsh won his world title victory before his home crowd in Basildon, Essex, in March 1987.

Charges dropped in John Stalker affair

Jan 18. The row involving John Stalker, the ex-deputy chief constable of Manchester, was revived today when fraud charges against his friend Kevin Taylor, the businessman at the centre of the affair, were dropped amid talk of police dishonesty. Although he had no criminal record, Taylor was named in a 1986 police report claiming that Stalker associated with known criminals. It led to Stalker's suspension at a crucial time in his inquiry into an alleged "shoot-to-kill" policy operated by Northern Ireland police in 1982 (→ 25).

A fifth fail to pay Glasgow's poll tax

Jan 15. Evidence of massive resistance to payment of the poll tax came today from Scotland, where the tax was introduced in April 1989, a year ahead of the rest of Britain. Strathclyde Regional Council applied for summary warrants against 252,067 tax defaulters – including one-fifth of the adult population of Glasgow. Defaulters – all at least three months in arrears – have a fortnight before the council can call in sheriffs to arrest wages or bank accounts and in the last resort remove personal property for public auction. A spokesman for the Scottish Nationalists snarled: "It's now a war of attrition" (→ 18).

Gorbachev confronts warring factions

Troops enter the Azerbaijani town of Shaumyan, north of Nagorny Karabakh, the scene of fierce fighting.

Jan 18. President Gorbachev has sent thousands of army and special troops to Azerbaijan to try to put a stop to the murderous undeclared war between the Azeris and the Armenians. At the same time the Soviet authorities are poised to put down a separatist insurrection by nationalists in Azerbaijan who are defying martial law restrictions.

The crackdown in the capital, Baku, follows four days of bloody ethnic clashes between local Azeris and Armenians which have taken dozens of lives. The tensions that have been building in Soviet Transcaucasia for months erupted at a nationalist rally. In the ensuing pogroms in Baku, Armenian homes were set on fire and looted. Some 60 Armenians were killed and 200 injured. More than 10,000 have fled by boat from the republic. In the disputed Azerbaijani region of Nagorny Karabakh, where Armenians are in the majority, roads are blocked and trains are not running.

Announcing the dispatch of at least 11,000 army and special troops to Baku, Gorbachev argued that the state now had to show it would use force against "extremists, criminals and vandals". The Soviet interior ministry said that there had been dozens of raids on its armouries and offices in both republics in the past few days.

The warring factions were said to be well armed through supplies arriving from abroad, and the authorities have now closed the borders with Turkey and Iran. The Soviet army now faces a thankless task. Hated by extremists, it risks being caught in the crossfire (→ 22).

Bhagwan Rajneesh, free love guru, dies

Jan 19. Bhagwan Shree Rajneesh, the guru who taught that celibacy was a crime against nature, has died from a heart attack at his commune in Poona, India. He was 58. At one time Rajneesh – who stressed that it was "natural for sexual energy to need expression" – had half a million disciples keen to put his teachings into practice. But he was also famous for his extravagance, owning nearly 100 Rolls-Royce cars. Barred from more than 20 countries as an undesirable alien, the Bhagwan was recently expelled from the United States, and his commune in the state of Oregon was closed down.

Rajneesh: controversial cult figure.

Washington mayor arrested for drugs

Jan 19. Marion Barry, the mayor of Washington and one of America's best-known black politicians, was secretly filmed smoking "crack" – the highly addictive form of cocaine – FBI agents said today. The filming took place after Barry was lured to an hotel room in the city by a girlfriend. The popular mayor now faces a possible prison sentence. Despite his denials – "I don't know how folks use that stuff" – the 53-year-old Barry has long been suspected of using illicit drugs. America's black leaders are concerned that his arrest may damage the image of black politicians elsewhere in the US.

Barry: victim of a crack "sting".

January
1990

Su	Mo	Tu	We	Th	Fr	Sa
	1	2	3	4	5	6
7	8	9	10	11	12	13
14	15	16	17	18	19	20
21	22	23	24	25	26	27
28	29	30	31			

21. E Germany: Egon Krenz is among 14 former politburo members ousted from the Communist Party (→ 28).

21. India: Security forces in Kashmir fire on crowds demanding independence from India, killing at least 30 (→ 25).

22. N Ireland: A police inspector is shot dead in his house in Armagh city.

23. UK: GEC says that it will buy Ferranti Defence Systems for £310 million.

24. USSR: The Soviet navy opens fire on Azerbaijani ships blockading Baku (→ 14/2).

24. UK: Ford manual workers accept a 10.2 per cent pay rise.

24. Melbourne: Ivan Lendl wins the Australian Open after Stefan Edberg retires hurt; McEnroe was disqualified.

25. India: Indian troops enter Srinagar, the capital of Jammu and Kashmir, as separatist tensions mount (→ 20/3).

25. Pakistan: Benazir Bhutto becomes the first head of state to give birth while in office.

25. UK: John Stalker hands new documents concerning his "shoot-to-kill" inquiry to the home office (→ 4/4).

26. Romania: Accusing the ruling National Salvation Front of Stalinist methods, Dimitru Mazilu resigns as vice-president (→ 28).

26. S Africa: Police chase protesters in Kimberley as the English rebel cricketers start their first match (→ 30).

26. Adelaide: Australia's first war crimes trial opens, with Ivan Polyukovich accused of mass murder in the Ukraine during the Second World War.

27. UK: A Mori opinion poll gives Labour a 12-point lead over the Conservatives (→ 25/2).

27. Yugoslavia: At least ten Albanians are killed in fighting with the security forces in Orahovac and Pec (→ 30).

DEATHS

21. Barbara Stanwyck, US actress (*1907).

25. Ava Gardner, US actress (*24/12/22).→

Democratic reform engulfs Yugoslavia

Jan 22. The tide of democratic reform sweeping through Eastern Europe entered Yugoslavia today with a landslide vote to abandon the one-party system. Only 27 of the 1,600 delegates at an extraordinary congress of the Communist Party opposed an amendment abolishing the party's "leading role" in society after its 45 years of unchallenged dominance.

Rajko Novak, who proposed the motion, told the delegates: "If the party does not give up its monopoly there will inevitably be a bloody end." The amendment is expected to become law before elections are held in the spring (→ 27).

Air disaster kills 73 on Long Island

Jan 25. The quiet of a secluded residential area of Long Island was shattered tonight when a Boeing 707 jet crashed in fog, killing 73, including the pilot. More than 80 passengers survived. The plane, which was circling New York City before landing at Kennedy airport, appears to have run out of fuel. The death toll would have been much higher had the plane come down in densely populated Manhattan, just 25 miles (40 kilometres) away.

Baku crowds mourn Red Army victims

Up to one million Azeris pack the streets of Baku to mourn their martyrs.

Jan 22. Mikhail Gorbachev and his generals set about re-establishing communist rule in Baku, the capital of Azerbaijan, today as the republic buried its dead after the Soviet army's bloody takeover. An estimated one million people were present at the funerals of some 60 people who were killed when tanks and troops smashed their way into Baku at the weekend.

The Red Army quickly secured key strategic points. Officially 83 people died, including 14 soldiers. But Azeri nationalists insist that hundreds, if not thousands, were killed. The Popular Front claims that the authorities were planning to dispose of hundreds of corpses at sea surreptitiously.

The decision to occupy Baku by force represents a major setback to Gorbachev's policy of solving all problems by political means. When he went on television to explain why he sent in the troops he looked like a man who had just suffered a tremendous personal defeat. But he could argue that the outbreak of virtual civil war in the region had created a special situation calling for tough action. The Azeri nationalists now have dozens of martyrs to comfort them in what seems certain to be a long campaign of civil disobedience (→ 24).

Moscow agrees to pull out of Hungary

Jan 23. The Red Army is to leave Hungary after 45 years. An announcement in Moscow today said that Soviet troops would leave "at the earliest possible time". The timetable for the withdrawal of the 52,000 soldiers will be arranged by Hungarian and Soviet officials "in the next few days".

Miklos Nemeth, the Hungarian prime minister, told his parliament today: "I have spoken with Prime Minister Ryzkhov twice in recent weeks and we agreed that the stationing of Soviet troops is the result of fully outdated political and military concepts and there is no political or military reason to have them here any longer" (→ 26/2).

Jan 25. Hollywood great Ava Gardner dies. Her role in "The Barefoot Contessa" (1954) secured her fame as "the most beautiful animal in world".

Record trade gap fuels economic gloom

Jan 26. Britain's trade deficit for 1989 hit an all-time high of £20.31 billion. However, in December the unfavourable gap between imports and exports was lower than in any month for more than a year.

In the wake of these announcements, the chancellor, John Major, tonight offered little hope to borrowers and mortgage payers. He warned that interest rates – now at 15 per cent – must stay high "for some time to come" in order to curb inflation and check import growth. He tried to sound bullish as

he told MPs: "We are turning the corner." But a tough budget in March is generally expected. John Smith, Labour's shadow chancellor, contrasted present trade performance with past rosy talk about an economic miracle.

City analysts forecast a marked improvement in Britain's balance of payments this year provided there is a fiscal and monetary squeeze. At parliament's mid-term the burning question is: can the economy be got right before the Tories face the next election? (→14/2).

Snatched baby returned to her parents

Jan 27. Alexandra Griffiths was reunited with her parents today over two weeks after her abduction from St Thomas's hospital, London. The newborn baby was taken from her cot by a woman posing as a health visitor. Alexandra's mother, Dawn, helped police to draw up an artist's impression of the kidnapper.

Following a hunt that stretched to mainland Europe and Australia, police learnt that a woman answering the abductor's description had been seen in the Cotswolds. Late last night they swooped on the village of Burford and recovered the baby from a holiday cottage. A 35-year-old woman, who had claimed that she was pregnant, was taken to a local hospital (→29).

Mother and baby: ecstatic reunion.

Jobs for the boys keep women down

Jan 23. Women are still being kept out of top jobs by the old boy network, says a report out today. They face discrimination in parliament, the judiciary, industry and universities. At Oxford and Cambridge, where almost all senior academic and administrative posts are filled by men, women are simply regarded as "not good chaps". *Women at the Top*, by the Hansard Society, shows that Britain has the worst record in Europe on this issue. Only six per cent of MPs and five per cent of judges are women. Four out of five places in the public appointments system go to men, and women are still largely excluded from the boardroom.

Jan 22. An Oxford cinema owner is fined £1,000 for refusing to remove a 25-foot-high fibreglass shark from the roof of his house.

Storm toll reaches 46

Kew Gardens counts the cost: England and Wales lost some three million trees.

Jan 26. Hurricane-force winds, gusting to over 100mph (160kph), brought death and chaos to southern Britain yesterday. At least 46 people are known to have died – many when uprooted trees crashed onto their vehicles – and hundreds have been injured by falling masonry and flying debris. At Swindon, in Wiltshire, a girl of 11 was killed when her school's roof blew off. Another child died when a conservatory collapsed at a Bristol school. Gordon Kaye, the star of the TV comedy *'Allo 'Allo*, was critically injured when a piece of an advertising hoarding crashed through his car windscreen in central London.

Rail, road and sea travel was severely disrupted. London's Euston station was closed for much of the

day as pieces of glass crashed down from the roof onto the concourse. Main-line services were virtually non-existent as railway workers battled to clear lines of fallen trees.

Road travel was badly affected, with motorways littered with overturned cars and lorries. "They were thrown about like toys," said one policeman. Thames Valley police said: "There has been so much storm-related damage that our control room has been unable to monitor it."

The west of England took the brunt of the hurricane. Hundreds of thousands of homes have been left without electricity and are likely to remain so for several days as power workers struggle to replace miles of broken cables (→29).

Police rehearsing for a charity event meet unexpected weather on the Thames.

January
1990

Su	Mo	Tu	We	Th	Fr	Sa
	1	2	3	4	5	6
7	8	9	10	11	12	13
14	15	16	17	18	19	20
21	22	23	24	25	26	27
28	29	30	31			

28. E Germany: It is agreed to bring forward the country's first free elections by two months, to mid-March (→ 28/3).

28. Londonderry: An IRA bomb explodes accidentally during a republican parade, killing a 17-year-old boy.

28. UK: The *Independent on Sunday* newspaper is launched.

28. Bangladesh: About 150 people are feared drowned after a overcrowded river ferry collides with another vessel and sinks.

28. Indonesia: At least 131 people are killed in widespread flash floods and landslides.

29. UK: The US announces plans to reduce its military presence in Britain by about 2,650 people (→ 31).

29. UK: The Church of England publishes a report criticizing the "injustices" of government social policy.

29. UK: Janet Griffiths is remanded in custody charged with the abduction of baby Alexandra Griffiths.

29. New Orleans: The San Francisco 49ers beat the Denver Broncos 55-10 to win the Super Bowl XXIV.

30. USSR: Gorbachev acknowledges the likelihood of future German reunification.

30. London: Guy's hospital performs the world's first successful heart surgery on a baby in its mother's womb.

30. UK: Many thousands of people across the country demonstrate in support of the ambulance unions (→ 23/2).

30. Channel: Nineteen crew members of a Greek-registered freighter are feared drowned after their ship sank.

31. US: President Bush proposes reducing US and Soviet troop levels in Europe to 195,000 on each side (→ 9/2).

31. USSR: Gorbachev firmly denies reports that he intends to step down as Communist Party general secretary (→ 27/2).

31. Belfast: Four senior members of the Ulster Defence Association are jailed for a total of 36 years for extortion.

Cricket tour sparks riots in South Africa

Jan 30. More than 100 people were injured, many by anti-riot birdshot, when police turned on a crowd opposed to Mike Gatting's "racist" cricket tour in Bloemfontein today. The arrival of the 16 rebel England cricketers sparked off 24 hours of what was described as the worst rioting in South Africa since the troubles of 1986.

Earlier, at Kimberley, with an all-white audience hardly filling the tiny grandstand, the cricketers completed their second day's play – as police fired tear-gas and rubber bullets at 1,500 anti-tour demonstrators outside the ground. Violence flared when an Afrikaner hurled a bottle at young blacks beyond the perimeter fence. Three protesters were hurt (→ 14/2).

Anti-tour protesters in Cape Town.

Scheme for football ID cards jettisoned

Jan 29. A controversial scheme to force football fans to carry identity cards has been shelved by the government. The decision is a blow to Mrs Thatcher, who instigated the plan in the face of vigorous Tory backbench and Labour opposition.

Confirmation of the move comes on the day that Lord Justice Taylor publishes his report into last year's Hillsborough stadium disaster, in which 95 died. The report expresses "grave doubts" about the feasibility of a national membership scheme and its impact on safety. It recommends that all English and Welsh clubs should convert to all-seater stadiums by 1999 – at an estimated cost to football of £130 million.

Sunday Times editor wins token damages in Pamella libel case

Neil hails "victory for new Britain".

Jan 30. The case of the newspaper editors and the alleged call-girl Pamella Bordes ended in a blaze of publicity when Andrew Neil of the *Sunday Times* won £1,000 libel damages against the *Sunday Telegraph* and its ex-editor Peregrine Worsthorne. Times Newspapers was awarded 60p. Neil had accused the *Telegraph* of implying that he was unfit to edit a quality newspaper and that he had known that Bordes, a former Commons researcher, was a prostitute at the time of his affair with her in 1988. At the trial Neil, who had met Mrs Bordes in Tramp nightclub, claimed that Worsthorne was part of a mafia centred on the Garrick club.

Worsthorne derides low damages.

Kosovo riots kill 27

Jan 30. Twenty-seven people have died in anti-government rioting by ethnic Albanians in the Yugoslav province of Kosovo during the past week. In an effort to stop the bloodshed, Yugoslav federal leaders rushed to Kosovo today and are expected to issue tough new laws to curb the violence. Meanwhile the rioting continues, with rock-throwing mobs erecting barricades and attacking buses. The police are using helicopters to drop tear-gas, and reports say that they have opened fire on rioters in the regional capital of Pristina (→ 1/2).

Jan 31. A Soviet soldier samples the delights of Moscow's first McDonald's burger restaurant.

Gales lash Britain

Jan 29. High winds and gales punished Wales and the West Country today for the second time in five days, and in the West Midlands there was severe flooding as the river Severn reached its highest level in 20 years. Cornish coastguards reported a gust of 95mph (150kph) at Falmouth, where they are still mopping up after last week's storms, and in Worcester many houses were flooded and roads closed. Meanwhile 36,000 homes in Cornwall, Devon, Avon and Somerset are without power for the fourth successive day (→ 7/2).

Anarchy rules in Bucharest as mobs clash

Jan 28. Greeted with so much joy, the Romanian revolution has gone sour. Bucharest is gripped by mob rule as a trial of strength develops between supporters of the ruling National Salvation Front and members of opposition parties seeking to share power in the run-up to free elections in May.

The situation deteriorated today after an opposition rally in the city centre when a crowd of 40,000 tried to storm the government building. They were beaten off by hundreds of police, soldiers and paratroopers. Meanwhile, thousands of National Salvation Front supporters were rushed by lorries to Victory Square to relieve the siege of the Front's headquarters with the use of sticks and chains. Hundreds of people were hurt (→ 2/2).

Troops and tanks prevent marchers from storming the parliament building.

Ulster "dirty tricks" campaign revealed

Jan 30. Reopening an inquiry into the dismissal of Colin Wallace, a former army press officer in Ulster, the government admitted tonight that a disinformation policy against the IRA was operated in Northern Ireland in the early 1970s. Opposition MPs called for the inquiry to be widened to cover Wallace's allegations that the "dirty tricks" campaign had been directed at Protestants and MPs, and that there had been an attempt to destabilize the Wilson government. Wallace was sacked in 1975 for leaking a restricted document to the press.

Pauline Collins strikes a blow for women's freedom in "Shirley Valentine" and wins the "Evening Standard" film award for best actress of the year.

Commonwealth Games scarred by ban on British weightlifters for illicit drug-taking

England's Adrian Moorhouse powers to victory in the 100m breaststroke.

Jan 31. Two Welsh weightlifters were flown out of New Zealand in disgrace today after it was found that they had used performance-enhancing drugs. Ricky Chaplin and Gareth Hives, who had been competing in the Commonwealth Games in Auckland, were stripped of medals won earlier in the games and banned for life from the sport.

On a happier note for Wales, Bobby Morgan yesterday secured the first Welsh diving gold since 1974 when he took first place in the platform diving event, and Louise Jones triumphed in the 1,000 metres cycling sprint. Earlier, Colin Jackson broke the Commonwealth and European record to win the 110 metres hurdles in 13.08 seconds.

Wales stand in fifth position in the medals table after the first week. England are third, behind Australia and Canada. Adrian Moorhouse got England off to a good start, leading the swimming team to a gold, silver and bronze victory in the 100 metres breaststroke. Kriss Akabusi and Sally Gunnell won a golden double in the 400 metres hurdles. Linford Christie ran the fastest time of his life to take the 100 metres sprint in 9.93 seconds.

Australian women scooped the swimming prizes. Hayley Lewis, aged 15, won five swimming gold medals – the greatest achievement by a woman in Commonwealth Games history – while "supermum" Lisa Curry-Kenny came back from retirement to win four gold medals (→ 3/2).

Gunnell wins the 400m hurdles.

Hives: disgraced Welsh weightlifter.

13

February
1990

Su	Mo	Tu	We	Th	Fr	Sa
				1	2	3
4	5	6	7	8	9	10
11	12	13	14	15	16	17
18	19	20	21	22	23	24
25	26	27	28			

1. UK: Nine Iranians, including the London bureau chief of Iranian state TV, are deported.

1. Yugoslavia: Federal troops and tanks are sent into Kosovo to quell ethnic clashes.

1. Bulgaria: The communist leaders quit to make way for a broad-based coalition (→ 25).

2. Romania: Four leading members of the Ceausescu regime are jailed for their part in the December revolt (→ 18).

3. New Zealand: Australia comes first and England second in the Commonwealth Games medals table.

4. Moscow: At least 100,000 people demonstrate in favour of multi-party democracy.→

4. New Zealand: The New Zealand cricketer Richard Hadlee becomes the first man to take 400 Test wickets.

5. Costa Rica: Rafael Angel Calderon, of the centre-right Social Christian Unity Party, is elected president.

6. UK: The government proposes a package of criminal justice reforms to keep minor offenders out of jail.

7. W Germany: A new "German Unity" committee holds its first meeting.

7. UK: With several areas of Britain suffering from serious floods, forecasters warn of more severe storms (→ 26/2).

8. UK: The House of Lords votes to allow experiments on human embryos to continue (→ 5/4).

9. UK: Labour outlines its alternative to the poll tax – a property tax based on people's ability to pay.

9. USSR: The Soviet Union and the US agree to destroy a "significant" part of their chemical weapon stockpiles.

10. UK: Thatcher argues that Britain should keep its nuclear deterrent as a protection against hostile countries in the Middle East.

DEATH

8. Del Shannon, US rock singer (*30/12/39).

Nigel Lawson takes two jobs in the City

Feb 5. Nigel Lawson, who resigned as chancellor last October after a row with the prime minister over her former economic adviser, Sir Alan Walters, starts work today as a main board director and part-time consultant at Barclays Bank. The appointment was made last Thursday, at a salary reported to be £100,000. Meanwhile, Mr Lawson is embarking on a second private-sector job, joining the board of GPA of Ireland, the world's largest aircraft leasing company, as a non-executive director at a salary of up to £40,000. GPA was founded in the mid-1970s, by the son of a Tipperary train driver, with $50,000 of share capital, and now leases a $3 billion fleet of aircraft.

RSC closes theatres

Feb 8. Britain's best-known stage company is being forced to close its two London theatres to save money. Terry Hands, the artistic director of the Royal Shakespeare Company, announced today that the RSC will close the Barbican and the Pit theatres for four months from November, saving £1.4 million. He said that it was "a black day" for the RSC, which has a deficit of £4.7 million. The cumulative fall in its government subsidy since 1984 amounts to £5.7 million.

De Klerk opens new era

Black South Africans rejoice in de Klerk's lifting of the ban on the ANC.

Feb 2. President F W de Klerk opened a new era in South African politics today by lifting the 30-year-old ban on the African National Congress (ANC) and the South African Communist Party and ending restrictions on over 30 other anti-apartheid organizations.

Speaking to South Africa's white parliament in Cape Town, de Klerk promised that the imprisoned ANC leader Nelson Mandela would be freed as soon as red tape would allow – probably within a fortnight. He said that other political prisoners would also be released, and announced a government decision to lift press restrictions and suspend the death penalty.

De Klerk's dramatic initiative goes a long way towards creating the sort of climate in which negotiations between blacks and whites on South Africa's future can begin. The ANC welcomed the speech, but insisted that it was only the beginning of a long road towards ending apartheid and white minority rule in the country. The ultra-right-wing Conservative Party expressed outrage at the reforms, while in Johannesburg police fired tear-gas at blacks celebrating the news (→ 11).

Beirut fighting between rival Christians claims almost 200 lives

Rocket-fire lights up the night sky as bloody fighting again engulfs Beirut.

Feb 4. The war between the rival Christian forces of General Michel Aoun and Samir Geagea raged on for the sixth day today with artillery shells, rockets and automatic fire echoing through the ruined streets of east Beirut. It is now thought that some 200 people, most of them civilians, have died in this fratricidal conflict.

Tonight, as the weary, frightened people huddle in their cellars without heat, light or water, the smoke from burning oil tanks casts a black shadow over the city. The power station is out of action. Only the rival radio stations, which spew out hate-filled propaganda, seem to be working – apart, that is, from the ever-eager guns.

FEBRUARY 1990

Attack on Egyptian bus kills 15 Israelis

Feb 4. Fifteen people died and eight were injured in an attack on an Egyptian bus carrying Israeli tourists late this afternoon. Some 40 miles (65 kilometres) east of Cairo, two gunmen drew alongside the bus ordering it to stop. Shots were fired through the windows, and the attackers boarded the vehicle, which carried no Israeli identification, firing automatic weapons and throwing grenades. Wounded travellers are being treated at Heliopolis, near Cairo. A little-known group called the Organization for the Defence of the Oppressed in Egypt's Prisons claimed responsibility. It said that the attack was carried out in response to the torture of fundamentalists jailed in Egypt.

Schools under fire

Feb 5. Teaching is bad, books in short supply and accommodation inadequate in many British schools, says an inspectorate report issued today. Some 30 per cent of work done in schools is poor or very poor, according to the schools' senior chief inspector, Eric Bolton. The figures could represent "a large number of pupils and students getting a raw deal" said Mr Bolton, with the less able more likely to lose out. The shortage of qualified teachers is also worsening.

Pro-democracy demonstrators rally in Moscow before the momentous meeting.

Central committee backs end of 72-year monopoly rule of Soviet Communist Party

Feb 7. The Soviet Communist Party today agreed to push through the most revolutionary changes to the Soviet system since 1917. The party's central committee voted to abandon the communists' guaranteed monopoly on power, and called for a genuine presidential system of government. Effectively the Soviet Union is now well on the road to a system of competing parties and free votes – and the potential removal of the government.

The change was approved after three days of fiery debate on Article Six of the party's constitution. It was agreed that the party would no longer claim "full authority in government". The amendment will have to be approved at a party congress later this year, and by the Congress of People's Deputies, the country's supreme parliament.

The vote is a victory for President Gorbachev as well as for the entire reformist cause in the Soviet Union. The only dissenting vote came from Boris Yeltsin, the radical former Moscow party chief, who said that the change did not go far or fast enough down the road to real democracy. But Gorbachev was also criticized by some party hardliners (→ 13).

Iran renews threat against Rushdie

Feb 9. Ayatollah Ali Khamenei, the Iranian leader, today reaffirmed the death sentence pronounced a year ago on the British writer Salman Rushdie. "Ayatollah Khomeini's *fatwa* against the author of the blasphemous book, *The Satanic Verses*, is still valid and must be carried out," he said in Tehran.

Rushdie, who remains in hiding, last Sunday broke a year's public silence by publishing a 7,000-word essay in defence of his novel *The Satanic Verses*. Later in the week, in a lecture at the Institute of Contemporary Arts in London – delivered on his behalf by the playwright Harold Pinter – Rushdie made a plea for "the little room of literature" to be kept open.

Pinter delivers Rushdie's lecture.

England trounce France 26-7 in five nations' championship

England's Mike Teague keeps possession, aided by Probyn (l) and Rendall.

Feb 3. England swept to a 26-7 rugby win against France at the Parc des Princes today in the five nations' championship – their greatest margin of victory for more than 70 years. Two penalties from Simon Hodgkinson were followed by a scorching try from Rory Underwood in the 18th minute, giving England a score from which France never recovered. With the tally at 22-7, the England captain, Will Carling, sealed the match with a try in the second minute of injury time. England are now looking forward with confidence to winning their first grand slam in a decade.

In Dublin, Scotland opened their five nations' programme with a 13-10 win over Ireland (→ 19/2).

Romania racked by dire health woes

Feb 7. As part of a Western relief effort, Britain is to send a million syringes to Romania, following reports about the catastrophic health situation there after years of privation. Between 400 and 500 children are known to have contracted Aids from infected blood and syringes, and dirty syringes are a main source of rapidly spreading hepatitis. Romania's infant mortality rate is the highest in Europe; it also has the highest death rate among underfives, the highest maternal mortality rate and the highest death rate from cardiovascular diseases. Over 500 women have been dying each year from botched abortions.

15

Su	Mo	Tu	We	Th	Fr	Sa
				1	2	3
4	5	6	7	8	9	10
11	12	13	14	15	16	17
18	19	20	21	22	23	24
25	26	27	28			

11. W Germany: On his return from talks in Moscow, Chancellor Kohl says German unification will not take long (→9/3).

11. UK: Norman Fowler, the former employment secretary, urges tax relief on child-care provision by employers.

12. Perth: Carmen Lawrence is named Western Australia's first woman premier.

13. Ottawa: At a meeting of Nato and Warsaw Pact foreign ministers, the USSR agrees to President Bush's proposals for troop cuts in Europe.

13. UK: Margaret Thatcher signals her support for lifting a ban on new British investment in South Africa (→23).

13. US: James "Buster" Douglas is recognized as world heavyweight boxing champion.

13. USSR: Gorbachev issues a radical democracy programme for the Communist Party (→20).

14. S Africa: The England rebel cricket tour is cut short by two weeks.

14. UK: Mortgage rates are raised to 15.4 per cent, an all-time high.

15. Madrid: Britain and Argentina restore full diplomatic relations, eight years after the Falklands conflict.

16. France: A court order that Eurotunnel must hand over £62 million in unpaid fees to Transmanche Link jeopardizes the Channel Tunnel (→21).

16. Kenya: The burnt body of Robert Ouko, the foreign minister, is found four miles from his home (→23).

16. UK: A National Opinion Polls survey finds that 73 per cent of voters disapprove of the poll tax (→28).

17. Czechoslovakia: The Communist Party expels 22 of its former leaders, including Gustav Husak.

DEATHS

12. Harold McCusker, deputy leader of the Ulster Unionist Party (*7/2/40).

14. Norman Parkinson, British photographer (*21/4/13).→

Douglas denied title after busting Tyson

The referee counts out Mike Tyson, floored by Douglas in the tenth round.

Feb 11. James "Buster" Douglas of the US caused one of the biggest upsets in boxing history today by knocking out his compatriot Mike Tyson in a world heavyweight championship fight in Tokyo. But he was immediately relieved of the title in a row about the result.

Tyson's supporters claimed that he was the true victor in the fight after knocking out Douglas in the eighth round. A videotape recording showed that Douglas was on the canvas for 12 seconds because the referee conducted the count wrongly. Douglas, who said he "clearly heard eight" as he got up, went on to win the next round before flooring his opponent with a four-punch combination in the tenth.

The presidents of the World Boxing Council and the World Boxing Association said that the result would not be recognized until their executive committees could get to the bottom of the controversy (→13).

Ethnic bloodshed mounts in Tajikistan

Pro-Soviet sympathies on show at a rally in the republic's capital, Dushanbe.

Feb 14. A state of emergency took effect today in the Central Asian republic of Tajikistan, where ethnic, and anti-Soviet, riots have claimed nearly 40 lives. The unrest was triggered by resentment over the arrival in the republic's capital, Dushanbe, of Armenian refugees from Azerbaijan, and reports that they were being given preferential treatment to obtain housing.

Gangs of young Tajiks have roamed through Dushanbe harassing people of other ethnic groups, particularly Russians, and there has been widespread looting.

Airbus bursts into flames, killing 92

Feb 14. An Indian Airlines Airbus burst into flames as it came in to land at Bangalore in southern India today, killing 92 of the 146 people on board. Grazing a clump of trees on its final approach, the plane crashed 50 yards short of the runway. Officials are trying to establish how the new Airbus-320 could crash with no prior indication of an emergency. It has been claimed that pilots were not properly trained in the use of the sophisticated flight-control system.

Safer sex promoted by "condom fairy"

Safer sex poster aimed at teenagers.

Feb 13. Explicit posters promoting safer sex and a "condom fairy" to encourage the use of sheaths will feature in a lively Aids education campaign launched today. The promotion, "Get set for safer sex", targets young heterosexuals and injecting drug users – the two groups judged to be most at risk from a second wave of the epidemic.

A range of six posters carrying legends such as "No risk in a kiss" and "As safe as playing on your own" are intended to encourage non-penetrative sex. They will be displayed in colleges, bars and nightclubs, while an accompanying video stars the "condom fairy" with its crown of rolled condoms. The campaign responds to what teenagers have said they want to know about HIV infection and Aids.

Students lash out at Hong Kong deal

Feb 16. Some 3,000 students marched through Hong Kong today protesting against Britain's agreement to China's proposals to limit democracy in the colony after the Chinese takeover in 1997. The students chanted slogans attacking the "secret deal" and burnt copies of the "Basic Law" constitution outside the Chinese news agency. The protest was triggered by Douglas Hurd's speech to the House of Commons, in which the foreign secretary outlined proposals for the direct election of only one third of the members of the colony's legislative council. He argued that it was better to reach agreement with China than to seek conflict (→ 27).

Perrier withdrawn in chemical scare

Feb 14. The discovery of traces of benzine in its carbonated mineral water has led the Perrier company to withdraw its entire stock of 160 million bottles from the world market. The chemical, which is thought to induce cancer, was originally found in bottles examined in the US, but has since been traced in supplies to Denmark, Japan and Britain. The contamination was apparently caused by dirty filters at the Perrier plant at Vergeze, in southern France.

Freed Mandela vows to pursue fight

Feb 11. Nelson Mandela, dignified but defiant, left Victor Verster prison near Cape Town this afternoon – a free man for the first time for 27 years. The African National Congress (ANC) leader walked from the last of his many jails about two hours later than planned. He was greeted by 2,000 people – as many as the authorities had allowed – but in Cape Town itself 50,000 had gathered outside the flag-bedecked city hall. A huge banner said it all: "Nelson Mandela – the nation welcomes you home".

Frustration with the delay was transformed into unbounded jubilation when Mandela, white-haired and grey-suited, finally appeared, flanked by his wife, Winnie. In his first words in public for a quarter of a century he said: "I greet you in the name of peace, democracy and freedom for all." He thanked those who had campaigned for his release, and praised President F W de Klerk as a man of integrity, but he endorsed the ANC's recent calls to continue the "armed struggle" and intensify political protest.

Unfortunately, before he arrived, some people on the fringes of the crowd looted shops and threw bottles and stones at police, who responded with shotguns, tear-gas and rubber bullets. Four people are believed to have died. Elsewhere 15 people died, mainly in Natal, where there were clashes between pro- and anti-ANC agitators (→ 13).

Mandela and his wife, Winnie, salute supporters outside Victor Verster prison.

Soweto welcomes its most famous citizen

Feb 13. Around 100,000 people crammed the Soccer City stadium in Soweto, near Johannesburg, today to welcome home the black township's most famous citizen after his absence of nearly three decades. Nelson Mandela told the happy crowd that it filled his heart with joy to be back, but his pleasure at returning home was marred because his people "are still suffering under an inhuman system". He went on to condemn black internal problems – inter-communal strife, thuggery in the name of the liberation struggle and crime – while laying the blame for these ills squarely at the door of the apartheid system. Unity and discipline among blacks, he said, would help guarantee a fast and peaceful end to "the dark hell of apartheid" (→ 27).

Navy wives say no to Wrens on warships

Feb 16. Royal Navy wives marched through Plymouth and Portsmouth today to oppose a ministry of defence decision to allow Wrens to go to sea. Their protest follows a claim that, when the US Navy put women on ships, 35 per cent of them became pregnant within the first year of service. The objectors said that they were not against Wrens going to sea, but that they should be on their own ships. The commanding officer of HMS *Drake* at Plymouth, who received a 300-signature petition, said he understood the wives' worries: "Boys will be boys and girls will be girls, of course, but we have a rigid system of discipline and none of that will change."

Wrens prepared for the ocean wave.

A famous royal study by the photographer Norman Parkinson, who died on 14 February; he was a pioneer in fashion photography and portraiture.

17

February
1990

Su	Mo	Tu	We	Th	Fr	Sa
				1	2	3
4	5	6	7	8	9	10
11	12	13	14	15	16	17
18	19	20	21	22	23	24
25	26	27	28			

18. UK: Mrs Thatcher admits German unification is inevitable, but says Nato must stay in Germany.

18. Melbourne: Greg Norman wins the Australian Masters golf chamionship.

19. Nepal: During a general strike for multi-party democracy, police open fire on a crowd, killing five (→ 23/4).

19. UK: John Ryan resigns as Welsh rugby coach and chairman of the selectors after his team's record 34-6 defeat by England (→ 17/3).

20. USSR: A draft law allows republics to break away from the Soviet Union after a simple referendum (→ 24).

20. UK: Environmentalists attack government plans to proceed with a £12.4 billion road-building programme.

21. UK: The high court declares unlawful local cash limits on grants and loans to the poor from the Social Fund.

21. UK: Beaches along a 15-mile stretch of the Sussex coast are closed after six containers of potassium cyanide are washed ashore.

23. UK: Tourism and new investment sanctions against South Africa are lifted.

23. UK: Parts of Britain have their hottest February day this century; central London temperatures reach 64F (18C).

23. Kenya: The suspicious death of the foreign minister, Robert Ouko, sparks country-wide riots.

24. USSR: The first genuine multi-party elections since 1917 are held – for a new Lithuanian parliament (→ 25).

24. Mediterranean: A gunboat flying a Syrian flag fires on a ferry off Lebanon, killing one person and injuring 18.

DEATHS

19. Michael Powell, British film director (*30/9/05).→

23. Jose Napoleon Duarte, former president of El Salvador (*25/11/25).

24. Malcolm Forbes, US publisher (*19/9/19).

Leukaemia threat haunts nuclear workers

Feb 21. Male workers at Britain's nuclear plants may be advised not to have children. The alert comes after the revelation of a firm link between exposure to radiation at the Sellafield plant in Cumbria and the incidence of leukaemia in the children of men working there. The government has set up an inquiry.

Dr Roger Berry, the health and safety director at British Nuclear Fuels (BNF), which runs Sellafield, was asked at a press conference what advice he would give to a male employee worried about the risk.

"Workers who want individual counselling can get it; if they are so worried the advice could be: don't have children," he said. "It is not something, however, that I hope would be widespread advice."

Dr Berry's remarks were condemned by environmental pressure groups. A spokesman for Greenpeace said: "It is outrageous that Dr Berry can even consider advising parents not to have children. It is not for the workers to change their ways but for BNF to stop its dangerous practices."

Singing awards go to Collins and Lennox

Collins and Lennox at the ceremony.

Feb 18. The British record industry celebrated its biggest evening of the year tonight with the presentation of the Brit Awards. Phil Collins was named best male singer and won a prize for his single "Another Day in Paradise". Annie Lennox was voted best female singer. Fine Young Cannibals won the best group and best album awards, the latter for *The Raw and the Cooked*. Simon Rattle and the London Philharmonic Orchestra were awarded the best classical album prize for *Porgy and Bess*.

In a specially recorded interview before the presentation, Margaret Thatcher revealed that two of her favourite tunes were "How Much is That Doggie in the Window?" and "Telstar".

Hizbollah boss calls for hostage release

Feb 23. Sheikh Mohammed Fadlallah, the spiritual leader of the Hizbollah group thought to be holding 18 western hostages in Beirut, today called on the kidnappers "to free all the hostages and to abandon the practice of hostage-taking". This surprising development comes just one day after a Tehran newspaper suggested that the western hostages should be freed without preconditions. The importance of these statements is that both the newspaper, the *Tehran Times*, and the sheikh support Iran's President Rafsanjani, who is committed to bringing his country back into the international community (→ 10/4).

Tory MP breaches Commons rules

Browne: failed to declare interests.

Feb 19. John Browne, the debonair Tory MP for Winchester, was today declared guilty of breaking House of Commons rules by failing fully to register outside business interests. The verdict came from an all-party parliamentary committee.

Mr Browne now faces a period of suspension. His offence was inadequate disclosure about his dealings with a Saudi Arabian bank, Lebanese businessmen and Britain's satellite television industry. An $88,000 payment from the bank was involved.

Mr Browne said: "This has never been a matter of dishonesty. I wish to continue serving my constituency." It is unlikely that Winchester Tories will re-select him for the next general election.

Freed convict says police framed him

Feb 23. A 35-year-old Caernarvon man was freed by the appeal court today after serving 14 months of a 15-year jail term for armed robbery. On his release Hassan Khan described how he was beaten and intimidated by detectives from the West Midlands serious crimes squad – since disbanded – who then fabricated evidence against him. He was convicted of robbery on the basis of four alleged confessions, apparently concocted after he refused to do a "deal" with police.

Feb 20. Sparks fly at night as East German engineers demolish the Berlin Wall from the Brandenburg Gate to Checkpoint Charlie.

Liberal Democrats triumph in Japan

Feb 19. The tainted but still powerful Liberal Democratic Party (LDP) has been comfortably returned to power in Japan under its "clean" leader, Toshiki Kaifu, winning 275 seats in the election for the lower house.

The Japan Socialist Party, led by the charismatic woman politician Takako Doi, made great gains in the election, as had been expected, winning 136 seats against 85 in the previous parliament; but it did not do as well as it might have done, given the vulnerability of the LDP.

This vulnerability stemmed from the implication of a dozen senior members of the party in a scandal in which they were offered undervalued shares in the Recruit company in exchange for favours. This was too much even for the liberal attitude that the Japanese normally adopt towards their politicians' business activities.

What remains to be seen now is whether Mr Kaifu, having won the election, can survive the plots of his colleagues.

Mixed reception greets ambulance deal

Poole hails "staggering" increases.

Feb 23. After 20 hours of talks, ambulance union leaders have agreed a formula with management to end their long-running dispute, which saw police and troops manning emergency services. Roger Poole, the chief union negotiator, described the package as delivering "staggering" pay increases. "We have driven a coach and horses through the government's pay policy," he said. The deal – reached early this morning after six months of disruption – will now be put to a ballot of ambulance workers.

Some crews are furious about the lack of a long-term pay mechanism – one of their key demands – in the planned settlement. Accusing their leaders of betrayal, workers on Merseyside voted for an indefinite strike from Monday. Others were suspicious of the enthusiasm with which Duncan Nichol, the chief executive of the health service, and Kenneth Clarke, the health secretary, greeted the deal.

The two-year package will, according to the government, put just 13 per cent on the pay bill; while the unions say that the basic pay of qualified ambulance staff will be 17.6 per cent higher at the end of the deal. Extra allowances will give paramedics in London an increase of 23.4 per cent over two years. Kenneth Clarke said the agreement was simply a "repackaging" of what was already on offer (→ 26).

Rebels take control of Romanian HQ

Feb 18. A furious crowd fought its way into the HQ of the Romanian provisional government today demanding the removal of President Ion Iliescu and his prime minister, Petre Roman. The politicians were not in the building. Wielding iron bars, the mob smashed double-glazed windows and roamed free in the building, throwing communist literature to a crowd of 10,000 in the square below. Vice-president Jelu Voican, a dissident under Ceausescu, was cornered with his two bodyguards and carried to the balcony, where rioters threatened to throw him to the ground. He was saved by moderates chanting "No violence!" (→ 20/3).

Protesters storm the government HQ.

Socks and shares at odds as crisis hits high-street retailing

Feb 20. Sock Shop International, the loss-making "niche" retailer once seen as a major success story of the eighties, today called in insolvency administrators after the suspension of its shares on the stock exchange at 34p and a failure to secure re-financing. The shares of Sock Shop, controlled by Sophie Mirman and her husband, Richard Ross, hit a peak of 325p just 18 months ago. The company's fortunes began to decline last summer as hot weather and transport strikes cut profits in Britain, where it has 105 outlets, while an attempt to export the formula to the US ran into mounting problems. Sock Shop's troubles are the latest in a series of crises to hit the retail trade. Tie Rack and Filofax, also "niche" marketing ideas, are both now suffering huge losses. Among other high-street names to regret the passing of the eighties are Dixons, Next and Sir Terence Conran's Storehouse Group.

A scene from "Black Narcissus", directed by Michael Powell, who died on 19 February. Among his other classic films were "The Red Shoes", "The Life and Death of Colonel Blimp" and "The Battle of the River Plate".

Boardroom shuffle salvages Chunnel

Feb 21. A financial crisis at Eurotunnel, which will operate the Channel Tunnel, has been averted by a last-minute boardroom shuffle. The contractors, Transmanche Link, have agreed to a deal removing Alistair Morton, Eurotunnel's chief executive, from direct daily management of the scheme. The pact allows Eurotunnel to draw on bank credit to keep the project going until April. Had agreement not been reached, work would have stopped in a week's time (→ 21/4).

Three wounded in Leicester bombing

Feb 20. A bomb explosion rocked Leicester city centre today, at the height of the evening rush-hour. The device, attached to an unmarked army van, went off in a side street, injuring the driver, a woman sergeant, and two passersby. Another sergeant who was in the van escaped unhurt from the blast, which shattered windows along Rutland Street. Police have denied a claim by the local MP, Keith Vaz, that it was caused by an army bomb that had fallen out of the van.

February
1990
Su	Mo	Tu	We	Th	Fr	Sa
				1	2	3
4	5	6	7	8	9	10
11	12	13	14	15	16	17
18	19	20	21	22	23	24
25	26	27	28			

25. UK: A Mori opinion poll puts Labour 17 points ahead of the Conservatives.

25. UK: Jonathan Sacks is appointed to succeed Lord Jakobovits as chief rabbi.

25. Bulgaria: Up to 200,000 demonstrate in Sofia against the ruling Communist Party.

26. UK: Ambulance workers on Merseyside start an all-out strike (→ 13/3).

26. UK: The Rover Group agrees to cut its working week from 39 to 37 hours.

26. S Africa: Magnus Malan, the defence minister, says that a white Swapo official executed last year was a South African army intelligence agent.

27. USSR: Parliament agrees to the creation of an executive presidency giving Gorbachev widely expanded powers (→ 3/3).

27. US: Exxon Corporation and Exxon Shipping are indicted on five criminal counts relating to the 1989 Alaskan oil spill.

27. Poland: Diplomatic relations with Israel are formally resumed after a 23-year gap.

27. UK: As violent storms again sweep Britain, the total damage bill for recent gales rises to £2.5 billion.

27. UK: The Advertising Standards Authority promises a tougher line on sexist ads.

28. USSR: A law is passed allowing individuals to own their own land for the first time since the 1920s.

28. Nicaragua: Chamorro calls for the immediate demobilization of the Contras.

28. India: Rajiv Gandhi's Congress Party (I) faces its second poll disaster in three months, in state elections.

DEATHS

25. Sandro Pertini, former president of Italy (*1896).

26. Les Ames, England cricketer (*3/12/05).

27. Greville Wynne, British electronic engineer and spy (*1919).

28. Colin Milburn, England cricketer (*23/10/41).

Tebbit spearheads Hong Kong revolt

Feb 27. Norman Tebbit, the former Conservative Party chairman, is leading a revolt against the government's plans to give about 225,000 Hong Kong citizens the right to settle in Britain after the Chinese take over the colony in 1997. He has strong support among Tory MPs opposed to allowing so many immigrants to enter Britain. More than 80 have signed a letter stating that they cannot support the government's bill. Mrs Thatcher was told about the strength of the revolt at a meeting with "deeply unhappy" backbenchers today. They are making their stand on the principle of election promises to curb immigration (→ 19/4).

Olympic medallist wins big damages

Tessa Sanderson with Derrick Evans.

Feb 28. Tessa Sanderson, the Olympic javelin gold medallist, has won £30,000 libel damages over claims that she stole another woman's husband. Her ordeal in court was, she said, like "the last throw of the Olympics", but it was well worth the experience to clear her name. In articles published in the *Sunday Mirror* and the *People* in March 1989, Jewel Evans had accused the athlete of luring away her husband of nine years. But Ms Sanderson said that her affair with Derrick Evans began only after the break-up of his marriage. Mirror Group Newspapers must now foot the bill.

Mandela given hero's welcome in Zambia

PLO embraces ANC: Yasser Arafat greets Nelson Mandela in Lusaka.

Feb 27. Few heads of state can have received the sort of welcome which greeted Nelson Mandela today when he arrived in Zambia on his first foreign trip since his release.

Lusaka airport resembled a carnival as Mandela was greeted by the presidents of Zambia and five other southern African states, together with Yasser Arafat, the Palestine Liberation Organization leader, Sonny Ramphal, the Commonwealth secretary-general, Mahathir Mohamed, the Malaysian prime minister, and Joe Clark, the Canadian foreign minister. Mandela thanked Kenneth Kaunda, the Zambian leader, for giving refuge to exiled African National Congress leaders for ten years (→ 16/3).

Soviet troops depart from Czechoslovakia

Feb 26. Twenty-one years after the Warsaw Pact invasion of Czechoslovakia, Mikhail Gorbachev has agreed to withdraw Soviet troops from the country. By July next year, all 73,500 will be gone, the Czechoslovak president, Vaclav Havel, announced in Moscow today. Most of the troops will be out of the country by the end of May in time for the country's elections in June. The rest will leave in phased movements. Hungary has reached a similar agreement on Soviet troop withdrawals, expected to be signed in March.

Soviet tanks loaded onto a train for their departure from Czechoslovakia.

Ortega suffers shock election defeat

Tory council rebels over high poll tax

Feb 26. Confounding all expectations, President Daniel Ortega of Nicaragua today conceded victory to Violeta Chamorro in the country's first truly free poll since his Sandinista movement took power in 1979. Ortega said that he and the Sandinistas "will respect and heed" the outcome of the election, which was promised as part of a general peace plan for Central America. With nearly 80 per cent of the votes counted, the Sandinistas remain the largest single party in Nicaragua, with 40.9 per cent support. But 55.2 per cent of the vote has gone to Chamorro's National Opposition Union (Uno), an alliance of anti-Sandinista parties ranging from far left to far right (→ 28).

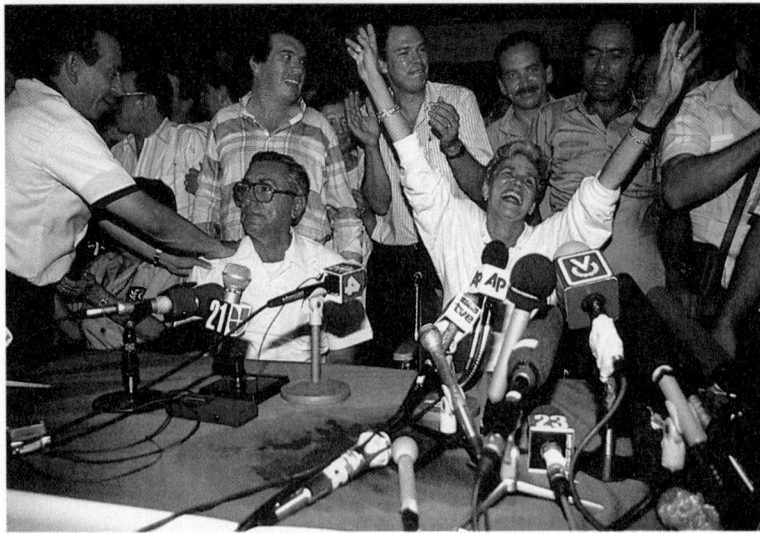
Violeta Chamorro rejoices in her stunning victory over the Sandinistas.

Feb 28. Resentment over the poll tax exploded today in the once true-blue English shires when 18 Oxfordshire councillors resigned the Tory whip. This shook the government as well as ending automatic Tory control of the county council. The rebels' leader, David Walker, protested: "We are a frugal local authority and we've had enough." Whitehall has forced the council to set the poll tax at £412 a head instead of its own proposed £253. Morale is now low among Tory activists across the country. But Mrs Thatcher again insisted: "The community charge will be an electoral asset." Some colleagues groaned (→ 9/3).

Pro-democracy rallies sweep Soviet cities

Lenin is symbolically torn asunder as marchers urge full political pluralism.

Feb 25. Tens of thousands took to the streets of Moscow and several other major Soviet cities today demanding more political and economic reforms. There were unprecedented security precautions, but all these pro-democracy rallies passed off peacefully.

In Moscow the rally took place in the face of a sustained scare campaign by the authorities about possible violence. Security forces ringed government buildings, and roads to the Kremlin were blocked off by riot police. Some 200,000 people were estimated to have taken part in what was seen as the biggest non-official rally in Moscow since the Bolshevik revolution.

Leaders of the inter-regional group of reformist deputies in the Soviet parliament called for full political pluralism and for a "round table" of official and unofficial reformists backing *perestroika*. A speaker also demanded that the army, the KGB and the interior ministry "categorically rule out" the use of force against protesters.

Demonstrations were also held in cities in the Ukraine and Byelorussia, where Communist Party conservatives face defeat in forthcoming elections, and in Georgia. In the Baltic republic of Lithuania, the nationalist Sajudis movement was said to be heading for a landslide election victory (→ 3/3).

Nature sites threatened by development

Feb 27. One of the most famous beauty spots in southern England is to have a six-lane motorway built across it. A two-and-half-mile (four-kilometre) section of the M3 – work on which will start in 1991 – will cut through Twyford Down near Winchester. The new road will cross a designated area of outstanding natural beauty and pass close by a site of special scientific interest. Cecil Parkinson, the transport secretary, dismissed demands from protesters that a tunnel be built to carry the extension under Twyford Down: "The advantages of a tunnel scheme do not outweigh the substantial additional costs and extensive delay in completing the M3."

The announcement comes on the day that plans were approved to build a £2 billion film studio and theme park on London's largest site of special scientific interest, beside the Thames at Rainham, in Essex. The site is a significant area of marshland and salt mudflats supporting important wildlife.

Feb 26. Tempestuous seas batter the promenade at Weston-super-Mare, as storms across Britain claim at least 14 more lives. Two thousand people were evacuated from Towyn, in north Wales, after huge waves smashed a 200-yard hole in the sea wall, threatening hundreds of homes (→ 27).

March
1990

Su	Mo	Tu	We	Th	Fr	Sa
				1	2	3
4	5	6	7	8	9	10
11	12	13	14	15	16	17
18	19	20	21	22	23	24
25	26	27	28	29	30	31

1. Cairo: At least 16 die in a fire in the Sheraton hotel.

1. UK: The north Wales town of Towyn is hit by fresh floods.

1. N Ireland: A passenger train hits two cars in County Antrim, killing three people.

2. Lusaka: Nelson Mandela is elected deputy president of the ANC (→ 12).

2. UK: Tory-controlled Wandsworth council sets a poll tax of £148 per head – the lowest in the country.→

3. USSR: Up to ten people die in renewed violence against Meskhetian Turks in the republic of Uzbekistan.

4. UK: Peter Walker, the Welsh secretary, says that he will leave the cabinet (→ 14).

4. S Africa: Army officers seize power in a bloodless coup in the homeland of Ciskei (→ 7).

5. UK: The government says that Britain will end the dumping of sewage sludge in the North Sea by 1998.

6. Afghanistan: A curfew is imposed on Kabul after a failed coup against president Najibullah.

6. USSR: Parliament passes a law sanctioning the ownership of private property (→ 13).

7. S Africa: Police fire on demonstrators in Bophuthatswana, killing 14 (→ 26).

7. UK: The Tory MP John Browne is suspended from the House of Commons for a month for failing to declare certain business interests.

8. UK: The number of people in Britain with fully-developed Aids has exceeded 3,000 (→ 11/4).

9. Berlin: Talks start on German reunification (→ 18).

9. UK: Customs officers seize 116lb (53kg) of heroin – Britain's biggest-ever haul.

10. Haiti: President Prosper Avril is ousted 18 months after seizing power in a coup.

DEATH

10. Lord (Michael) Stewart, British Labour politician (*6/11/06).

Iraqis sentence reporter

March 10. An Iranian-born reporter working for the *Observer* newspaper was sentenced to death today by an Iraqi military court after being found guilty of espionage. Farzad Bazoft, aged 31, who had been invited to Iraq with a number of other journalists, was arrested last year when he tried to penetrate an Iraqi military base to check reports of a devastating explosion in which 700 were alleged to have died. He later "confessed" on videotape to spying. Daphne Parish, a 52-year-old British nurse who drove him to the base, was sentenced to 15 years in prison. The editor of the *Observer*, Donald Trelford, described the sentences as "barbaric and unjust" (→ 11).

After seven weeks spent in isolation, Bazoft "confesses" to being a spy.

Separatists secure Lithuanian poll win

March 3. Lithuania's elections have resulted in a landslide victory for the pro-independence movement, Sajudis. When the Baltic republic's new supreme soviet, or parliament, next meets it is expected to make a formal declaration of its intent to leave the Soviet Union. Sajudis won 72 of the 88 seats, while the Lithuanian Communist Party, which has broken away from the Soviet Communist Party, took 12. The remaining four seats went to Soviet Communists still loyal to Moscow.

Lithuania decided to advance its elections in the face of impending new powers for the Soviet leader, Mikhail Gorbachev, who opposes the republic's secession (→ 11).

England notch up historic cricket victory against West Indies

March 1. Ending a time-honoured tradition of the national game would not normally bring joy to the hearts of the English cricketing classes. But Graham Gooch's youthful band of players achieved just that today when they became the first England side in 16 years and 29 matches to send the West Indies packing, and that by a stinging nine wickets. England now lead 1-0 in their five-test Caribbean tour. Gooch – whose test side included, for the first time in recent memory, neither Ian Botham nor David Gower – admitted that there was "a long way to go" to take the series. For the moment, though, he felt only "elation" (→ 10/4).

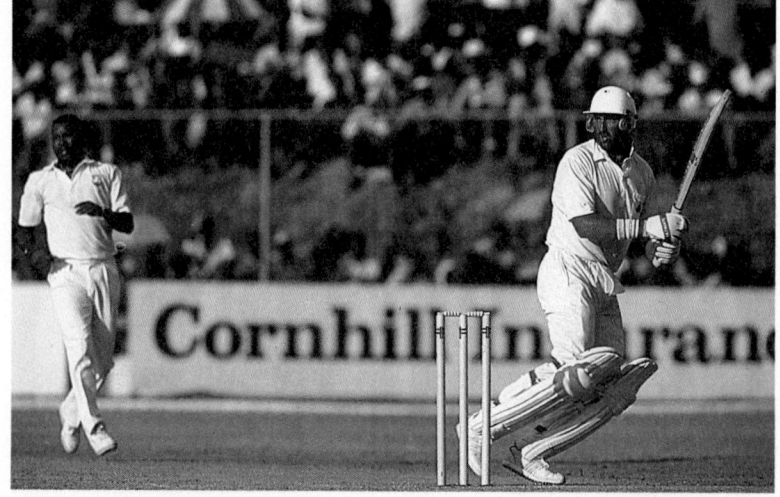

Despite a modest personal score, Gooch leads his team to a superb triumph.

"Workers for Freedom" bring colour to London Fashion Week.

Strike cash claims denied by Scargill

March 5. Arthur Scargill, the leader of the National Union of Mineworkers, has strongly denied that he used union strike funds to pay off personal debts. The *Daily Mirror* newspaper and ITV's *The Cook Report* today claimed that, during the 1984-5 miners' strike, Scargill diverted some £60,000 out of £163,000 donated by Libya's Colonel Gadaffi to pay off his own mortgage and the personal loans of two NUM officials. Scargill says the transactions were legitimate.

Glasgow's feast of culture is launched

March 2. A multi-cultural feast of the arts opened in Glasgow today as the Queen officially inaugurated the city's year as Cultural Capital of Europe. The title was handed to the city's lord provost by Jacques Chirac, the mayor of Paris. The ambitious arts programme, which will cost about £43 million, is to include everything from the Leningrad Symphony Orchestra and American football to a "greenhouse" of growing crystals and a festival of Asian artistes.

Fayeds accused of lying and cheating

Mohamed Fayed: in the firing line.

March 7. The Fayed brothers lied and cheated their way into ownership of the House of Fraser group of stores, according to a department of trade and industry (DTI) report completed in July 1988 but published only today.

The DTI's inspectors say that the Fayeds lied about "their origins, their wealth, their business interests and their resources" to beat a rival bid for the chain by Lonrho in late 1984. Lonrho now considers its long campaign against the Fayeds to have been vindicated.

However, Nicholas Ridley, the trade and industry secretary, has rejected demands that he use his powers to disqualify the Fayeds as directors of House of Fraser. "I do not think it would be in the public interest," he said.

Poll tax uproar sweeps English towns

Violence and mass arrests mar rallies

March 9. Police sealed off Brixton, in south London, tonight as a rally marking Lambeth council's meeting to set its level of poll tax disintegrated into violence.

The demonstration had started peacefully, but when the meeting closed after failing to reach agreement on a tax level the protesters marched off up the road. Police made attempts to direct and disperse the crowd, and then mounted baton-charges amid a volley of missiles. There were 37 arrests, and ten police officers were injured.

The trouble marks the end of a week of often violent demonstrations across England and Wales as councils set their poll tax rates. On Tuesday night in Bristol, police came into conflict with 700 protesters and arrested 21 who had tried to force their way into the council chamber. The Labour-controlled council set a rate of £490.

Loud protests from the public gallery forced Norwich city council to abandon its meeting; similar episodes have disrupted town halls this week in Maidenhead, Birmingham, Bradford, Reading, Newcastle, Gillingham, Plymouth, Leeds, Stockport, Lewisham, Haringey, and many other places.

Some of the worst scenes occurred yesterday evening, when police

Tory councillors grapple with a protester at a Southampton council meeting.

baton-charged a crowd of 5,000 demonstrating outside Hackney town hall in east London. Fifty-six people were arrested and one protester's leg was broken when a police vehicle ran into him. The situation degenerated into a riot; shop windows were smashed and there was widespread looting.

Police say that the violence has been caused by small groups of extremists who have taken advantage of legitimate political protests to make trouble. Most of those at the demonstrations were ordinary people, young and old, who came to make a peaceful stand against what they regard as an unfair tax (→ 23).

Grassroots feeling on show in Bristol.

Kohl blunders into Polish border gaffe

March 6. Chancellor Kohl of West Germany has retreated from a row which threatened to undo decades of reconciliation between the Germans and their neighbours. Three days ago Kohl said that a united Germany could guarantee its postwar border with Poland only if the Poles stuck to a pledge not to claim war damages and guaranteed the rights of ethnic Germans in Poland. This apparent attempt to bargain over the Polish frontier caused such outrage – in Germany and abroad, but especially in Poland – that Kohl has had to apologize (→ 9).

Lambeth burns a Thatcher effigy.

Political enemies unite to criticize unrest

March 9. Margaret Thatcher and Neil Kinnock, the Labour leader, joined today in condemning this week's poll tax riots. The violent demonstrations had an inevitable political spin-off as they led the chorus of denunciation.

The prime minister blamed Britain's militant left. With Tony Benn and some other Labour MPs supporting civil disobedience protests, Mr Kinnock moved swiftly to show his respectable credentials by emphasizing his backing for the police.

Mrs Thatcher calculated that the rioters had provided ammunition for the government in the increasingly bitter controversy over the tax, and Labour feared that she was right. Top Tories tonight demanded an independent public inquiry into alleged links between the Militant Tendency and the Labour Party, which has already outlawed this extremist group. The opposition now plans further moves against Militant sympathizers, who include a few Labour MPs.

Mrs Thatcher's difficulties grew this week with the announcement that Peter Walker, the secretary for Wales, has decided to quit the cabinet. He is the longest-serving "wet" in the Tory hierarchy. A party cynic said: "Another horse for her hearse." (→ 24)

23

Su	Mo	Tu	We	Th	Fr	Sa
				1	2	3
4	5	6	7	8	9	10
11	12	13	14	15	16	17
18	19	20	21	22	23	24
25	26	27	28	29	30	31

11. UK: Margaret Thatcher appeals personally to Iraq's President Saddam Hussein to spare Farzad Bazoft.→

12. Stockholm: Nelson Mandela is reunited with his political ally Oliver Tambo after 30 years of separation (→ 16/4).

12. UK: Record retail sales figures for February are announced – they rose 2.4 per cent in a month (→ 20).

13. USSR: Parliament votes to institute a powerful executive presidency and throw open the doors to a multi-party system.→

13. US: Economic sanctions against Nicaragua are lifted (→ 19/4).

13. UK: Simon Jenkins is appointed editor of *The Times*.

14. Libya: A suspected chemical weapons plant at Rabta is reported to be on fire (→ 9/4).

14. UK: David Hunt is named as the new Welsh secretary, to succeed Peter Walker.

14. UK: The House of Commons is adjourned on the grounds of grave disorder for the first time in 30 years.

15. Israel: The premier, Yitzhak Shamir, loses a vote of confidence in the Knesset (→ 25/4).

15. UK: The lord provost of Edinburgh has his bank account frozen for non-payment of the poll tax (→ 20).

15. UK: Charges are dropped against 14 policemen involved in the 1986 Wapping disturbances.

16. USSR: Gorbachev delivers an ultimatum to Lithuania to rescind its declaration of independence (→ 22).

17. Paris: The Bastille opera opens with a performance of Berlioz' *Les Troyens*.

DEATHS

12. Rosamond Lehmann, British writer (*3/2/07).

12. Jane Grigson, British cookery writer (*13/3/28).

13. Bruno Bettelheim, Austrian-born psychoanalyst and author (*28/8/03).

Lithuania declares itself independent

The flag of freedom is raised outside the parliament building in Vilnius.

March 11. The tiny Baltic republic of Lithuania today declared itself independent, dropping the words "Soviet Socialist" from its name and raising the flag used during its independence between the two world wars. The Vilnius parliament voted unanimously to restore the state's 1938 constitution and elected a new leader, Vitautas Landsbergis, aged 58, a musicologist.

Workmen also started removing the stone hammer and sickle – the emblem of Soviet power – from the face of the parliament building. This is an unprecedented challenge to the Soviet leader, Mikhail Gorbachev, as it may set an example to other restless republics. Under the new presidential powers he is seeking, he could impose a clampdown on the republic (→ 13).

Vitautas Landsbergis assumes his new role as leader of the rebel state.

Gorbachev elected executive president

March 15. Mikhail Gorbachev was today elected the first executive president of the Soviet Union. Standing as the only candidate, he won 60 per cent of the vote in a secret ballot. The announcement of the result was greeted with only lukewarm applause. In an acceptance speech, Gorbachev promised fast and radical action to secure a "breakthrough" in tackling the Soviet Union's urgent economic and ethnic problems. He ruled out independence talks with Lithuania, but said there could be a "respectful dialogue" with the republic (→ 16).

Gorbachev promises radical action.

Ambulance workers vote for pay deal

March 13. Ambulance crews have voted by four to one to accept the two-year pay package agreed in February between their leaders and health service managers to end six months of dispute. All staff are expected to be working normally by the end of the week. Roger Poole, the chief union negotiator, said the deal would give staff an eventual 17.6 per cent increase; although the unions have failed to win a pay formula for future years, he insisted that this was still on the agenda.

Scotland beat England at Murrayfield to take grand slam

March 17. Scotland scored a major upset over their English rivals this afternoon to carry off the grand slam in rugby's five nations' championship. The two sides began on equal terms, each having won their games against Wales, Ireland and France, but with England heavily tipped for the victor's crown. In 80 minutes of feverish play at Murrayfield, David Sole's Scottish team constantly outmanoeuvred, outscrummaged and outran their opponents. A brilliant English try by Jeremy Guscott was the exception rather than the rule, and Scotland ended with a comfortable 13-7 win.

Scotland's Cronin is beaten at the line-out as England fight to keep on terms.

No extradition for IRA Maze escapers

March 13. In a blow to relations between London and Dublin, the Irish supreme court today refused to allow the extradition to Northern Ireland of two IRA men who escaped from the Maze prison in the mass breakout of 1983. The court said that Dermot Finucane and James Pius Clarke should not be sent back to the North because of "a probable risk" that prison staff would assault them – a claim strongly denied by Britain. The decision has provoked outrage among Tory and Ulster Unionist MPs, and Downing Street called the judgement "deeply offensive". But a spokesman for Mrs Thatcher said that the Irish government could not be blamed for the decisions of an independent court (→6/4).

Democratic leader takes over in Chile

Patricio Aylwin at the inauguration.

March 11. Augusto Pinochet, the ruthless dictator who once claimed that "not a leaf stirs in Chile unless I move it", was showered with rotten fruit and coins today as he drove to Congress to hand over power to a democratically-elected leader. The general watched impassively as the presidential sash was placed on his successor, Patricio Aylwin, a 71-year-old lawyer who heads a broad coalition embracing interests from left to centre. A joyful front-page headline in *La Epoca* announced that "The great day of democracy has come".

Farzad Bazoft hanged for spying

Bazoft's friends and colleagues hold a vigil outside London's Iraqi embassy.

Daphne Parish in her Baghdad cell.

March 15. Farzad Bazoft, the *Observer* journalist found guilty of spying, was hanged today in Baghdad. Before he died he was visited by Robin Kealy, the British consul-general, and spent his last minutes giving the diplomat farewell messages for his family and friends. Daphne Parish, the nurse sentenced with Bazoft, remains in jail.

The reporter's death has shocked colleagues, who insist that he was only doing his job, and angered the British government, whose clemency pleas were spurned by the Iraqis. "Thatcher wanted him alive," said one official in Baghdad. "We gave her the body." In a subdued House of Commons, the prime minister described the killing as "an act of barbarism which is deeply repugnant to all civilized people".

Bazoft's hanging was in keeping with the ruthless brutality with which President Saddam Hussein rules Iraq. He crushes all opposition, both real and imagined. One of his most shocking acts was to

Saddam Hussein's legacy: victims of chemical warfare against Iraqi Kurds.

order the use of poison gas against Iraq's Kurdish minority, who were resisting forcible deportation from their homes on the border. Tens of thousands of Kurds were killed in their villages by the deadly gases. Photographs of women still cud-dling their babies in their death agonies shocked the world two years ago. A recent Amnesty International report also gives horrifying details of tortures practised in Hussein's jails against those accused of defying his tyrannical rule (→28).

Israel's ruling coalition collapses after Shamir sacks Peres

March 13. The Israeli coalition government split apart today after weeks of self-destructive argument between its opposing Likud and Labour members over America's proposals for talks between the Israelis and the Palestinians.

The prime minister, Yitzhak Shamir, the leader of the right-wing Likud party, has prevaricated for weeks over the US plan, which was largely backed by the Labour Party. Asked by the Americans to give a yes or no answer, he refused to put the issue to a cabinet vote.

He then wrote an end to his turbulent 15 months of "unity government" by sacking the Labour Party leader, Shimon Peres, from his post as deputy premier.

All the Labour ministers resigned, and Israel now faces a period of political turmoil during which Likud and Labour will both attempt to gain the support of the minority parties in order to form a government (→15).

Su	Mo	Tu	We	Th	Fr	Sa
				1	2	3
4	5	6	7	8	9	10
11	12	13	14	15	16	17
18	19	20	21	22	23	24
25	26	27	28	29	30	31

18. UK: Temperatures reach 70F (21C), as a March heatwave continues.

18. Glasgow: A student is killed and seven others are injured when a man fires on people leaving nightclubs.

19. W Germany: The Deutschmark soars in value following the right-wing election victory in East Germany (→ 26).

19. UK: BP makes over 1,000 employees redundant (→ 27).

20. Romania: Tanks are sent into the town of Tirgu Mures to quell ethnic riots.

20. US: Imelda Marcos, the widow of the ex-dictator of the Philippines, goes on trial for racketeering, embezzlement and bribery.

20. UK: The chancellor, John Major, delivers his first budget.→

20. Belfast: Two IRA bombs explode injuring five people at Shorts' missile plant (→ 9/4).

20. UK: Nine more Tory councillors, from a village near Hull, resign the party whip in a poll-tax protest.→

21. UK: A new, limited police inquiry into the Birmingham pub bombings is announced.→

21. US: The Australian entrepreneur Alan Bond sells Van Gogh's *Irises*, which he bought for £30 million in 1987, to the Getty museum (→ 17/5).

22. Japan: The Nikkei share index closes nearly 1,000 points down after a day of wild trading.

23. Brussels: Helmut Kohl, the West German chancellor, calls for rapid moves towards full political union within the European Community (→ 28).

23. UK: The Duchess of York gives birth to her second daughter.

24. UK: An opinion poll gives Labour a record 27-point lead over the Conservatives (→ 16/4).

DEATH

21. Lord (Victor) Rothschild, British scientist, author and collector (*31/10/10).

Right-wing triumphs in East German poll

Campaigning in East Germany: Chancellor Kohl (r) holds a press conference with Alliance for Germany leaders; Lothar de Maiziere is second from left.

March 18. Parties of the right won a clear victory today in the first genuinely democratic election to be held in East Germany. The conservative Alliance for Germany secured 49 per cent of the vote, while its nearest rival, the Social Democratic Party, lagged well behind, with 21 per cent. The outcome can be seen as a resounding vote of confidence in Chancellor Helmut Kohl of West Germany, who campaigned on behalf of the Alliance.

Lothar de Maiziere, the Alliance leader, said: "This is clearly an amazing result for us. Just as we said amazing when the borders opened on 9 November, so we say amazing again." He is expected to become East Germany's next prime minister and handle negotiations for a reunified Germany.

An overjoyed Mr Kohl said the result was "historic for Germany". He called for the new government to be formed quickly so that talks could begin on the introduction of currency union – a key factor in staunching the flow of migrants from East to West Germany. The election has created the optimum conditions for the West German government to control the pace and direction of reunification (→ 19).

Police saw "real" bombers, says MP

March 24. Chris Mullin, a Labour MP, claimed tonight that the five "real" Birmingham pub bombers were all questioned by West Midlands police within a year of the 1974 bombings, and then released. Mullin, a driving force behind the campaign to free the Birmingham Six – who have spent 15 years in jail for the crime – says he knows the identity of the five men who were genuinely responsible, one of whom is still at large in England. Two of the bombers are in prison for other offences; two live in Ireland. One of those involved helped to plan further bombings. Granada Television intends to name all five men in a drama-documentary to be broadcast next week.

Moscow steps up war of nerves with rebel Lithuanians

March 22. The Soviet leadership's war of nerves with Lithuania took a new turn today when President Gorbachev ordered the Baltic republic to disband the unofficial militias set up to guard its frontiers. He gave Lithuania – which has declared independence from Moscow – two days to halt the enrolment of volunteers.

The Soviet move is one of a series over the past few days designed to make the Lithuanians change their minds over the break with Moscow. Gorbachev has also decreed that all firearms must be handed over, and the KGB has tightened border controls. Soviet armoured cars and trucks periodically roll through the streets of the capital, Vilnius.

But, despite the warnings and ultimatums, Lithuanians maintain that all their decisions have full legal validity and that Moscow's claims to the contrary are null and void. Meanwhile, in Vilnius itself everything is outwardly normal. People seem to think that Moscow's huffing and puffing is no more than that.

Soviet government spokesmen are insisting that the crisis will not be resolved by force, but they point to increased tension (→ 30).

March 20. Namibia wins independence after 105 years of colonial rule: President F W de Klerk of South Africa transfers power to the new president, Sam Nujoma of the South West African People's Organization.

Budget dogged by Scottish poll tax row

March 22. Two days ago John Major, the chancellor of the exchequer, introduced his first, fairly neutral budget. It received a broad welcome from Neil Kinnock, the Labour leader. Then came the unexpected.

Scottish MPs exploded with rage. The budget had included the political sweetener of doubling – to £16,000 – the savings limit up to which poll tax rebates and housing benefit would be payable. The Scots demanded: "Will this be retrospective, because our constitu-ents have already been poll-taxed a year ahead of the English and Welsh?" No backdating for Scotland, the government said. Amid the fury, Malcolm Rifkind, the Scottish secretary, hinted that he might resign from the cabinet. He had not been consulted about the budget announcement.

Tonight the government said that it would provide ex-gratia payments to Scottish councils to ease poll tax demands. Opposition parties talked of ignominious retreat and government shambles (→ 23).

Major on his way to present the budget; it was the first to be televised.

Havel drops Semtex bombshell in London

March 21. The Czechoslovak communist regime sold Libya 1,000 tons of Semtex, according to Vaclav Havel, the new Czech president, who is paying a state visit to Britain. He told a press conference that enough of the odourless explosive – which may have caused the Lockerbie plane disaster – was sold to supply the terrorist world for 150 years. He said that Czechoslovakia had now ceased exporting Semtex, but that it was still being produced for industrial purposes.

President Havel said that his country must learn from Britain's tradition of democracy and from its industrial revolution. But he insisted that – keen to spare its children from the burden of repaying past debts – Czechoslovakia did not want loans from the West. Under the old regime, which was swept away last year, the president was a leading human rights campaigner.

Havel inspects a guard of honour before lunch at Buckingham Palace.

Hawke hangs on to power in Australia

March 24. Bob Hawke's Australian Labor government has scraped in for a fourth term in today's cliffhanger election, pushing Andrew Peacock and the Liberals back into political oblivion. The possible eight-seat majority, reduced from 13, has been won from a public disenchanted with an economic downturn teetering on the brink of recession.

Labor lost nine seats in Victoria, where the losses of the State Bank and costly financial bungling have the state government reeling. Angry voters even stripped 13 per cent from Hawke in his heart-land seat of Wills. But a pro-Labor vote in Queensland, the successful containment of potential electoral damage in a Western Australia beset by financial scandals, and a National Party slump, all helped to save the Government. Electoral bridesmaid Peacock is now likely to

Bob and Hazel give a victory wave.

give way to rising star John Hewson as Liberal leader. Two other party leaders, Janine Haines of the Democrats and the Nationals' Charles Blunt, failed to make it back to Canberra.

Paperwork burden "is stifling teachers"

March 22. Britain's second-largest teaching union today painted a disastrous picture of overworked teachers struggling to implement the requirements of the national curriculum. The National Association of Schoolmasters/Union of Women Teachers said that administering the new assessment system soaks up too much teaching time. A survey of 550 teachers found that they worked an average 51-hour week, of which only 23 hours were taken up with actual teaching. The union is urging members not to let the mounting paperwork take them away from their most important task (→ 16/5).

Labour gains bring Conservative jitters

March 23. Labour has won its most spectacular by-election victory for more than half a century, capturing a once-safe Tory seat with a 9,449 majority and 49 per cent of the vote. Results from yesterday's Mid-Staffordshire poll showed a massive 21 per cent swing away from the Conservatives. The triumphant Labour candidate, Sylvia Heal, whooped: "The dark age of Thatcherism is drawing to a close."

A wave of jitters spread through the Tory ranks. Feverish speculation erupted about whether Mrs Thatcher can keep the premiership with the government is deep in the doldrums. The prime minister was defiant. "We are not for trimming and turning," she said (→ 24).

March 18. John Thaw is named Best TV Actor in the BAFTA awards for his portrayal of Inspector Morse. "Dead Poets' Society" won Best Film.

March
1990

Su	Mo	Tu	We	Th	Fr	Sa
				1	2	3
4	5	6	7	8	9	10
11	12	13	14	15	16	17
18	19	20	21	22	23	24
25	26	27	28	29	30	31

25. USSR: In a resurgence of violence, Armenian nationalists kill nine people in Azerbaijan.

26. E Germany: Ibrahim Bohme steps down as Social Democratic Party leader over his alleged links with the Stasi, the former secret police (→ 1/4).

26. US: Julio Gonzalez is charged with arson and murder following the New York disco fire.

26. S Africa: Eight people are killed in clashes with police in Sebokeng township, south of Johannesburg (→ 2/4).

27. UK: Cecil Parkinson, the transport secretary, scraps £2 billion worth of road projects for London.

27. UK: Ford announces 3,000 job losses at its Halewood plant (→ 2/5).

28. Hungary: No clear winner emerges in the first free polls in decades (→ 9/4).

28. UK: Luke Rittner resigns as chief executive of the Arts Council over government plans for arts funding.

28. N Ireland: The Irish People's Liberation Organization, a republican splinter group, is banned.

29. Australia: Rob Jolley, the Victorian treasurer, resigns in the wake of massive losses incurred by the state-owned Tricontinental Bank.

29. UK: Norman Tebbit says that he will stand for the leadership if Mrs Thatcher steps down.

29. UK: Lord Linley wins £30,000 libel damages against the *Today* newspaper over its suggestion that he behaved like a "lager lout" (→ 3/5).

30. USSR: Soviet security forces take over Lithuania's main publishing house in the capital, Vilnius.→

30. UK: Omar Latif, an Iraqi accused of attempting to smuggle nuclear triggers to Baghdad, is deported (→ 2/4).

30. UK: The Pearson Group pays £60 million for Alton Towers amusement park.

31. UK: Oxford win the 136th Boat Race by over two lengths.

Eighty-seven die in New York disco fire

Rescue teams worked through the night to retrieve the dead and injured.

March 25. It took no more than a few horrific minutes for 87 people – 66 men and 21 women – to die in an inferno that swept through a windowless New York discotheque tonight. Firemen from a neighbouring station extinguished the blaze quickly, but entered the Happy Land in the Bronx, one of 700 un-licensed and illegal social clubs in the city, to find the dance floor covered with bodies.

Most of the dead – many of them illegal immigrants from Honduras and the Dominican Republic – had been asphyxiated. "It was so tightly packed that all the oxygen was consumed by the fire within seconds," said a policeman. Others were engulfed by flames as they fought to escape up a staircase so narrow that two people could not pass on it. The only survivor was Happy Land's disc jockey, who emerged with more than 50 per cent burns to his body.

Police suspect arson. Two men were observed arguing over a woman shortly before the blaze started, and shots were fired before one of them drove away. A man has been arrested.

The owners of the discotheque were served with an eviction notice in December, but the order was never enforced (→ 26).

Runcie says he will quit as archbishop

March 25. Robert Runcie revealed today that he will retire as arch-bishop of Canterbury on 31 January 1991, some eight months before his 70th birthday. The unexpected news has caused intense speculation about his replacement as leader of the world's 70 million Anglicans. The prime minister, who will make the final decision, must reconcile the wishes of her party with those of the church. A candidate from outside the Church of England might be the preferred choice. Robin Eames, the primate of All Ireland and archbishop of Armagh, has been named as one of the strongest contenders (→ 25/7).

Runcie with Cardinal Basil Hume.

Day Lewis wins Oscar for "My Left Foot"

March 27. A low-budget Irish film took the Hollywood elite by storm last night when Daniel Day Lewis won an Oscar for Best Actor and Brenda Fricker secured the Best Supporting Actress award for their performances in *My Left Foot*. The film tells the story of Christy Brown, the severely handicapped Dublin writer and painter, and his courageous mother.

Jessica Tandy, a British-born octogenarian, was named Best Actress for *Driving Miss Daisy*, which also won the Best Film award. A special Oscar went to the Japanese director of *Rashomon*, Okira Kurosawa, on his 80th birthday. More than a billion people across the world watched the ceremony via satellite television.

March 27. The actress Glenda Jackson is selected as Labour's prospective parliamentary candidate for the London constituency of Hampstead and Highgate.

Day Lewis carries off the prize.

Police battle protesters in West End

Soviet troops round up army deserters

March 31. The Soviet army intervened in the Lithuanian crisis today by rounding up deserters and taking over the headquarters of the local Communist Party. The moves were quickly condemned by the Lithuanian president, Vitautas Landsbergis, as a gross violation of sovereignty. At the same time he accused the West of "collusion" in a fresh betrayal of Lithuania by not putting pressure on President Gorbachev to leave the tiny republic in peace. Some 20 young Lithuanians who had left their army units and taken refuge in a psychiatric hospital were seized in the raid by Soviet paratroopers (→ 17/4).

Estonia votes to break with Moscow

March 25. Estonian communists today voted to follow Lithuania in breaking with the Soviet Communist Party. A congress in Estonia's capital, Tallinn, set a six-month transition period on the split – in the hope that the Soviet party will agree at a vital meeting in July to allow the republics to become a loose federal structure of autonomous organizations. More than 200 Russian delegates to the congress refused to vote and drowned out an attempt to read a telegram of support from the congress to the Lithuanian comrades (→ 8/5).

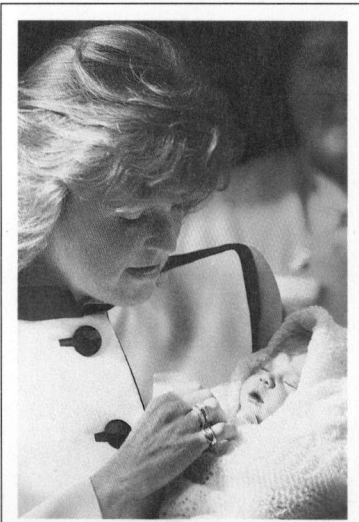

The Duchess of York and Eugenie Victoria, her second daughter.

Police clash with demonstrators in Trafalgar Square as a peaceful protest is "hijacked" by political extremists.

March 31. A huge march and rally to protest against the introduction of the poll tax has ended in a full-scale riot across central London involving widespread looting and damage to property. There were 341 arrests and dozen of injuries.

An estimated 300,000 people had gathered in London's Trafalgar Square to chant "We won't pay the poll tax" and hear speakers, including the Labour MPs Tony Benn and Dave Nellist, call for a campaign of civil disobedience to make the poll tax unworkable. A similar rally in Glasgow, which passed off peacefully, attracted about 40,000.

The trouble started when small groups of demonstrators staged sit-down protests in Parliament Square and Whitehall. Police made a series of unsuccessful attempts to clear the protesters. Tempers rose on both sides, and running fights soon broke out.

As the rally ended in Trafalgar Square, mounted police moved in to disperse the crowds, some of whom responded by throwing missiles. Buildings and cars were set on fire, shopfronts were smashed, and by 7pm the fighting had reached the streets of Soho. Shocked tourists and Saturday night revellers were caught up in the violence, which lasted until midnight and spread as far as Tottenham Court Road and Oxford Circus (→ 3/4).

Huts on a building site are set ablaze.

Nuclear devices bound for Iraq stopped by Heathrow security

March 28. Forty thimble-sized capacitors, which could be used in the trigger mechanism of a nuclear weapon, were seized at Heathrow today in a joint Anglo-US "sting" operation against Iraq.

The devices – dummies substituted by US customs officers – had been ordered from a Californian electronics company and were being staged through London on their way to Baghdad when British customs arrested their carrier, an Iraqi called Omar Latif. He is being held for deportation, and a number of other people are being questioned.

The capacitors, also known as "krytons", are super-fast switches which deliver electrical pulses in a fraction of a second and ensure the simultaneous explosion of a nuclear trigger's charges. Iraq's eagerness to acquire them demonstrates President Saddam Hussein's obsessive determination to arm himself with the most sophisticated modern weapons (→ 30).

Su	Mo	Tu	We	Th	Fr	Sa
1	2	3	4	5	6	7
8	9	10	11	12	13	14
15	16	17	18	19	20	21
22	23	24	25	26	27	28
29	30					

1. E Germany: West German proposals to use an exchange rate of two Ostmarks to one Deutschmark in the currency union with East Germany stir a storm of protest (→ 24).

2. Iraq: President Saddam Hussein says he will retaliate with chemical weapons if Israel attacks Iraq (→ 11).

2. UK: An earth tremor of 5.2 on the Richter scale damages buildings in many towns and cities.

2. Australia: A ship illegally lands over 200 Cambodians at Broome; they paid the crew A$100,000 for the trip.

2. S Africa: President F W de Klerk says that troops will be sent into black townships to quell unrest (→ 9).

3. Bulgaria: Petar Mladenov is elected president of a new, non-socialist republic.

3. India: At least 32 people are killed in the Punjab by a bomb believed to have been planted by Sikh separatists.

4. UK: The Hong Kong Nationality Bill provides for Hong Kong people to be issued with British passports on a points system (→ 19).

4. Belgium: King Baudouin steps down temporarily to allow the passage of a bill legalizing abortion.

4. UK: The home office denies that new evidence shows a collusion to remove John Stalker, the ex-deputy chief constable of Manchester, from the 1986 shoot-to-kill inquiry in Ulster.

5. UK: An inquiry into the Strangeways riot, led by Lord Justice Woolf, is announced.→

6. Nepal: Hundreds are reported killed or wounded after security forces fired on marchers in Kathmandu (→ 8).

7. US: John Poindexter, the former national security chief, is convicted of conspiracy in the Iran-Contra case.

DEATHS

2. Peter Jones, British radio sports commentator (*7/2/30).

3. Sarah Vaughan, US jazz singer (*27/3/24).

Poll tax cuts forced on 20 local councils

April 3. By government decree, 20 local councils – none run by the Tories – will have to cut their proposed poll tax levels. Chris Patten, the environment secretary, named them in parliament today and called his budget reductions "reasonable and appropriate". Labour MPs protested angrily and accused the government of "a blatant political fix": some higher-spending Tory councils had been exempted from the "capping" exercise.

The government is now considering whether to introduce annual county council elections, in the hope that this might stop the upward surge in spending seen in some places immediately after the present four-yearly contests (→ 10).

Kidney transplant doctor is struck off

Raymond Crockett after the verdict.

April 4. A doctor was struck off the medical register today for using kidneys from Turks who had been paid to donate them. Dr Raymond Crockett was found guilty by the General Medical Council of serious professional misconduct and forbidden to practise. The case, in which four Turkish men received between £2,400 and £3,360 for giving kidneys for Dr Crockett's patients at London's Humana Wellington hospital in 1988, involved two surgeons. They were also found guilty today but were allowed, on strict terms, to carry on practising.

Danish ferry blaze claims some 150 lives

The "Scandinavian Star" – still on fire – in the Swedish port of Lysekil.

April 7. A major investigation is under way in three Scandinavian countries tonight following a devastating fire on board the roll-on, roll-off ferry *Scandinavian Star* as she sailed from Norway to Denmark. The ferry caught fire this morning. Some 150 people are feared to have died in the blaze.

As the crippled vessel was towed, still smoking, into a Swedish port, questions were being raised about the crew's competence to cope with the emergency. Survivors have complained that fire alarms failed to work, inadequate signposts made it hard to find exits, and that many of the mainly Filipino and Portuguese crew appeared to panic as the blaze spread. Unconfirmed reports have spoken of passengers sleeping in their cars – strictly against the rules in this type of ferry.

The Swedish Seafarers' Union claims that the disaster was the result of "dangerous conditions" on board the Bahamian-registered ship. The captain, Hugo Larsen, said he believed that the fire was the work of an arsonist.

"Pollard willows and setting sun" by Vincent van Gogh, on show in Amsterdam at one of the major exhibitions to mark the centenary of his death.

30

Riot erupts in Strangeways prison

Dublin court fuels extradition dispute

April 6. In another controversial decision, the Dublin supreme court has refused to allow the extradition of a suspect wanted in Northern Ireland. The court said that it would not hand over Owen Carron, the former Northern Ireland republican MP, on the grounds that the firearms offence for which he is wanted in Ulster is linked with the "political" offences of another man.

A passenger in Carron's car was carrying arms when it was stopped by police in Fermanagh in 1985; both men were charged with possession of firearms. The passenger was convicted and jailed, but Carron absconded before his trial.

The decision is in line with the landmark case last month involving Dermot Finucane, in which the supreme court reversed earlier rulings that republican suspects could not avoid extradition by claiming political motive. It has worsened London-Dublin relations and fuelled Unionist calls for the Anglo-Irish pact to be scrapped (→ 27).

Brisk Mr Frisk runs to National record

April 7. Mr Frisk knocked 14.1 seconds off the Grand National record today, winning the classic steeplechase in eight minutes 47.8 seconds. The horse, ridden by the amateur jockey Marcus Armytage at 16-1, finished ahead of Durham Edition (9-1), Rinus (13-1) and the favourite, Brown Windsor (7-1).

Mr Frisk (l) and Uncle Merlin.

Strangeways inmates contradict claims that up to 20 prisoners died in the riots.

Rebels hold out on the "A" wing roof.

April 1. A pall of smoke hangs over Manchester's Strangeways prison tonight after a day of rioting in which more than 50 inmates, prison officers and policemen were injured. Seven hundred prisoners remain on the loose in the jail, many of them on the roof, where slates have been ripped out for use as missiles against police and staff in full riot gear below.

First reports speak of atrocities against "rule 43" prisoners – most of them sexual offenders segregated in "E" wing of the vast Victorian prison. Prison officers and firemen have reported seeing between three and 12 bodies lying in the smoking debris. About 500 inmates have been evacuated.

Prison staff had been aware of growing tension in overcrowded Strangeways – where many prisoners, even those on remand, have been "banged up" for as long as 23 hours a days in their cells.

The riot began in the prison chapel when a prisoner grabbed a microphone and shouted: "This is our opportunity." The rioters seized keys from their escorts and broke their way into the main blocks, opening cells for more than 1,000 men to join them. The chapel and gymnasium were set on fire.

Friends and relatives watched as prisoners, some wearing staff uniforms and hats, swarmed onto the roof. One used a loudspeaker and threatened to jump. "We are having no more," he shouted (→ 5).

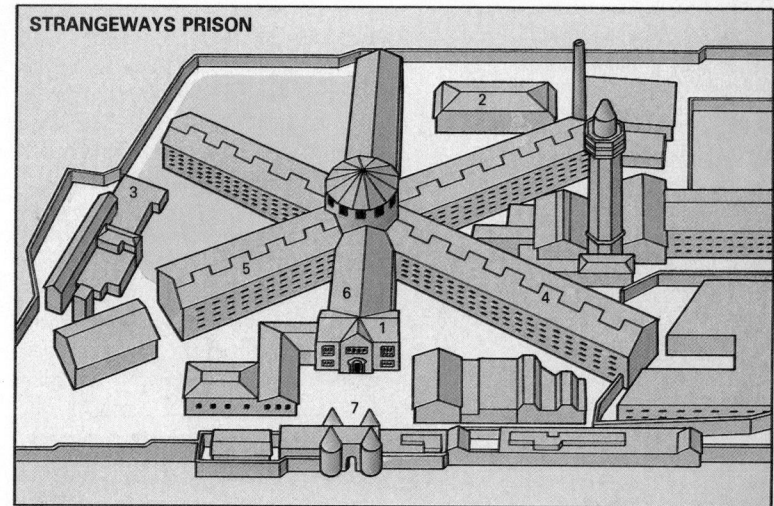

STRANGEWAYS PRISON

(1) prison chapel – where the riot broke out; (2) gymnasium – set on fire; (3) prison hospital – raided for drugs; (4) "E" wing – sex offenders attacked; (5) "A" wing and (6) "F" wing – controlled by inmates; (7) main gate.

Governor condemns "explosion of evil"

April 6. As lurid accounts of hangings and "kangaroo courts" seeped from embattled Strangeways prison, the governor, Brendan O'Friel, described the uprising by more than 1,000 inmates as "an explosion of evil". The destruction was of a magnitude hard to comprehend, he said, but added that there had been no firm evidence of fatalities. One evacuated prisoner has died in hospital, however. Derek White, an alleged sex offender on remand, suffered head and chest injuries when prisoners attacked the segregated inmates of "E" wing on Sunday.

With rioters remaining in control of two wings and two landings, barricades of scaffolding are making it increasingly difficult for prison officers to storm the besieged jail. A police helicopter siren is being used to drown rooftop protests. Events took an ominous turn today when one young inmate was led onto the roof, his hands tied and a makeshift noose around his neck. His captors later took him back inside the jail.

With the disturbance in its sixth day, most inmates have surrendered to the authorities; only 39 men are continuing to hold out (→ 10).

April
1990

Su	Mo	Tu	We	Th	Fr	Sa
1	2	3	4	5	6	7
8	9	10	11	12	13	14
15	16	17	18	19	20	21
22	23	24	25	26	27	28
29	30					

8. Nepal: King Birendra agrees to demands to end Nepal's feudal-style monarchy and lift a 30-year ban on political parties (→ 19).

9. S Africa: Troops enter Natal to halt weeks of black factional fighting that has left some 400 people dead (→ 15).

9. Libya: An alleged fire at the Rabta chemical weapons plant is reported to have been a hoax.

10. Barbados: The West Indies beat England in the fourth test, to level the series 1-1 (→ 16).

10. UK: The London borough of Lambeth is named as the 21st council to be subject to poll tax capping (→ 1/5).

10. UK: William Goodwin, a trainee journalist, is fined £5,000 for refusing to reveal his source for confidential leaked information.

11. Greece: Constantine Mitsotakis is sworn in as prime minister (→ 4/5).

11. Belfast: Charles Haughey makes the first official visit by an Irish premier in nearly three decades.

11. UK: It is reported that the number of people who have developed Aids from heterosexual intercourse has nearly doubled in a year.

12. UK: Inflation rises to 8.1 per cent (→ 11/5).

12. E Germany: Lothar de Maiziere is appointed prime minister (→ 4).

13. USSR: It is finally admitted that Soviet secret police massacred nearly 15,000 Polish officers during the Second World War, including those killed at Katyn.

13. UK: Sheffield Forgemasters, the makers of the alleged "supergun", say that 44 tubes have already been delivered to Iraq (→ 18).

14. USSR: Two hundred deputies in the Russian parliament back Boris Yeltsin's candidature for the republic's presidency (→ 30/5).

DEATH

8. Doreen Sloane, British actress (*24/2/34).

Abu Nidal frees French hostages in Beirut

Houtekins, Valente and their daughter are reunited with family and friends.

April 10. The Palestinian terrorist boss Abu Nidal today freed the French hostage Jacqueline Valente, her lover, Fernand Houtekins, and their daughter, Sophie, who was born in captivity. Another child, a boy called "Palestine", died soon after he was born in Abu Nidal's camp. Valente and Houtekins, a Belgian, were among eight people seized in October 1987 from a converted fishing boat while cruising the Mediterranean. Much has been made of the role played by Libya's Colonel Gadaffi in securing their release. The whole affair is, however, wreathed in disinformation. It is, for example, believed that they were captured not by Abu Nidal, who has no navy, but by the Libyan navy, which is said to have handed them over to the terrorist. It is also apparent that they were freed not because of Gadaffi's "noble" act or Abu Nidal's magnanimity but because the French government has done a deal with the Libyan leader. Houtekins's brother, his wife and two children remain in captivity. They are Belgian and the Belgian government has not yet met Gadaffi's terms (→ 30).

Faldo hangs on to his US Masters title

April 9. Nick Faldo, Britain's top golfer, added another trophy to his hoard today when he followed Jack Nicklaus to become only the second player to win the US Masters golf tournament twice in succession.

Faldo, aged 32, took the coveted Green Jacket prize – worth about £7 million in winnings and sponsorship deals – after a sudden-death play-off with the US veteran Ray Floyd, aged 47. He clinched the game when Floyd dropped into the water at the notorious 11th hole on the Augusta National course.

Faldo poised to drive at the eighth.

Traditionalists take power in Hungary

April 9. After decades of communist rule, Hungarians voted today, in the final round of free elections, in favour of the traditionalist Hungarian Democratic Forum. A majority for the Forum – together with its allies, the Christian Democratic People's Party – is assured in a new parliament. Its president, Joszef Antall, is expected to be the country's next prime minister. Antall said that one of his main priorities would be to take the country into Europe. "We shall do everything we can to gain access to the European Community, in the first place as associate members," he promised, adding that Hungary would try to maintain ties with the Soviet Union (→ 21/6).

April 11. The Vatican announces that Mother Teresa of Calcutta, aged 79, who won the 1979 Nobel peace prize, is retiring as head of her Missionaries of Charity order.

Four soldiers are killed in IRA bomb blast

April 9. Four members of the Ulster Defence Regiment died instantly today when an IRA bomb, thought to have contained over 1,000 pounds of explosive, was detonated beneath their Land-Rover on a country road in County Down.

Mrs Thatcher linked the killings to a recent Irish decision not to extradite three republicans to the North. "We need all the help we can get to fight people who attempt these murders and those who succeed," she said. In the run-up to a controversial visit to Belfast by the Irish premier, Charles Haughey, her comments added further strain to Anglo-Irish relations (→ 11).

Troubles mushroom in Britain's prisons

April 10. As 19 men continue to hold out at Manchester's Strangeways jail, a rash of unrest has hit Britain's troubled prison system. Dartmoor was among the first to suffer, when 103 inmates refused to return to their cells. One man was later found dead in his burnt-out cell. Extensive damage is reported.

At Cardiff, 130 prisoners destroyed furniture, windows and lavatories, injuring two staff members, and at Bristol reinforcements were called in when 200 rioting prisoners took control of a wing at Horfield.

Eighteen prisons have been affected – with, in some cases, men transferred from Strangeways acting as ringleaders. At Durham, a prison officer was held at knifepoint until his captors were overpowered.

A Prison Officers' Association spokesman likened jail conditions to "unsupervised anarchy" (→ 16).

Novelist wins first round of Peru poll

April 9. Mario Vargas Llosa, the eminent novelist and leader of a right-wing alliance, has won the first round of Peru's presidential election – but he may find that his slender majority makes government impossible. Vargas Llosa has offered an olive branch to his chief rival, Alberto Fujimori, the son of Japanese immigrants, whose Democratic Front secured 30 per cent of the vote (→ 11/6).

Vargas Llosa in a shower of rice.

Iraqi "supergun" parts intercepted

The Iraq-bound "Gur Mariner" (top) and "gun" parts unloaded at Teesside.

April 11. Customs officers at Teesport have seized what are alleged to be parts of a barrel for a "nuclear cannon" bound for Iraq. The 140-ton barrel, 130 feet long – described as "petroleum piping" – was packed in eight crates. A supergun with such a barrel would be capable of firing a three-foot-diameter nuclear shell for hundreds of miles. It could also be used for launching rockets into space.

The officers who carried out "Operation Bertha" removed documents from Sheffield Forgemasters, the firm which made the barrel. A company spokesman said later that "after the initial approach was made by someone on behalf of the Iraqis, the company was given the green light by the department of trade and industry".

Azmi al-Salihi, Iraq's ambassador to Britain, denied all knowledge of the gun. "This is just another fabricated story," he said (→ 13).

Murdered expert who invented gun

April 13. Dr Gerald Bull – a Canadian scientist murdered in Brussels ten days ago by two bullets in the back of the neck – is now known to be the wayward genius who invented the Iraqi "supergun". Bull was obsessed with building a gun which could fire projectiles for hundreds of miles. He did not care in what cause the gun was used, as long as he had the cash to finance his dream. He first developed his ideas as head of Harp, the US Army's High Altitude Research Project, which used naval guns to fire projectiles to the edge of space. He later served a jail term for supplying South Africa with banned ammunition, but it was his work for South Africa in developing a brilliant field gun which brought him to Iraq's attention. Someone then decided that he was too clever to live.

Bull and the Quebec premier at a space research station in 1965.

Thatcher and Bush hold talks in Bermuda on Europe's future

April 13. It was a "very upbeat" President Bush who flew into an atypically downbeat Bermuda rainstorm today for talks with Mrs Thatcher on the future of Europe and the Nato alliance.

Despite the wind and the dark clouds there was nothing gloomy about the tone both leaders set for this mid-Atlantic summit, called in the wake of the dramatic changes in Eastern Europe and the Soviet Union. The president claimed that he and the prime minister were "very close" on their responses to the developments of recent months, while a spokesman for Mrs Thatcher said that the British side has "lots of ideas" about a changing US-European relationship.

Central to these ideas is the whole question of Nato's role as defender of Western Europe. Is it logical or sensible to update Nato's European arsenals while the supposed threat from the East grows less likely by the week?

April
1990

Su	Mo	Tu	We	Th	Fr	Sa
1	2	3	4	5	6	7
8	9	10	11	12	13	14
15	16	17	18	19	20	21
22	23	24	25	26	27	28
29	30					

15. UK: Nelson Mandela meets Archbishop Trevor Huddleston, the president of the Anti-Apartheid Movement.→

15. India: At least 100 people are feared dead in a fire on a commuter train near Patna.

16. UK: A Mori opinion poll puts Labour 17 points ahead of the Conservatives.

16. UK: Three prisoners involved in the Strangeways siege surrender after suffering from food poisoning (→25).

17. USSR: Moscow imposes an economic blockade on Lithuania.→

18. Beirut: Eleven children are killed in a school-bus attack.

18. UK: The government admits that the tubes seized by customs last week on their way to Iraq are parts of a gun (→19).

18. Yugoslavia: Emergency measures are lifted in Kosovo, where 56 people have died in a year of violent clashes (→15/5).

19. UK: It is reported that Iraq's supergun was part of a £4 million ballistics testbed.→

19. UK: More than 600 south Wales miners become the first victims of a round of pit redundancies.

19. Nicaragua: The Contra guerrillas agree to a ceasefire with the outgoing Sandinista government (→30/5).

20. UK: British Satellite Broadcasting shelves a big advertising campaign for its satellite TV service because of delays in equipment delivery (→29).

21. UK: Stephen Wright becomes the fifth worker to die on the British side of the Channel Tunnel (→8/5).

DEATHS

15. Greta Garbo, Swedish-born actress (*18/9/05).→

15. Lord (Jock) BruceGardyne, British journalist and politician (*12/4/30).

20. James Chipperfield, British circus proprietor (*17/7/12).

21. Romain de Tirtoff (Erte), Russian-born artist and designer (*23/11/1892).→

Greeks arrest driver of "supergun" lorry

The British truck driven by Paul Ashwell: impounded by Greek customs.

April 20. Paul Ashwell, a 25-year-old long-distance lorry driver from Northamptonshire, was arrested at the southern Greek port of Patras today when customs officials discovered that his truck was loaded with parts for the Iraqi "supergun".

A Greek customs officer described the confiscated components as a vast cylinder with a base enabling it to be connected to a gun carriage. He said that the cargo was falsely described as steel tubing. It seems likely, however, that the Greek authorities had been tipped off to watch for the lorry.

Ashwell, who was arrested because no permit had been sought for the transport of the weaponry, insisted that he was only a driver and had no idea that his cargo was part of a gun (→11/5).

Freakish rainfall floods out Australians

April 21. Floods have swamped more than a million square miles of Queensland, New South Wales and Victoria and have brought mass evacuations from country towns. Some communities have taken to the high ground and are relying on flights with emergency supplies as flood-waters course through their homes. Fodder is being dropped to stranded sheep and cattle, but there have been huge stock losses in areas which were affected by drought only a few weeks ago. The people of the New South Wales town of Nyngan are fighting for survival, building a wall of 300,000 sandbags against the floodwaters.

Ever-enigmatic film legend Garbo dies

April 15. "I want to be alone," she said in the 1932 movie *Grand Hotel*, and so she seems to have remained until the end. The Swedish-born actress Greta Garbo died today at the age of 84, after a lifetime of studied seclusion. A labourer's daughter, Garbo was discovered in a Stockholm department store. She captivated Hollywood in the 1920s, making 24 films before her last role in *Two-Faced Woman* in 1941. She won a special Oscar in 1955.

Garbo takes time off between films.

Nelson Mandela attracts massive crowd to Wembley concert

ANC supporters celebrate before the Nelson Mandela concert at Wembley.

April 16. Nelson Mandela's two-day Easter visit to Britain reached a jubilant and tumultuous climax tonight when he and his wife, Winnie, were guests at a huge pop concert in their honour at Wembley stadium in London. Thousands of mainly young people packed into the stadium to welcome the African National Congress leader – freed earlier this year after more than 27 years in prison. When the cheering had died down, Mandela thanked his friends in Britain for all their support, but also struck a serious note; in a thinly veiled jibe at Mrs Thatcher, he said that Pretoria should not be given "rewards and carrots" while the main pillars of apartheid remain (→4/5).

Test series ends in win for West Indies

Gordon Greenidge makes his 149.

April 16. What began with a bang ended with a whimper in Antigua today when England's cricketers failed to save a test series which had started so promisingly for them.

The West Indians saw England off by an innings and 32 runs to take the fifth and final test of the tour, winning the series 2-1 with two matches drawn. However, England won the first test and if the weather had not wiped out the third test in Trinidad things might have been different. Graham Gooch, England's captain, agreed: "After coming out here as no-hopers, we took them into the last game," he said. There is optimism yet.

"Les enlacements de la flamme", a 1926 creation by the Russian-born artist and designer Erte, who died in Paris on 21 April, aged 97.

Tory revolt against Hong Kong bill fails

April 19. One of the biggest revolts against Mrs Thatcher's government failed tonight when a bill giving British citizenship to 50,000 key Hong Kong people and their dependants won a Commons majority of 97. Forty-four Tory MPs voted against their party line, but the government was guaranteed victory through a divided opposition and the support of minor parties.

The rebels accused ministers of betraying past pledges about limiting immigration. Their leader, the ex-cabinet member Norman Tebbit, warned of "social upheaval" if there is a big influx from Hong Kong. David Waddington, the home secretary, retorted that the legislation is needed to maintain confidence within the colony in the run-up to China's takeover in 1997.

Whitehall does not expect an immediate rush to take up residence rights in Britain.

Baroness is jailed

Susan de Stempel: found guilty.

April 21. Baroness Susan de Stempel was jailed for seven years today for masterminding a series of thefts and forgeries to defraud her senile aunt, Lady Illingworth, of her £500,000 fortune. Left penniless at the age of 84, Lady Illingworth spent the last two years of her life in an old people's home paid for by the state. Even her wish to be buried beside her husband was ignored. Baron Michael de Stempel, the baroness's husband, was jailed for four years, and her children Sophia and Marcus Wilberforce for 30 and 18 months respectively.

Baltic state blockaded

Lithuanian printing workers protest after Soviet troops take over their plant.

April 20. Soviet troops stormed a printing plant in the Lithuanian capital, Vilnius, today as Moscow tightened its economic blockade of the rebel republic. About 50 soldiers with truncheons and rifles rushed into the plant operated by the breakaway Lithuanian Communist Party, beating workers. Thousands of onlookers jeered and chanted "Fascists, fascists!".

The economic blockade was imposed on Tuesday in an attempt to bring the Baltic state to heel over its independence declaration. The first step was to shut off oil supplies to Lithuania's only refinery. Then deliveries of gas were cut to barely 15 per cent of normal. New reports say that food consignments intended for the republic have been diverted.

The Lithuanian government met in emergency session to decide how to cope with the threatened energy shortage. Officials attacked Moscow for resorting to "coercion and economic war against a neighbour" and said the moves sprang from a "major crisis" in the Soviet Union.

Prunskiene contemplates freedom.

Lithuania is entirely dependent on Moscow for its oil and gas, and Kazimiera Prunskiene, the state premier, has flown to Norway to seek alternative supplies. The Lithuanians have also asked the US for help in beating the blockade (→ 23).

Attempted child abduction cases mount

April 20. Detectives in Manchester launched an investigation today into another case of attempted child abduction which bears the hallmarks of numerous similar incidents in two other areas of the country. There have been 14 comparable cases over the past three months in Humberside, South and West Yorkshire, and Somerset. The latest kidnapping attempt was made by a woman posing as an NSPCC inspector who called at a house in Salford, criticized the condition of a nine-month-old haemophiliac boy and said that he would be taken into care. The baby's mother asked the woman to leave.

April

1990

Su	Mo	Tu	We	Th	Fr	Sa
1	2	3	4	5	6	7
8	9	10	11	12	13	14
15	16	17	18	19	20	21
22	23	24	25	26	27	28
29	30					

22. Nigeria: An attempted coup against President Ibrahim Babangida fails.

22. Lebanon: The US hostage Robert Polhill is freed by his captors, Islamic Jihad for the Liberation of Palestine.→

23. USSR: Lithuania's one oil refinery closes as Moscow's blockade bites deeper (→4/5).

23. UK: Pucklechurch remand centre near Bristol is hit by rioting.→

24. Bonn: The West and East German leaders set 2 July as the date for economic union between their countries.→

24. US: The Californian financier Michael Milken, the creator of "junk bonds", pleads guilty to six violations of securities laws.

25. Space: The revolutionary Hubble space telescope is launched from the US shuttle *Discovery* (→27/6).

25. Israel: Shimon Peres, the Labour leader, concedes failure in his attempt to form a coalition government that excludes Likud (→11/6).

26. Australia: An area the size of Western Europe is reported to be under water after floods.

27. S Africa: Five eminent ANC figures, including Joe Slovo, the Communist Party leader, return home after 30 years' exile (→4/5).

28. Dublin: The 12 EC leaders agree to pursue political union (→29).

29. USSR: Gorbachev rules out Soviet acceptance of a unified Germany within Nato (→1/5).

29. UK: British Satellite Broadcasting launches its satellite TV service.

30. UK: An RAF Shackleton crashes on the Hebridean island of Harris, killing all ten of its crew.

30. Tibet: Beijing lifts martial law in Tibet, 14 months after sending in troops to crush anti-Chinese demonstrations.

DEATH

23. Paulette Goddard, US actress (*3/6/05).

Abortion and foetal research reviewed

April 25. Anti-abortionists have failed in a bid to slash the time limit for abortions from 28 to 18 weeks.

In a free vote early today MPs came out strongly in favour of cutting the present 28-week upper limit to 24 weeks – after rejecting proposals to set it at either 18, 28, 20, 26 or 22 weeks. The rejection of 22 weeks was a particular blow to anti-abortion groups, which had hoped that it might be accepted as a compromise. Later, MPs voted in effect to remove the upper time limit for abortion to prevent "grave personal injury to the physical and mental health of the pregnant woman" or risk of serious foetal handicap. The result means the first change in the law since abortion was made legal in 1967.

The vote took place as part of the debate on the Human Fertilization and Embryology Bill, and comes two days after the Commons decided by a majority of 173 to allow research to continue on human embryos up to 14 days old. Professor Robert Winston, the head of a pioneering test-tube baby clinic, described this as "a massive vote of confidence in British science and a boost for childless couples".

Last prisoners surrender at Strangeways

The five remaining prisoners are lowered from the roof on a platform hoist.

April 25. The inglorious siege of Strangeways prison came to a near-comical end today as the remaining five rebels, defiant to the end, were brought down from the roof by mechanical hoist. They danced and waved to cheering supporters and were even applauded by riot squad officers as they touched down.

The last man off the roof was Paul Taylor, aged 28, the alleged ringleader of the protest, who has frequently harangued police and spectators during the 25-day siege.

As engineers entered the shattered prison, the inevitable inquest began. A high court judge, Lord Justice Woolf, is inquiring into the disturbances at Strangeways and other jails; but already a war of words is under way between prison officers and the home office.

Staff claim that Strangeways could have been stormed within 24 hours of the uprising. David Waddington, the home secretary, retorted that "the end result justified the tactics employed" (→1/5).

Hendry's snooker triumph crowns gripping weekend of sport

April 29. Twenty-one-year-old Stephen Hendry put the seal on a great sporting weekend tonight when he beat Jimmy White at Sheffield's Crucible theatre to become the youngest-ever world snooker champion. His win, by 18 frames to 12, puts him first in world rankings.

Victor's laurels also went tonight to Britain's Nigel Benn, who took the world middleweight boxing championship from Doug DeWitt of America in Las Vegas. The World Boxing Organization fight was stopped in the eighth round.

Oldham Athletic's dreams of glory ended gallantly today when Nottingham Forest kept the Littlewood's Cup by the smallest margin. Forest's Nigel Jemson scored the only goal of the match at Wembley. Mean-

Hendry: youngest champion.

Jemson takes action for Forest.

while, Liverpool yesterday won their 18th League championship, seeing off Queen's Park Rangers 2-1 at Anfield.

Wembley was also the scene yesterday of Wigan's 36-14 point trouncing of Warrington in the

Silk Cut Rugby League Challenge Cup final, which they have won for a record three times in a row. Wigan are the first side to win the Challenge Cup, Regal Cup and League championship in a single season.

German leadership challenger stabbed

April 25. The man tipped by many to become the first chancellor of a reunited Germany is fighting for his life after an assassination attempt at an election meeting in a suburb of Cologne. Oskar Lafontaine, the popular deputy leader of the West German Social Democrats and the party's candidate to challenge Chancellor Kohl in the general election scheduled for December, was accepting some flowers and a book of poetry from a woman when she suddenly produced a long knife and plunged it into his neck. The motive for the attack is a mystery, but the woman is believed to be mentally ill (→4/5).

US hostages released

Polhill arrives in West Germany.

Reed in Damascus after his release.

April 30. Frank Reed, the US college administrator held hostage by the pro-Iranian Islamic Jihad group since September 1986, was freed into Syrian custody in Beirut today. He is expected to be flown to the US base at Wiesbaden in West Germany for medical checks.

His release, following that of Robert Polhill eight days ago, gives hope that all the Western hostages might soon be freed. The Iranians are making it clear that much depends on President Bush's response to their "gesture of goodwill".

Mr Bush has already expressed thanks to Syria for facilitating Reed's release, saying: "We would also like to thank the government of Iran for using its influence." Iran is likely to be looking for a more solid reward, such as the freeing of Iranian assets frozen by the US since the occupation of the American embassy in Tehran in 1979.

When Reed appeared on Syrian TV this evening the effects of his long ordeal were only too apparent. He said that he had been blindfolded for much of his captivity. He told a news conference: "I am not prepared to answer questions ... simply because there are other hostages there and I do not want to say anything that harms them or their way of life there" (→3/5).

Appeal court sets Irish prisoners free

April 27. Remarks made by Tom King, the former Northern Ireland secretary, during the trial of three Irish people accused of plotting to kill him meant that their convictions were unsafe, the appeal court ruled today. John McCann, Finbar Cullen and Martina Shanahan all refused to give evidence at their trial in October 1988. During the trial, Tom King warned that the government was planning to allow juries to infer guilt from defendants who remained silent. Releasing the three – who will be expelled from Britain – the appeal judges said that King's announcement could have influenced the jury (→21/5).

Britain found guilty of abusing rights

Harriet Harman: civil rights activist.

April 25. A European tribunal has found Britain guilty of breaching human rights over a secret MI5 operation to spy on civil liberties and nuclear disarmament activists.

The ruling, announced today by the Committee of Ministers of the Council of Europe, will fuel calls for tighter controls on the intelligence service. The case was brought by two former key figures in the National Council of Civil Liberties, Patricia Hewitt and the Labour MP Harriet Harman, after revelations in 1985 by an ex-MI5 officer that they were targets of a covert operation against "subversives" going back to the late 1970s.

Great train robber shot dead in Spain

April 24. Charles Wilson, the most enigmatic of the great train robbers, was shot dead at the side of his Marbella swimming pool today. His killer, believed to be a professional "hit man", escaped on a bicycle after shooting Wilson's dog. Police suspect a drugs connection, although Wilson and his wife have been living quietly on the Costa del Sol for the past three years. Wilson – "the silent man" – was sentenced to 30 years in 1963.

Long-term consequences of Chernobyl accident start to emerge

April 27. The fourth anniversary of the Chernobyl nuclear accident has been marked this week by tens of thousands of people in the Soviet republics of Ukraine and Byelorussia, the two regions worst affected. An estimated 300 people, mostly power station workers, have died of nuclear-related causes since the explosion, which cost 31 lives at the time. There has also been a disturbing rise in the number of children contracting thyroid cancer. The republics are seeking billions of roubles to continue cleaning up radioactive contamination blown by the wind over a far wider area than was first realized. There are plans for the urgent evacuation of up to 200,000 more people from contaminated zones (→24/5).

Marchers' banners read "Mamma, I want to live" and "Go, radioactive hell".

37

Su	Mo	Tu	We	Th	Fr	Sa
		1	2	3	4	5
6	7	8	9	10	11	12
13	14	15	16	17	18	19
20	21	22	23	24	25	26
27	28	29	30	31		

1. Westminster: Mrs Thatcher restates her claim that Labour councils are to blame for high poll-tax bills.→

1. UK: Liverpool beat Derby County 1-0 to win the Football League championship.

1. Nepal: Thousands march through Kathmandu celebrating May Day for the first time since 1961.

1. UK: Representatives of the Prison Officers' Association walk out of talks with the home office over the future of Strangeways prison (→11/6).

1. Cairo: Fifteen people die when the authorities clamp down on religious extremists.

1. UK: A four-year-old girl receives over 200 stitches after being savaged by two pet dogs.

1. UK: Lou Macari, the former manager of Swindon football club, is questioned over tax fraud (→28).

2. UK: The home office warns that any English football supporters convicted of hooliganism in Italy during the World Cup will face a two-year ban on all English matches abroad (→8).

2. UK: Complaints against the police have risen by 11 per cent since last year.

3. UK: The government states that it is ready "in principle" to meet Iran, with a view to securing the release of the British hostages.→

2. Perth: Robert Maxwell's bid for a West Australian newspaper is thwarted.

4. Bonn: Talks on the future of a united Germany begin between the two Germanies and the four wartime victors (→6).

4. Sydney: Four people die when a steam train on a jazz outing is hit by an express.

4. Greece: Constantine Karamanlis becomes president.

5. Twickenham: Bath defeat Gloucester 48-6 to win the Rugby Union Cup.

DEATH

3. David Rappaport, British actor (*23/11/52).

Jeering crowds humiliate Gorbachev

May 1. The May Day celebration on Red Square – that most hallowed of Soviet occasions – was transformed today into a jeering parade against Mikhail Gorbachev and his reform policies. The humiliating scene ended only after the Soviet president and his colleagues, with catcalls and whistles ringing in their ears, abruptly abandoned their places of honour on the balcony of the Lenin mausoleum and retreated to the peace and quiet of the Kremlin.

For decades the May Day event has been a carefully-orchestrated festival of loyal Moscow workers. But this year – in line with the new freedoms gained under Gorbachev – the authorities allowed a march organized by the pro-democracy Moscow Voters' Association. Taking part in this demonstration was a cross-section of opposition groups, ranging from Baltic and Russian nationalists to fledgling non-communist political parties.

Banner messages displayed by marchers alluded to "70 years of excrement on the people" and demanded "Gorbachev – hands off Soviet power". The protest clearly irritated the Soviet leader. Radical politicians said that the demonstration reflected the mood of millions of ordinary citizens (→25/5).

A retired military officer joins the anti-Gorbachev protest in Red Square.

Enough is enough: the embarrassed president prepares to retreat from the scene.

May 4. A campaign to prevent the sale abroad of Canova's "Three Graces" succeeds when an export licence is denied. The statue is on show at London's V&A museum.

Job losses coming, warn businessmen

May 2. The years of falling unemployment are over. That is the bleak message from the latest quarterly survey issued today by the Confederation of British Industry. The CBI estimates that 18,000 jobs are being lost each month as firms are squeezed by high interest rates, inflationary wage pressures and tough competition. Despite signs of a buoyant export market, the CBI describes its findings as "deeply worrying". David Wrigglesworth, the chairman of its economic situation committee, said: "Britain is not in good shape compared with its European and other overseas rivals." One in three firms expect to lay off workers in the next four months, with largest firms the hardest hit (→16).

City mugger grabs £292 million bonds

May 2. There were rich pickings from a morning's mugging today when – a stone's throw from the Bank of England – 58-year-old John Goddard was relieved of his briefcase at knifepoint.

Mr Goddard is a messenger for Sheppards, a City money-broking firm, and the case which he was forced to part with contained 292 bearer bonds worth no less than £1 million each. The lucky thief was described as about 25 years old and 5 feet 10 inches tall.

The Bank of England acted swiftly to try to prevent him turning any of his new-found wealth into usable currency. By lunchtime, all the major financial centres around the world had been warned that the certificates were stolen.

Historic Cape Town talks end in unison

A light moment before talks begin.

May 4. "The realization of a dream" was how Nelson Mandela described his historic talks with South Africa's president, F W de Klerk, which ended today. When the two leaders sat down in Cape Town three days ago it was the first time that the government had spoken to the African National Congress since the movement was founded in 1912; and, with Mandela in jail and the ANC banned, dialogue was unthinkable until very recently. In a communique issued at their joint press conference today – another historic event – the two men declared that both sides had agreed on key points aimed at creating a peaceful climate for negotiations on South Africa's future (→ 6).

Tories suffer local election battering

May 4. Labour has confirmed its opinion-poll lead over the Conservatives with sweeping victories in yesterday's local elections. Neil Kinnock's euphoria has been muted by notable Tory triumphs in London, however, allowing Mrs Thatcher to hail the results in Wandsworth and Westminster especially as a vindication of the poll tax (or community charge).

These two boroughs, which each set poll-tax rates well below the national average, witnessed large swings to the Conservatives. The Tories advanced elsewhere in London, too, although the trend was by no means consistent, with Labour notching up gains as well as losses. However, statistical niceties failed to deter either Kenneth Baker, the Tory chairman, or Mrs Thatcher from claiming that Labour's large lead in the opinion polls had been confounded. "The message about the community charge is beginning to work," said the prime minister.

Conservative MPs with marginal seats outside the capital were less convinced. Overall, Labour made net gains of 304 seats and 14 councils; with a swing averaging 11 per cent this would be sufficient to win a general election. Labour did particularly well in southern England while maintaining its hold on the north and Scotland. The Liberal Democrats were also pleased, taking 18 per cent of the total vote and emerging clearly ahead of their third-party rivals, the Greens and the dwindling SDP (→ 11).

Wandsworth MP Mellor at the count.

Latvians poised to seize independence

May 4. The Baltic state of Latvia today voted for independence from the Soviet Union. It changed its name and reinstated a pre-war constitution. The result was cheered by thousands of champagne-guzzling supporters who had gathered outside the parliament in Riga to toast the decision to weaken ties with Moscow. Latvia has now joined Lithuania and Estonia in challenging President Gorbachev to let the Baltic republics reassert their pre-war independence (→ 7).

Freed US hostage says Britons are alive

Frank Reed breaks the good news from his hospital balcony in West Germany.

May 4. Frank Reed, the US hostage released by his Hizbollah captors in Beirut on Monday, has confirmed that the British hostages John McCarthy and Brian Keenan are alive. Speaking from a hospital in West Germany, Reed said: "I have been with John and Brian since last October." He later spoke by telephone to Jill Morrell, the leader of a campaign to free John McCarthy.

Reed revealed that both McCarthy and Keenan, who has dual British and Irish nationality, were in good health and good spirits, but he had no news of Terry Waite. Nothing has been heard of the archbishop of Canterbury's special envoy since he was seized three years ago. Brian Keenan's sisters, Elaine Spence and Brenda Gillham, today flew to Washington to meet Reed on his return to the US. Mrs Spence said of his release: "I just hope this is the start of a process which will bring them all home."

Meanwhile, Iran and the US have settled more than 2,000 financial claims outstanding for more than a decade. Both sides insist that the agreement is not part of a deal involving US hostages in Lebanon. The settlement is seen, however, as going some way towards meeting Tehran's demand for a gesture of goodwill from the Americans in response to Iranian help in freeing Reed and Robert Polhill (→ 24/8).

May 5. The peace of Bournemouth's bank holiday weekend is shattered when football fans from Leeds clash with police. Twenty-five are arrested; Leeds win the match 1-0, and gain promotion to the First Division.

May
1990

Su	Mo	Tu	We	Th	Fr	Sa
		1	2	3	4	5
6	7	8	9	10	11	12
13	14	15	16	17	18	19
20	21	22	23	24	25	26
27	28	29	30	31		

6. USSR: Romanian day trippers flood into Soviet Moldavia as the border opens for the first time for 50 years (→ 21).

6. S Africa: P W Botha resigns from the National Party in protest at government talks with the ANC (→ 10).

6. Birmingham: Over 700 Asian youths are involved in violence after a festival marking the end of Ramadan.

6. Cardiff: Neath beat Bridgend 16-10 to win the Welsh Rugby Union Finals.

7. Oval: Lancashire score 863, the third highest first class total recorded in the UK.

7. USSR: Ivars Godmanis, the deputy chairman of the Latvian Popular Front, is elected prime minister (→ 15).

8. UK: Colin Moynihan, the sports minister, calls for an alcohol ban in Sardinia, the English football team's base in the World Cup (→ 25).

8. USSR: Estonia formally changes its name to the Republic of Estonia and reinstates its 1938 pre-war constitution (→ 13).

9. UK: The Monopolies and Mergers Commission opens an inquiry into the level of car prices in the UK (→ 31).

10. Paris: South Africa's President F W de Klerk meets Francois Mitterrand; it is the first time for 29 years that the presidents of France and South Africa have met (→ 20/5).

10. UK: Pan Am pays out £10 million in compensation to families living in Lockerbie (→ 17).

11. Greece: The British lorry driver Paul Ashwell is released from jail on £19,000 bail (→ 12).

11. UK: Robert Maxwell launches *The European* newspaper.

12. Rome: Italian police seize "supergun" parts consigned to Iraq and impound a further ninety tons in Naples (→ 21).

DEATH

8. Cardinal Tomas O Fiaich, Irish churchman (*2/11/23).→

Cardinal dies on Lourdes pilgrimage

Man of God and passionate Irishman: the outspoken cardinal in his prime.

May 8. Ireland is mourning the death in France of Cardinal Tomas O Fiaich, the Roman Catholic Cardinal Archbishop of All Ireland, who collapsed from a heart attack during a visit to Lourdes and died in a Toulouse hospital today. He was 66 and had been suffering from a heart condition for some years.

Tomas O Fiaich was a traditional Irish nationalist with a deep love for his country, its language, history and culture. Despite his warm and outgoing personality, some of his controversial remarks infuriated Ulster's nationalists – particularly his suggestion that 90 per cent of bigotry in Ireland came from Protestants. He also attracted protests when he said that people might be morally justified in voting for Sinn Fein (the political wing of the IRA) and that Britain should withdraw from Northern Ireland.

Charles Haughey, the Irish premier, described the cardinal as a "man of peace and a great Irishman". The Church of Ireland primate, Archbishop Robin Eames, talked of his "generous nature and concern for the good of his community and his people".

Kohl declares new start for Germany

May 6. Chancellor Helmut Kohl of West Germany today declared that the end of the post-war era was in sight, with nothing now standing in the way of German reunification. His optimism comes after the opening of talks in Bonn between the two Germanies and the four wartime Allies, who still technically occupy Germany. The "two-plus-four" talks aim to settle external aspects of German unity – which, essentially, boil down to whether or not a united Germany should be in Nato. The USSR insists it should not, although the Soviet foreign minister, Eduard Shevardnadze, remarked yesterday that the issue need not delay unification (→ 18).

South Koreans riot

May 10. Fifty thousand students battled with police on university campuses throughout South Korea today in spite of an appeal from President Roh Tae Woo for national unity. The students are protesting against the inauguration of Woo's "dictatorial and undemocratic" Liberal Democratic party. Fighting broke out in the capital, Seoul, as groups of up to 2,000 students occupied main streets and attacked the US cultural centre (→ 20).

Charles and Diana fly to Budapest for first royal visit since war

May 7. The Prince and Princess of Wales arrived in Hungary today on the first official visit by members of the British royal family since the Duke of Windsor – then Prince of Wales – went there in 1937.

The interim Hungarian president, Arpad Goncz, greeted the couple in English, which he learnt during a six-year spell in a communist jail. Later, Prince Charles laid a wreath at the tomb of the unknown soldier and met both the caretaker premier, Miklos Nemeth, and Jozsef Antall, his successor since last month's free elections. Tonight the prince spoke at a banquet at Budapest's school of economics – until recently a pillar of Marxist orthodoxy. He said "our hearts leapt for joy" when Hungary "cast aside" dictatorship (→ 16).

The Prince of Wales delivers his speech at Budapest's school of economics.

Sixth Briton is killed in Channel Tunnel

The tunnel: an engineering triumph – but must it cost so many lives?

May 8. Calls for immediate action to improve safety procedures in the Channel Tunnel have followed the third death in the tunnel workings this year. Billy Cartman, a 33-year-old grouter, died yesterday after being crushed by heavy machinery.

The British safety record on the tunnel is much worse than the French. Six British workers have been killed by industrial injuries since the tunnel started 18 months ago; just one French employee has died. Workers allege that they are routinely forced to break speed limits and safety regulations in order to meet deadlines.

Facing stiff financial penalties for overrunning its costs, Transmanche Link, the consortium of contractors building the tunnel, has tripled the rate of boring this year. It denies accusations that this is at the expense of safety (→31).

"Mad cow disease" blamed for cat's death

Infected cattle carcasses are burnt to reduce the spread of the disease.

May 10. The agriculture ministry revealed today that a cat put down five weeks ago in Bristol was suffering from a disorder similar to "mad cow disease" or, more properly, bovine spongiform encephalopathy (BSE). It is thought that the cat might have fallen ill because its food was contaminated with BSE agents. The fear is that the disease can be passed on from cattle to other animals, including humans, through the food chain. Keith Meldrum, the ministry's chief vet, denies that the human risk is any greater than it was before (→19).

Inflation hits new high

May 11. Inflation in Britain has hit an eight-year high, it was announced today; but the news sent shares rising on a stock exchange which had feared even worse figures. April prices were 9.4 per cent above what they were in the same month a year ago, bringing the retail price index to its highest level since May 1982 and not far below the 10.1 per cent figure which the government inherited in 1979.

Most City analysts still expect double-digit inflation before the end of the summer and John Major, the chancellor of the exchequer, did not rule out further rises when he blamed "council overspending" and higher budget excise duties for the April increase. The bad economic news comes amid mounting speculation on Mrs Thatcher's future as Tory leader – attacked as "hysteria" by the party chairman, Kenneth Baker. In the light of the government's recent poor showing in the polls and continuing public discontent over the poll tax, attention has focused in particular on the potential challenge from Michael Heseltine, the former minister who resigned in 1986 during the Westland crisis (→23).

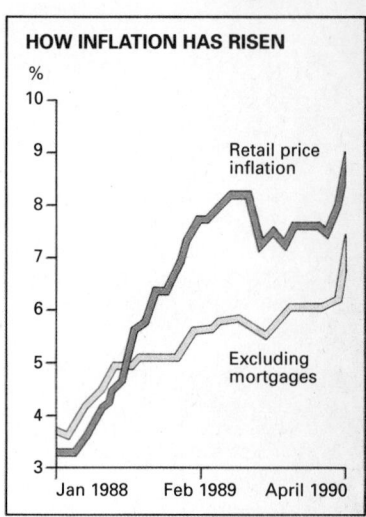

HOW INFLATION HAS RISEN

%
10
9 — Retail price inflation
8
7
6
5 — Excluding mortgages
4
3
Jan 1988   Feb 1989   April 1990

Waiting in the wings: could Heseltine be plotting to unseat Thatcher?

Aberdeen win Scottish Cup in shoot-out

May 12. Aberdeen today won the Scottish Cup after the first-ever final to be decided by a penalty shoot-out. Even then it took 20 shots to decide the match. Extra time had failed to separate Aberdeen and Celtic – or produce a goal – when the penalties began. Anton Rogan missed penalty 19 for Celtic, allowing Brian Irvine to hit the winning shot for Aberdeen.

South of the border, Manchester United and the underdogs Crystal Palace must meet again, following a thrilling 3-3 draw after extra time in the FA Cup Final (→17).

Irvine celebrates his winning goal.

May
1990

Su	Mo	Tu	We	Th	Fr	Sa
		1	2	3	4	5
6	7	8	9	10	11	12
13	14	15	16	17	18	19
20	21	22	23	24	25	26
27	28	29	30	31		

13. Bogota: Twenty-six people die when a car bomb explodes in a busy shopping centre (→ 27).

13. USSR: Lithuania, Latvia and Estonia join forces in their challenge for independence (→ 15).

14. Manila: Fifty-five people are injured when hundreds of protesters opposing the presence of US military bases fight police.

15. Yugoslavia: Borisav Jovic is appointed president.

15. Baltic: Anti-independence, pro-Soviet protesters attack parliament buildings in the capitals of Latvia and Estonia (→ 29/6).

16. UK: The government announces a £2.2 million advertising campaign to attract more students into the teaching profession (→ 1/6).

16. Budapest: Jozsef Antall, the prime minister, forms the first coalition government for 43 years (→ 21/6).

16. London: Four Underground maintenance men are killed by a runaway wagon on the Metropolitan line.

17. Wembley: Manchester United beat Crystal Palace 1-0 in the FA Cup Final replay.

17. India: Six hundred and eighty-eight people die when a cyclone hits Andhra Pradesh.

17. UK: Official figures show the first rise in unemployment for four years, from 1,200,000 to 1,605,600.

17. Ireland: The Irish Synod backs the ordination of women priests (→ 24/6).

18. N Ireland: David Trimble, the Ulster Unionist candidate, wins the Upper Bann by-election; the Tory candidate loses her deposit.

19. Space: The Soviet cosmonauts Alexander Balandin and Anatoli Solovyev are stranded on the Soyuz TM-9 space station.

DEATHS

16. Sammy Davis Jr, US entertainer (*8/12/25).→

18. Jill Ireland, British actress (*24/04/36).

Booby-trapped minibus kills army officer

May 16. IRA bombers struck again today, killing Sergeant Charles Chapman of the Queen's Regiment, when they blew up a minibus outside an army recruiting office half a mile from Wembley stadium.

The bomb, attached to an unmarked white Sherpa van carrying civilian number plates, exploded as Sergeant Chapman was moving the vehicle away from a wall behind the office in order to enable a woman colleague to get in. She was not badly hurt, but another sergeant sitting alongside Chapman suffered severe shrapnel wounds and shock.

The attack is part of the IRA's campaign against "soft" military targets. The dead man was aware of the danger following several similar attacks on recruiting offices and is known to have looked under the minibus before getting in.

It appears, however, that the bomb, attached by magnets, was skilfully planted and was not revealed by the normal cursory inspection. Forensic reports say it was the standard IRA car bomb, activated by a mercury tilt switch when the vehicle was moved. The minibus was completely smashed (→ 27).

Japanese tycoon splashes out on fine art

Renoir's hedonistic Parisians: worth a fortune the artist never dreamt of.

May 17. In his second spending spree of the week, Ryouei Saito, a Japanese paper manufacturer, has paid £46.5 million for the Renoir painting *Au Moulin de la Galette* at Sotheby's in New York. This is the highest sum ever paid for a Renoir.

Only three days ago, Saito bought van Gogh's *Portrait of Dr Gachet* for £49.5 million at Christie's, making it the world's most expensive painting. In a climate of ever-rising art prices, Renoir's painting of models and artists at a Montmartre dance hall was expected to exceed even this record sum; today's final price was greeted, therefore, with some disappointment. Total sales for yesterday's auction were £175 million.

All-day nursery children worry Thatcher

May 17. The prime minister today advised working mothers to stay at home and look after their children, rather than send them to an all-day nursery or playgroup. Her remarks, which some were surprised to hear from the lips of Britain's career woman *par excellence*, came during an interview on BBC Radio 4's *Woman's Hour*. Mrs Thatcher spoke of the "supremely important" early years and warned about the dangers of "a generation of creche children". Labour's Jo Richardson angrily riposted: "Women do not need to be lectured by someone who had a full-time nanny for her children."

Single currency for two German states

The German accord is sealed.

May 18. The two Germanies took their first formal step towards reunification today when they agreed to introduce economic and monetary union between the two countries from 1 July this year. On that date, East Germany will adopt the West German Deutschmark as its currency and will also take on the federal republic's monetary, economic and social laws.

A treaty sealing the accord was signed in Bonn today by the two German finance ministers, in the presence of Chancellor Helmut Kohl of West Germany and Lothar de Maiziere, the East German prime minister (→ 30/6).

May 15. Oil from the tanker "Rose Bay", holed after she collided with a trawler three days ago, washes ashore in Devon.

Politicians row over closure of steel mill

May 16. Government ministers are tonight embroiled in a fierce political row over the future of the Ravenscraig steel plant in Motherwell. British Steel plans to close its hot-strip mill, causing the loss of 770 jobs and arousing fears that the plant will close altogether with the loss of further jobs.

Ravenscraig, which was built in the 1950s by the then publicly-owned steel corporation, has long been a litmus test of government attitudes to Scotland's industrial heartland. Malcolm Rifkind, the beleaguered Scottish secretary, today deplored the planned closure. Not all of his colleagues see any reason to interfere, however (→28).

"Global warming" agreement signed

May 16. Britain was among 34 countries which today took the first joint steps towards fighting global warming, the so-called "greenhouse effect". A declaration signed by environment ministers at the end of the United Nations Environmental Conference at Bergen, in Norway, said that those who signed agreed to "anticipate, prevent and attack the causes of environmental degradation", including global warming and ozone depletion (→26).

Gummer says British beef is safe for all

Cordelia and John Gummer have no worries as they share a beefburger.

May 19. In an attempt to calm public fears that bovine spongiform encephalopathy (BSE), or "mad cow disease", can be passed on to humans, John Gummer, the agriculture minister, today bought a £1.60 beefburger and ate it in front of journalists at an Ipswich boat show. Gummer said his quarter-pounder was "delicious", and then bought another – this time for his four-year-old daughter, Cordelia.

It is not certain, however, that all Gummer's critics will be silenced by his gastronomic derring-do. Town councils in the Isle of Wight,

Sheffield, Wolverhampton and elsewhere have already withdrawn beef products, and some education chiefs are threatening to ban beef from school meals.

The ministry of agriculture is stubbornly refusing to pacify public concern. David Maclean, the junior minister, has ruled out both random testing of slaughtered cattle and a proposed ban on the use of certain offals in pet food. Meanwhile, Britain's largest burger chains, McDonald's and Burger King, report no drop in trade since the BSE scare started (→30).

Security leaks to loyalists confirmed

May 17. John Stevens, the deputy chief constable of Cambridgeshire, confirmed today that there had been collusion between Northern Ireland's security forces and loyalist terrorist groups. Stevens said, however, that his team – which has conducted an eight-month inquiry into accusations of collusion – had found that the leakage of information was "restricted to a small number of members of the security forces and is neither widespread nor institutionalized".

The inquiry was mounted after a claim by the loyalist UDA that it had used leaked official documents to target a Roman Catholic man for assassination.

Bomb report urges pre-emptive strikes

May 17. Pan American airline's security at Frankfurt airport was still "totally unsatisfactory" nine months after the Lockerbie bombing, a US presidential commission reported today. "All passengers flying out of Frankfurt on Pan Am are at great risk," the report continued. Controversially, the commission urges the US to adopt a "zero tolerance" to terrorism by engaging in pre-emptive and retaliatory strikes such as the 1986 raid on Libya.

Silent Paris marchers deplore desecration of Jewish cemetery

May 14. Tens of thousands of people marched through Paris today in a silent protest at last Wednesday's desecration of a Jewish cemetery in the southern French town of Carpentras. In an attack which shocked the country, 34 graves were vandalized and the corpse of a recently deceased 81-year-old man was dug up and impaled on an umbrella.

France is suffering from a resurgence of anti-Semitism and nationalism. Today's march, which was joined by President Francois Mitterrand, was a national expression of revulsion at all racial hatred. It brought together people of all faiths and politicians of all parties – except the neo-Nazi National Front.

President Mitterrand is welcomed by the enormous crowd of marchers.

May 16. Sammy Davis Jr, one of the greatest ever all-round entertainers, has died aged 64, after a long battle with throat cancer.

Su	Mo	Tu	We	Th	Fr	Sa
		1	2	3	4	5
6	7	8	9	10	11	12
13	14	15	16	17	18	19
20	21	22	23	24	25	26
27	28	29	30	31		

20. S Korea: Thousands clash with police in Kwangju in a march to commemorate the 1980 revolt.

21. UK: The Labour Party warns members not to support the All-Britain Anti-Poll Tax Federation, calling it a "Militant Front organization".→

21. USSR: President Dubcek meets President Gorbachev during his first Soviet visit since 1968.

21. Greece: The British lorry driver Paul Ashwell is cleared of all charges of transporting military equipment.

21. UK: An inquiry reports severe doubts about the validity of the evidence on which Anne Maguire and her family were convicted of conducting an IRA bombing campaign (→ 14/6).

21. UK: Gateway supermarkets will be the first employer to grant equal pension rights for men and women following a European court ruling.

21. Sydney: Australian TV networks report their first loss since TV started in 1956.

23. UK: The government announce a £1.8bn current account deficit for April.

23. Vienna: AC Milan beat Portugal's Benfica 1-0 to retain the European Cup.

23. UK: The General Medical Council allows doctors to advertise their services for the first time for 130 years (→ 7/6).

24. USSR: The Soviet Union hosts its first anti-nuclear congress.

25. Romania: Nicu Ceausescu, the youngest son of Nicolae Ceausescu, goes on trial on charges of inciting genocide in the December revolution which overthrew his father (→ 14/6).

26. UK: Leading scientists warn that the ozone layer over Europe is depleted (→ 29/6).

DEATHS

22. Max Wall, British comedian (*1908).

22. Rocco Barbella (Rocky Graziano), US boxer (*01/01/21).

Police fire on mine town mass meeting

May 20. South African police today shot dead three blacks at a mass meeting in the mining town of Welkom in the Orange Free State. Dozens were injured in the incident – which occurred, ironically, just as the meeting agreed to suspend a boycott of local white businesses. The police claim they were forced to open fire with tear-gas, rubber bullets and shotguns when the crowd got out of hand, but black eye-witnesses say no warning was given. The killings will escalate racial tension in the area, already dangerously close to boiling point after the murder last week of two whites at a mine outside the town (→ 13/6).

Bobby Robson will go Dutch after Cup

May 25. Bobby Robson led his England football team into Sardinia today and away from the controversy over his decision to quit his job as England manager after the World Cup to take over the Dutch side PSV Eindhoven. Robson had intended to announce the news after the World Cup, but the news leaked and there were angry exchanges between the manager, officials and reporters yesterday. The players, Robson maintains, are unaffected by the row (→ 8/6).

Price rise plans spark Soviet panic buying

Soviet citizens stock up in an attempt to beat the inevitable price rises.

May 25. The Kremlin's package of economic reforms, which includes some massive price rises, today provoked unprecedented panic buying. Tens of thousands of Soviet citizens went berserk, scraping together every rouble and buying any goods they could get their hands on. They waited for hours outside stores across the country, only to be confronted by empty shelves.

The price rises for a host of basic products were announced by Nikolai Ryzhkov, the prime minister, in a report to parliament. They will be introduced in stages, as government subsidies are progressively phased out to create a "regulated market economy." Bread, which has cost the same since 1955, will triple in price from 1 July. Sugar will double next year, and the price of meat will go up by 130 per cent.

At the moment, bread is so cheap that farmers feed it to cattle when fodder is short and boys can be seen using loaves of bread as footballs. The price rises will not be popular. The government is dismantling a long-established social contract which has guaranteed full employment, excellent public transport, and cheap food and accommodation for all the people of the USSR. A referendum on the economic reform package is likely to be held after parliament has debated the proposals (→ 30).

Accident verdict on M1 aircrash victims

May 22. The coroner's jury today returned a verdict of accidental death on the 47 people who died in the M1 air crash on 8 January last year. The accident occurred when the pilot of the British Midland Boeing 737-400, faced with a fire in the port engine, shut off the starboard one by mistake.

The coroner, Philip Tomlinson, said that airlines must take steps to avoid such an accident happening again. They should improve communications between cabin crews and pilots, and fit TV cameras to aircraft tails to enable pilots to double-check the information on the instrument panel.

In Nicolas Roeg's "The Witches", Anjelica Huston plays the Grand High Witch, fiendishly planning to turn the children of England into mice. Rowan Atkinson takes a memorable role as a barmy hotel manager.

Palestinians massacred

Israeli paramedics try to save the lives of those injured by the maniac.

May 21. Seven Palestinian workmen were murdered today and nine wounded by a deranged Israeli who mowed them down with a Galil assault rifle as they waited at a crossroads near Rishon LeZion to be picked up to work for Israeli contractors.

The workers, from Gaza, were ordered by a young man wearing army uniform to show their identity cards and then to sit on the ground. They complied with what they thought was normal army harassment. The man emptied three magazines – 90 bullets – into them before commandeering a car and driving away. Police arrested him at his girlfriend's flat. The in-

cident has provoked fresh confrontations in the Occupied Territories and the worst violence since the Palestinian uprising began. In battles with Israeli soldiers, another seven Arabs have died and hundreds have been injured.

Yasser Arafat reacted bitterly, blaming Israel for "conducting a massacre", but Israeli politicians hastened to condemn the shooting. President Chaim Herzog said it was "abominable" and the prime minister, Yitzhak Shamir, called it "criminal lunacy". The opposition Labour Party, hitting at Shamir's intransigence, said the killing stemmed from a climate of violence and the stalled peace process (→ 30).

Labour erects new platform for election

May 24. Labour today unveiled a policy document which will be the blueprint for its election manifesto. Economic growth is seen as the key to fulfilling its programme for modernizing the education, health and social services. "Making comes before taking," said Neil Kinnock, the party leader, although top-rate taxpayers face increases to pay for

higher pensions and child benefits. Overall the document, *Looking to the Future*, reflects Labour's newly-minted moderation, with talk of private investment in transport, statutory strike ballots for unions, and a markedly friendly attitude to Europe. Tories dismissed it as no more than glossy packaging of old policies (→ 18/6).

Kinnock announces Labour's programme for government in the 1990s.

Lord Sutch's raving loonies beat the SDP

May 25. Nobody expected Labour to do anything other than win the Bootle by-election, and a majority of 23,517 was duly announced today. Yet nor did anyone expect the election to be a political graveyard. In seventh place, however, was Jack Holmes, the candidate of the Social Democratic Party, with just

155 votes. The SDP, led by Dr David Owen, was humiliatingly outscored even by the Monster Raving Loony party, led by the occasional rock singer and habitual election loser Lord David Sutch, with 418 votes. Lord Sutch has offered the SDP a merger. Dr Owen has yet to reply (→ 3/6).

Ion Iliescu wins landslide victory in Romania's free elections

May 22. The New Zealand yacht "Steinlager 2", captained by Peter Blake, wins the Whitbread Round the World Race after 128 days, 9 hrs, 40 min and 30 sec.

May 21. Ion Iliescu, who has led Romania's interim government for the last five months, today romped to victory in the country's first free elections for 45 years. His National Salvation Front party won nearly 70 per cent of seats in the new Parliament, with a two-year mandate to govern and write a constitution.

Mr Iliescu, aged 60, said that the country would have its own unique brand of democracy: "We will take the future step by step. We don't want to follow a pattern." But his triumph left the opposition with little political pressure to exert on him, and the debate has moved onto the streets. Chaos is being predicted for the next six months as the economy deteriorates (→ 25).

A gypsy family votes in Romania's historic, and controversial, election.

Su	Mo	Tu	We	Th	Fr	Sa
		1	2	3	4	5
6	7	8	9	10	11	12
13	14	15	16	17	18	19
20	21	22	23	24	25	26
27	28	29	30	31		

27. UK: Peter Elliott runs the world's fastest mile so far this year, in a time of 3 minutes 51.08 seconds.

27. Colombia: The presidential election takes place after nine months of bombing and killing (→ 28).

27. Belgium: The government suspends a £6 million aid package to its former colony Zaire after reports of student massacre by President Mobuto's men.

28. UK: Swindon Town FC is promoted to the First Division for the first time (→ 7/6).

28. Southampton: *Maiden*, the all-women yacht in the Whitbread Round the World race, comes home.

28. Burma: The National League for Democracy claims a victory in the first multi-party elections for 30 years.

28. Colombia: Cesar Gaviria becomes president (→ 15/7).

28. Heathrow: The Albanian football team steals £2,000 worth of goods from the duty-free shop.

29. Canada: President Gorbachev starts an official visit.→

29. UK: David Trippier, the environment minister, claims that water charges must rise by six per cent in order to achieve EC standards of drinking and bathing water (→ 3/6).

30. Peru: Over 115 people die when an earthquake buries four villages.

30. Nicaragua: Contra rebels agree to lay down their arms.

30. Malaysia: Eight Hong Kong residents convicted of drug trafficking are hanged.

30. UK: The BBC World Service ends broadcasts in Japanese and Malay.

31. UK: The Monopolies and Mergers Commission prevents David Sullivan, a sex magazine publisher, from taking a controlling interest in the *Bristol Evening Post*.

31. UK: Eurotunnel secures an extra £2.5 billion to continue the Channel Tunnel (→ 14/6).

IRA murders two Australian lawyers

May 28. Two Australian lawyers were machine-gunned down in the main square of Roermond (in Holland near the German border) last night. The IRA had mistaken Nick Spanos and Stephen Melrose, both aged 24, for British servicemen.

The lawyers, both of whom had worked in London for some time, were planning to spend the night in Roermond after visiting the van Gogh exhibition in Amsterdam. As they left their British-registered car to take photographs, a hatchback pulled up by them and two men opened fire. The women with them – Melrose's wife Lyndal and Spanos' girlfriend Vicky Coss – were unhurt. The IRA has admitted responsibility (→ 1/6).

The morning after: Dutch officials inspect the scene of brutal assassination.

Hundreds die in ethnic riots in Pakistan

May 30. Amid unprecedented security, a grim-faced Benazir Bhutto tonight arrived in Hyderabad, in southern Pakistan, where ethnic violence has claimed more than 200 lives in four days of near civil war. The Pakistani prime minister is under pressure to use her army to end the violence in which Mohajirs – Moslem migrants from India – are fighting ethnic Sindhis.

The populations of Karachi (the scene of further violence, in which 24 people were killed and 30 injured) and Hyderabad are dominated by Mohajirs, while the provincial government is controlled by Ms Bhutto's Pakistan People's Party which in turn relies on the Sindhis for support.

Ms Bhutto has threatened to introduce direct rule if the government cannot bring an end to the violence. She has blamed the Mohajir national party and Sindhi extremists of the *Jiye Sind* movement for backing the gunmen who have taken most of the lives (→ 10/6).

Friendly presidents debate new Europe

May 31. What shall we do with a reunited Germany? Presidents Bush and Gorbachev have spent most of today, the first day of their Washington summit, debating just that. Bush is adamant that Germany must stay within Nato, the western alliance; Gorbachev insists it pulls out. They say that they are moving towards a compromise. Their obvious mutual respect should help them to achieve it.

Palestinians stage an armed attack on Israeli holiday beaches

May 30. The Israelis foiled an attempt by the Palestine Liberation Front today to attack beaches crowded for the *Shavuot* holiday. Two assault teams landed from heavily-armed speedboats, but in a 30-minute gunfight in the dunes behind Nizzanim beach, near Tel Aviv, four of them were killed and seven captured.

Further north, another speedboat with five men on board was intercepted by the Israeli navy. All the speedboats were believed to have been launched from a Libyan ship. This incident will embarrass the Palestinian leader, Yasser Arafat: the PLF is commanded by his ally Abu Abbas, who was responsible for the hijacking of the Italian liner *Achille Lauro* (→ 11/6).

Israeli soldiers stand guard at the scene of today's terrorist attack.

France slaps a ban on British beef and live cattle imports

May 30. Despite repeated British assurances that beef is safe, France has announced a ban on all imports of potentially diseased beef and live cattle from Britain. Austria, West Germany and the Soviet Union already operate similar restrictions on British beef, while the EC countries and 14 other nations have stopped buying live cattle from Britain.

John Gummer, the agriculture minister, has described the French decision as "unwarranted, unjustified and contrary to EC law." Whether legal or not, the move will certainly hit British farmers hard: France accounts for over half of all United Kingdom beef exports. In 1989 this trade was worth over £180 million.

Henri Nallet, the French agriculture minister, says that he must do everything to reassure French consumers that the meat they buy is not infected with BSE, also known as "mad cow disease". The British government, however, is not convinced. Gummer believes that the ban has been imposed for domestic reasons: while French beef prices have remained stable British prices have dropped, undercutting the French market. Although feelings are running high in Whitehall no retaliation has yet been planned.

May 27. Ayrton Senna wins the Monaco Grand Prix, and heads the race to be world champion.

Russia opts for Yeltsin

Gorbachev's rival celebrates victory.

May 30. Boris Yeltsin, the popular Soviet politician and former ally of Mikhail Gorbachev, today emerged triumphant as the president of the vast Russian republic. His victory gives him the leadership of more than half the Soviet Union's 280 million people and a formidable power base from which to challenge the Soviet president.

Yeltsin, adored by crowds as the standard-bearer for the radicals in the Soviet parliament, defeated a candidate favoured by Gorbachev. But he said today that he intended to build a partnership with the Soviet leader, who sacked him two years ago as chief of Moscow's Communist Party, "not on confrontation but on dialogue". (→ 12/6)

Heavy earthquake sweeps eastern Europe

May 30. Several people died and hundreds were hurt today when Romania was hit by an earthquake which was felt as far away as Moscow and Istanbul.

The 'quake measured 6.9 on the Richter scale – as powerful as the one which struck Armenia in late 1988 – and was centred about 150 miles north-east of the capital, Bucharest, near the border with the Soviet republic of Moldavia. Most of the casualties occurred in Bucharest and the area to the north and east, where police said at least eight died and nearly 300 were injured. Serious damage and at least one death were reported in Moldavia, while a woman in Bulgaria is reported to have died of shock.

The epicentre of the earthquake was 60 miles [90 km] underground, so that surface damage was generally slight. Many of the injuries in Bucharest happened when people who recalled the 1977 Bucharest 'quake, which killed 1,500, jumped out of buildings in panic.

Siberian villagers meet Princess Anne

The princess visits a farm near Kiev.

May 29. Princess Anne, making the first royal visit to the Soviet Union since the 1917 revolution, visited a Siberian peasant village today. She met some 40 families, many of whom wore the national dress of the Buryat people. A Soviet official said: "This is probably the most exciting thing that has happened here since Genghis Khan swept through on his way to burn Moscow in 1238." The princess has also had talks in the Kremlin with the Soviet leader, Mikhail Gorbachev, about Anglo-Soviet relations.

Filthy British beaches fail EC standards: charges are threatened

May 28. Carlo Ripa de Meana, the European commissioner for the environment, has taken Britain to court over its polluted beaches. The proceedings relate to three Lancashire beaches – Southport, Formby and Blackpool – which fail to meet European Community minimum standards for clean bathing. More prosecutions could follow.

Acceptable maximum levels of pollution were laid down in a 1975 directive, which was implemented in 1985. Since then, the EC says, the government has consistently delayed and obstructed the commission in order to avoid legislation to clean up European waters. Britain continues to pump 300 million tons of sewage, much of it untreated, into the sea every year (→ 29).

Blackpool's Golden Mile: one of the most polluted beaches in Europe.

47

June
1990

1. Torquay: Delegates of the National Association of Head Teachers hiss John MacGregor, the education secretary, at their annual conference (→ 25).

3. UK: British & Commonwealth Holdings, a financial services group, becomes the biggest-ever British insolvency (→ 13).

4. Beijing: Violence marks the first anniversary of the Tiananmen Square massacre (→ 26).

5. Iran: Ayatollah Khamenei broadcasts that Salman Rushdie should "be handed over to British Muslims so that God's decree can be implemented" (→ 22).

5. UK: Only 29 beaches out of 440 are awarded the EC "Blue Flag" for minimum cleanliness (→ 29).

6. France: John Johnston, the driver of the British coach which crashed killing 11 holidaymakers, is charged with manslaughter.

6. Epsom: "Quest for Fame", ridden by Pat Eddery, wins the Derby.

6. Salisbury: Margaret Baskerville, a vet, is injured when a car bomb explodes (→ 8).

7. UK: The British Medical Association opposes proposals for hospitals to become self-governing bodies (→ 2/7).

7. UK: Swindon Town FC is demoted to the third division, following a scandal over unofficial payments (→ 13).

7. Australia: Bob Hawke upsets Beijing by promising to protect Chinese students.

8. London: Nicholas Mullen, an IRA "fixer", is jailed for 30 years for running a London arsenal (→ 16).

8. UK: Animal rights activists say that they carried out this week's car bomb attack (→ 10).

DEATHS

2. Sir Reginald Carey "Rex" Harrison, British actor (*05/03/09).→

9. Angus McBean, British photographer (*08/06/04).

Soldiers are attacked at Lichfield station

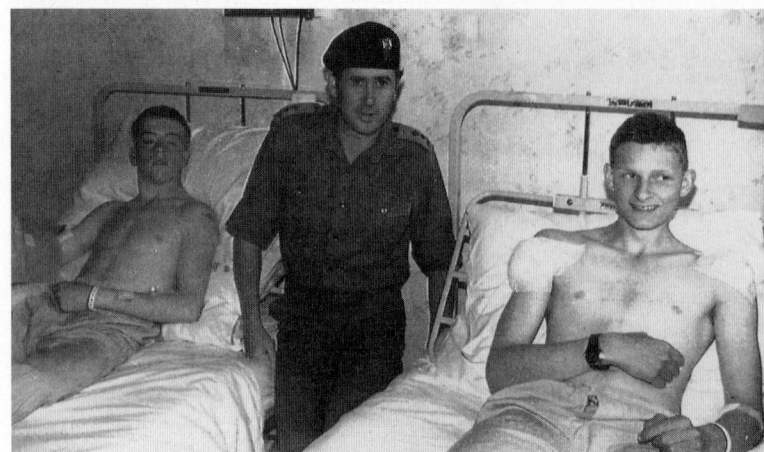

The wounded soldiers are visited by their commander in hospital.

June 1. Two gunmen, believed to be an IRA hit-team, shot dead an army recruit and wounded two others on Lichfield station today as they waited for a train to take them on their first leave. The soldiers, dressed in civilian clothes but perhaps recognizable by their haircuts, stood no chance.

"They were standing on the platform when these two men came up," said one witness. "I thought they were just messing about when there were six loud bangs. The soldiers collapsed. We did our best to staunch the blood. The two men ran across the line to get away."

The murdered soldier was Private William Davies, aged 19, from West Glamorgan. This attack could signal a switch in IRA tactics from bombs to bullets (→ 8).

Forty die in new wave of ethnic violence

Caught in the middle: a Kirghizian family surveys its ruined home.

June 3. The Soviet Central Asian republic of Kirghizia is gripped by a wave of bloody ethnic violence which has claimed at least 40 lives and injured several hundred people. Fighting has been going on for the last three days between the Kirghiz, about half the population, and the Uzbeks, who account for about 30 per cent. The trouble had developed after some 10,000 Uzbeks protested over the seizure by 1,500 Kirghiz of farm land near the city of Osh on which to build houses.

Troops in armoured cars are now patrolling the city's streets, trying to keep the two sides apart. Local leaders, appealing for calm, have declared a state of emergency and imposed a curfew.

Tour coach crashes and eleven perish

June 3. A British tourist coach crashed in France today, killing 11 passengers and injuring 60. It was travelling at 80 mph when a tyre burst, French police have claimed. The speed limit for coaches on French motorways is 55mph.

The passengers, mostly from the Midlands, were returning from a ten-day package holiday on the Costa Brava when the coach began to sway from side to side before crashing into a ditch. Eighteen of those hurt are in a serious condition. Some children are believed to be among the dead. The burst tyre has been removed for forensic examination (→ 6).

South African state of emergency lifted

June 7. In the latest move aimed at smoothing the process of political change in South Africa, President de Klerk today announced the lifting of the four-year-old state of emergency in three of the country's four provinces. It will remain in force in Natal because of continuing violence there, mainly between opposing black factions. De Klerk said that 48 political prisoners would be released and – presumably to allay white fears – 10,000 more policemen recruited (→ 13).

June 2. Rex Harrison has died. Here he relaxes with Elizabeth Taylor in "Cleopatra", his first major screen success, and a far cry from Professor Higgins.

David Owen calls it a day for ailing SDP

June 3. The Social Democratic Party is no more. With just 6,200 members, the nine-year-old party is too small to function properly. Dr David Owen and his colleagues in parliament, Rosie Barnes and John Cartwright, are now simply Independent Social Democrats.

When the SDP voted to merge with the Liberal Party and form the Social and Liberal Democrats in 1988, Owen and his followers stood aloof. Their party has since been sidelined by both the merged party and the resurgent Labour Party.

Owen claims that the SDP, launched in 1981 on a promise to "break the mould" of British politics, has encouraged the other parties to reshape their policies. But it never amassed enough votes to keep the Tories out of office. The final humiliation came at last month's Bootle by-election. The SDP polled 155 votes, the Monster Raving Loony Party 418.

Dr Owen, flanked by Barnes and Cartwright, announces the bad news.

Rebels' progress sparks Liberian exodus

June 7. British and American warships are standing by to evacuate foreign nationals as rebel troops advanced on the Liberian capital of Monrovia today. The country's president, Samuel Doe, has refused pleas to resign and leave Liberia, even though his position is seen as hopeless. Fearful of capture, he is sleeping each night in a different "safe" house. Leading churchmen have appealed to Doe to leave, but the president "seems to want to listen only to people who massage his ego", said one.

With Monrovia surrounded by disciplined troops of John Taylor's National Patriotic Front, Doe's army is in chaos. Soldiers are attacking and robbing civilians in the streets and fighting each other in the surrounding bush. Doe has appointed men from his own Krahn tribe as officers.

"There are colonels who cannot write their own names, intelligence officers who are illiterate and field commanders who cannot read a

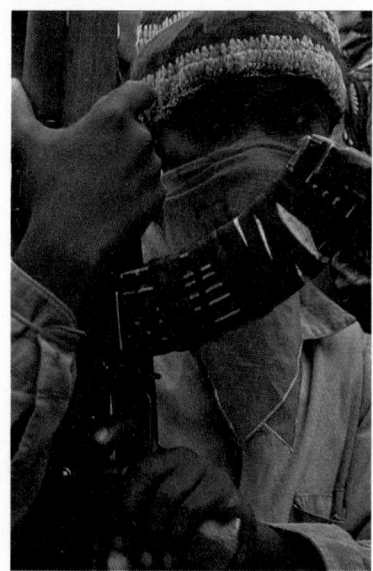

Well-armed: one of Taylor's men.

map," said a government official. With food running out – Monrovia's population is swollen by 40,000 refugees – hundreds are fleeing the country. Thousands of casualties are reported (→ 3/7).

Missile pact concludes US-USSR summit

Steering towards a deeper entente: the two presidents take a break.

June 3. The latest US-Soviet summit ended in Washington today with both sides hailing it as a a further move into a new era of friendship and cooperation. However, differences on a number of issues took some of the shine off the second Bush-Gorbachev meeting.

The core of the summit, a package of agreements on arms cuts, was signed two days ago despite an embarrassing last-minute argument centring on SS-18 missiles, the linchpin of the Soviet nuclear arsenal, which the USSR wants to modernize despite US objections. This is the key issue standing in the way of a full START (Strategic Arms Reduction Treaty) agreement, currently being negotiated in Vienna. On the other hand, deals were struck in principle on deeper cuts in nuclear and chemical weapons, and underground testing. The package also included broad agreement on the status of conventional [non-nuclear] forces in Europe.

The question of whether a united Germany should be in Nato (the West says yes, Gorbachev no) remains a sticking point. Differences over Lithuania also rocked the summit boat, as did today's unexpected warning by Gorbachev that he might curb the emigration of Soviet Jews unless Israel guaranteed that they would not be settled in the Occupied Territories (→ 12).

June 8. In the opening match of the 1990 World Cup, Cameroon humble the holders, Argentina, with a shock 1-0 defeat (→ 10).

June
1990

Su	Mo	Tu	We	Th	Fr	Sa
					1	2
3	4	5	6	7	8	9
10	11	12	13	14	15	16
17	18	19	20	21	22	23
24	25	26	27	28	29	30

10. Pakistan: Over 3,300 people are arrested in an attempt to curb the violence between Mohajirs and Sindis.

10. Bulgaria: The Communist Party wins a convincing victory in the first free elections for 50 years (→ 6/7).

11. Peru: Alberto Fujimori is elected president, beating the novelist Mario Vargas Llosa.

11. Manchester: The Woolf enquiry into the Strangeways riot opens, revealing that the home office vetoed early plans to storm the prison (→ 6/7).

12. UK: Investigators into the BA windscreen blast discover that the blow-out was caused by the fitting of wrong-sized bolts.

13. UK: Cable & Wireless announces the appointment of Lord Young, who as a minister oversaw its privatization, to the board of directors on a salary of over £400,000 (→ 27).

13. Strasbourg: Nelson Mandela asks the EC for money and requests that sanctions against South Africa are maintained (→ 20).

13. UK: A House of Commons select committee is told that British beef is safe to eat, provided that the offal is removed properly.

13. UK: Sunderland are named to be promoted to the first division instead of Swindon Town (→ 17).

14. Westminster: The home office announces that the Maguire Seven terrorist convictions cannot be upheld (→ 11/7).

15. London: The High Court rejects local councils' appeals against the government's poll tax capping (→ 29).

15. UK: The annual inflation rate reaches 9.7 per cent.

15. Donetsk, USSR: Miners call for a mass exit from the Communist Party, claiming that it no longer represents their interests (→ 19)

DEATH

16. Dame Eva Turner, British international opera star (*10/03/92).

High-speed Channel rail link is shelved

June 14. The government today finally shelved British Rail's plan for a high-speed rail link from the Channel Tunnel to London. The link, which would have cost an estimated £2.6 billion, was put forward by BR and its private sector partner Eurorail. The government originally ruled out putting any public money into the scheme, but the transport secretary, Cecil Parkinson, seemed at one stage to have changed his mind. Conservation groups in Kent are pleased, but tunnel travellers could yet be exasperated as their rapid progress through France slows to commuting pace (→ 27).

Hawks win in latest Israeli government

June 11. Israel's government took several steps to the right tonight. The Knesset gave its approval to Yitzhak Shamir's new coalition cabinet, which includes members of religious and other parties of the extreme right. The prime minister immediately confirmed that he would never cede any land to Palestinians as part of a peace deal, and attacked the US for opening a dialogue with the Palestine Liberation Organization. Shimon Peres, the Labour leader, retorted: "No tidings of peace, no chance of change, no reason for hope." (→ 9/7)

Uncompromising: Yitzhak Shamir.

Miners beat up protesters in Romania

Equipped with sticks and clubs, the miners roll into Bucharest on a digger.

June 14. Romania's still-fragile democratic institutions were under threat today as hundreds of coal miners terrorized innocent people on the streets of Bucharest as well as attacking centres of opposition. The death toll from mob violence has risen to at least 11, with scores of people injured. And the miners, who are meting out their brand of justice with clubs and coshes, are still in control of the city.

The miners were rushed by buses and trains to Bucharest from western Romania by President Ion Iliescu, whose National Salvation Front won last month's elections. Ostensibly his appeal to the miners was for help in dealing with students who had set fire to the interior ministry and police headquarters as part of their long-running anti-government demonstration.

Iliescu declared the student protest part of a fascist *coup* attempt and appealed for 10,000 miners to help save the government. The miners have been roaming the streets, beating up anybody suspected of being against the government. Offices of opposition parties have been ransacked. Some 460 people have been injured, and 1,000 arrested. The United States has signalled its concern by delaying signing some trade and cooperation agreements.

Belgian police catch up with IRA suspects

June 16. Two members of an alleged IRA cell were arrested on the Dutch-Belgian border today, and a manhunt is on for a third who escaped over the border into Holland despite being handcuffed.

The incident started when a farmer heard shooting in a wood near Turnhout. He called the police who surprised two men and a woman who had apparently been testing an arsenal of weapons which included a Kalashnikov assault rifle.

As they were being taken away the men ran off. One has been recaptured by the Dutch police. The woman, named as Donna Maguire, remains in Belgian hands, and the Belgians are convinced that they have broken up a cell responsible for attacks on British soldiers (→ 21).

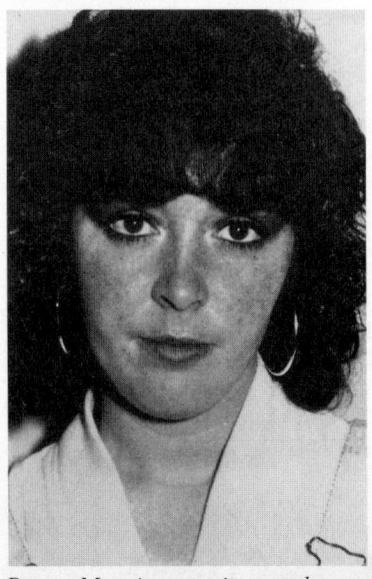
Donna Maguire, now in custody.

50

Blazing oil tanker threatens US coast

June 11. The United States coast-line is threatened with a major ecological disaster as firemen fight to quell a fire on a tanker carrying 38 million gallons of crude oil in the Gulf of Mexico. The Norwegian vessel *Mega Borg* has been blazing for two days, and thousands of gallons of water have been poured onto the ship in an attempt to cool down the red-hot hull.

Two seamen were killed in the original blast which happened as the ship was pumping oil into a smaller vessel. The tanker is carrying more than three times as much oil as the *Exxon Valdez* spilt in Alaska last year.

Fireships surround the Mega Borg.

Boris Yeltsin proclaims state sovereignty

The Russian president, Mr Yeltsin, holds an umbrella up to the Moscow rain.

June 12. The Russian Federation, the Soviet Union's largest republic, today proclaimed its state sovereignty. Its laws and constitution will now have priority over Soviet laws. The move was almost unanimously approved by the Russian parliament, whose president, Boris Yeltsin, hailed it as a significant achievement. The vote means that the battle by Russia, which stretch-es from Moscow through Siberia to the Pacific, to try to reap the benefits of its huge industrial, mineral and natural resources has begun in earnest. It has major implications for President Gorbachev and the Soviet Union as a whole. For example, Yeltsin has said that Russia will develop its own independent economic links with other states and republics (→15).

Animal rights bomb leaves baby injured

June 10. A 13-month-old baby was the chief casualty of a bomb planted beneath an animal researcher's car today. Little John Cupper suffered shrapnel wounds and nearly lost a finger. John's father was taking him to visit his mother in hospital when the bomb exploded as Dr Patrick Headley was driving past.

Dr Headley is a psychologist involved in animal research at Bristol University. He suffered minor injuries. Baby John was in a satisfactory condition after two operations.

Czech landslide for writer Vaclav Havel

June 10. Czechoslovak democrats have won a huge victory in the country's first genuine elections for 40 years. In a poll in which the pro-democracy movement had overwhelming backing, the playwright Vaclav Havel's Civic Forum and its Slovak allies, the Public against Violence, won over 170 seats in the 300-member parliament.

The Communists did surprisingly well, winning nearly 50 seats in a very high turnout of 95 per cent. The new parliament's main task will be to draft a constitution before elections in two years' time. In the meantime, it must steer the country through tough economic reforms designed to bring full capitalism. Hence its nickname: the "government of national sacrifice" (→30).

A Czech voter shows his support.

British jet pilot is sucked from 'plane

June 10. British Airways captain Timothy Lancaster was sucked half-way out of his cockpit when the windscreen blew out at 23,000 feet today. A steward then held him by the legs for 18 minutes until the co-pilot made an emergency landing in the BAe 1-11 jet at Southampton. Eight passengers refused to fly on to Malaga with flight BA5390 after the accident. Captain Lancaster is now recovering in hospital with frostbite and a broken elbow, wrist and thumb. An investigation has been launched (→12).

June 10. West Germany beat highly-rated Yugoslavia 4-1, and become favourites to win.
11. Scotland are defeated 1-0 by Costa Rica; in a lacklustre performance, England draw 1-1 with Ireland.
14. Cameroon, the outsiders, defeat Romania 2-1 and qualify for the last 16; the frontrunners Italy beat the US by only 1-0.
16. England draw 0-0 with the Netherlands; Scotland beat Sweden 2-1 (→17).

West Germany's Brehme dives low to tackle Yugoslavia's Stojkovic.

17. Swindon: Over 20,000 fans take to the streets to demonstrate support for their club's bid to remain in the first division (→ 2/7).

17. Belgium: The Battle of Waterloo is re-enacted by 2,300 enthusiasts, watched by over 100,000 spectators from ten countries.

18. UK: In an attempt to curb expenditure, the government announces defence cuts totalling £600 million (→ 19).

18. Australia: Adelaide wins race to be site of a new high-tech industrial city.

18. Westminster: Neil Kinnock promises that only seven per cent of basic-rate taxpayers will face increased income tax under a Labour government.

19. UK: The government promises to introduce criminal sanctions against squatters who occupy empty houses (→ 22).

19. France: President Mitterrand calls for the EC to give aid to President Gorbachev to help his economic reforms (→ 29).

19. Doncaster: A woman and two children are killed when they are hit by a train on a level crossing.

20. UK: A Commons committee severely criticizes the department of trade and industry for underestimating British Steel's profits prior to its privatization in 1988 (→ 28).

21. Hungary: The Budapest stock exchange reopens after 42 years.

21. London: "Bernadette" a newly-opened musical at the Dominion Theatre, is savaged by the critics as "banal" (→ 14/7).

21. London: RAF Stanmore is evacuated on the discovery of a bomb, which explodes causing only minor damage (→ 26).

22. UK: Michael Spicer, the housing minister, announces a £15 million initiative to help house the homeless.→

DEATH

20. Sir Tom Hopkinson, British journalist (*19/04/05).

Thousands die in Iranian earthquake

June 22. More than 40,000 people are believed dead, with at least 100,000 injured, in an earthquake that devastated 100 square miles of north-west Iran. The quake, measured at 7.7 on the Richter scale, hit the provinces of Zanjan and Gilan near the Soviet border. The shock was felt in distant Azerbaijan where some old buildings were damaged.

Despite Iran's avowed anti-western foreign policy, its president, Ali Akbar Rafsanjani, said that Iran would welcome aid "from whatever source". The greatest need was for cranes and heavy equipment to lift rubble, he said, as he declared three days of national mourning.

As teams of rescuers fought their way into the earthquake zone – where hundreds of villages have been cut off – the EC offered $1 million in instant aid.

Britain's overseas aid minister, Lynda Chalker, has set aside quarrels over hostages in Lebanon and Salman Rushdie to announce an "entirely humanitarian" aid package to Iran. British rescue workers, many of them veterans of the 1988 Armenian 'quake, are already on their way.

Tehran's hospitals are overflowing with victims, as aircraft fly a shuttle service from the stricken north-west. Iran's television is showing harrowing pictures of mass burials in communal graves and grief-stricken parents holding the bodies of their children (→ 26).

Destruction writ large: residents of Manjil pick their way through the rubble.

The human cost of the tragedy: a mother mourns her little children.

June 21. The summer solstice is greeted at Stonehenge, not by Druids but by policemen in anoraks. In a huge operation to keep out "hippies", police have set up a four-mile exclusion zone around the ancient monument.

Major floats plan for European cash

June 20. People travelling in Europe could end up paying for their hotel rooms in a new common European currency, if the chancellor of the exchequer, John Major, gets his way. In a speech to the Institute of Directors tonight, he unveiled what he called the "hard Ecu", to be used alongside existing currencies. The idea is to show European Community leaders meeting in Dublin that Britain is serious about monetary union. But it falls short of a single European currency, to which Mrs Thatcher is implacably opposed (→ 26).

New York welcomes Nelson Mandela

Harlem greets the ANC leader.

June 20. Nelson Mandela arrived in New York today to be greeted by the sort of welcome the city reserves for its heroes – a traditional ticker-tape snowstorm among the skyscrapers of Lower Manhattan.

Earlier in the day the deputy leader of the African National Congress arrived at New York's JFK airport to be met by a more formal red carpet and an array of dignitaries ranging from US politicians and civil rights leaders – including New York's first black mayor, David Dinkins – to 35, mainly African, UN ambassadors. The poor UN showing was down to the fact that Mandela is not a head of state – and protocol comes first.

An address by Mandela on the need to maintain sanctions was followed by the drive downtown. But his snowstorm nearly failed to happen – someone forgot that ticker-tape went out when computers came in. Luckily the sole remaining ticker-tape maker in the US was tracked down just in time (→ 4/7).

EC court challenges British constitution

June 19. Britain faces a constitutional shake-up after a ruling today by the European Court which gives British courts the power to overrule parliament in certain cases. Traditionally, while the judiciary can interpret and expose weaknesses in laws passed by the legislature, it is only parliament which has the right to repeal or alter laws.

Today's decision derives from a case brought by Spanish fishermen against the government over a 1988 act which banned Spanish ships sailing under British flags from fishing in UK waters and "plundering" Britain's European Community (EC) fish quotas. The House of Lords – Britain's highest court – said that it had no power to grant the Spaniards an injunction suspending the 1988 law while the European Court considered it.

The court said today that the Lords were wrong, because the alleged grievance to EC citizens remained while its cause was under judicial review, and the rights of citizens under EC law take precedence over national rules (→ 20).

Money promised to house the homeless

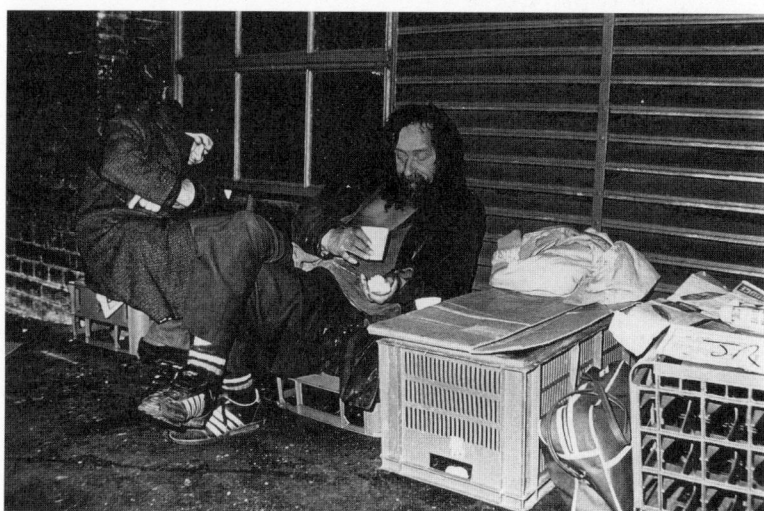

Victims of current housing problems wonder what the new deal really means.

June 22. Fifteen million pounds are to be spent on an attempt to wipe Britain's "cardboard cities" off the face of the land. Announcing the initiative today the housing minister, Michael Spicer, said: "The government is determined there should be no excuse for sleeping out on the streets."

The money will be used to fund extra accommodation and to help people in hostels to afford the deposits on longer-term housing. Mr

Spicer also hinted at measures to encourage private landlords.

Response from voluntary groups and the opposition has been mixed. The housing charity Shelter has made it clear that it blames the plight of the homeless on a housing shortage and not, as the government does, on the breakdown of family ties. A spokesman said: "Shelter remains to be convinced that these proposals will add up to more than a sticking-plaster."

England's Bull tackles Egypt.

June 17. Ireland draw 0-0 with Egypt, leaving all four teams in their group, including England, with identical records.
17. Colin Moynihan, the sports minister, backs the tough measures taken against English fans by the Sardinian authorities.
18. Luciano Pavarotti reaches no 3 in the UK pop charts with Puccini's aria *Nessun Dorma* – the BBC World Cup theme.
19. Colombia end West Germany's 100-per-cent winning record with a 1-1 draw.
20. Scotland lose 1-0 to Brazil and are out of the Cup.
21. England beat Egypt 1-0 to qualify for the second round; Ireland go through after drawing 1-1 with the Netherlands.
23. Cameroon beat Colombia 2-1 to reach the quarter-final of the competition.

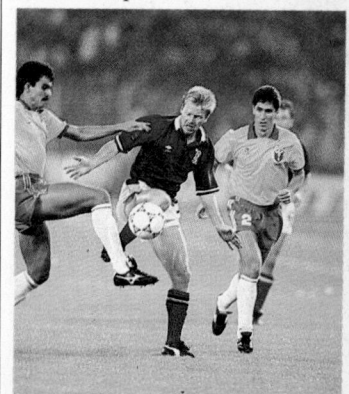

Scotland's Johnson and Brazil.

Meech Lake Accord to reform Canadian constitution collapses

June 22. Canada's three-year-old struggle to bring Quebec into the constitutional fold ended in failure today when the Manitoba and Newfoundland legislatures adjourned without agreeing on it. Today was the deadline for all Canadian provinces to ratify the 1987 Meech

Lake Accord, under which French-speaking Quebec was to be recognized as a distinct society under the Canadian constitution.

Intended to resolve the age-old quarrel between the Canada's anglophone and francophone provinces, Meech Lake angered many

Canadians. Indians criticized its failure to recognize that they, too, are a distinct society within Canada. Elijah Harper, the Cree Indian who blocked the accord in Manitoba, said it was a "great day for Canada and for the aboriginal peoples".

June

1990

Su	Mo	Tu	We	Th	Fr	Sa
					1	2
3	4	5	6	7	8	9
10	11	12	13	14	15	16
17	18	19	20	21	22	23
24	25	26	27	28	29	30

24. Australia: The Pyramid building society crashes, ruining thousands of small investors.

24. UK: Friends of the Earth leaks an official report showing the estimated final cost of the Sizewell B nuclear power station at over £2.6 billion, well above previous estimates.→

24. Zambia: A sharp increase in food prices causes widespread rioting and looting in the capital, Lusaka (→ 29).

25. UK: The Assistant Masters' and Mistresses' Association says that infant teachers are spending more time on administration than on teaching (→ 17/7).

26. UK: Salman Rushdie gives £5,000 to the Iranian earthquake appeal (→ 21/7).

27. USA: NASA says that its £1.5 billion Hubble space telescope has serious technical problems.

27. London: It emerges that the video cameras at the Carlton Club, which could have filmed the planting of yesterday's bomb, were not switched on (→ 17/7).

28. Cirencester: Prince Charles breaks his right arm in a polo match.

29. UK: Haringey Council announces huge cuts, including the loss of 800 jobs (→ 11/7).

29. Lusaka: Government troops raid the university campus, firing into rioters and killing a student.

29. UK: British Steel reveals that Sir Robert Scholey, the chairman, received a 79 per cent pay increase, to £308,541, last year (→ 26/7).

29. USSR: The republic of Lithuania votes to suspend its declaration of independence for 100 days (→ 13/7).

30. Prague: Czechoslovakia abolishes conscription, becoming the first Warsaw Pact country to do so (→ 5/7).

DEATHS

28. Robert Carvel, British journalist (*1/1/19)

29. Irving Wallace, US writer (*19/03/16).

Single currency unites the two Germanies

30 June. At midnight tonight the currencies of East and West Germany become one, in the most important step towards reunification since the hated Wall was breached last November.

The death of the *Ostmark* is not, however, being greeted with the same universal joy as the tearing down of the wall. Many West Germans fear that they will have to pay dearly to support the economic shambles prevailing in the East. At the same time the East Germans have no idea what to expect when the mighty *Deutschmark* rules in the East and all their subsidies are swept away.

All day today the shops in East Berlin have been selling their wares at rock-bottom prices, in preparation for the death of their failed socialist economy. Bars and restaurants are full of people drinking away their surplus *Ostmarks*.

Tomorrow will be hangover day with queues forming at the banks to draw their first *Deutschmarks*. But then, the East Germans have 40 years of queuing experience (→ 1/7).

Traffic halted for Queen Mother's parade

Her Majesty enjoys the celebrations, surrounded by her guard of honour.

June 28. The birthday celebrations for a special lady have started early. Central London was brought close to a standstill this evening as the official parade to mark the Queen Mother's 90th birthday made its way down Horse Guards Parade and the Mall. A cheering crowd of 16,000 lined the route. Among the special attractions were boxer Frank Bruno, an Aberdeen Angus bull and two royal racehorses. The Queen Mother's real birthday is not until 4 August.

Ozone deal signed by India and China

June 29. After 12 days of talks in London, China and India at last look set to ratify the 1987 Montreal Protocol, which calls for the phasing out of ozone-destroying chlorofluorocarbons (CFCs) by 2000. China and India, containing one-third of the world's population, have hitherto resisted all attempts to get them to cut their heavy CFC emissions. Environmental pressure groups say that today's agreement is still too little, too late.

Bush dumps main election guarantee

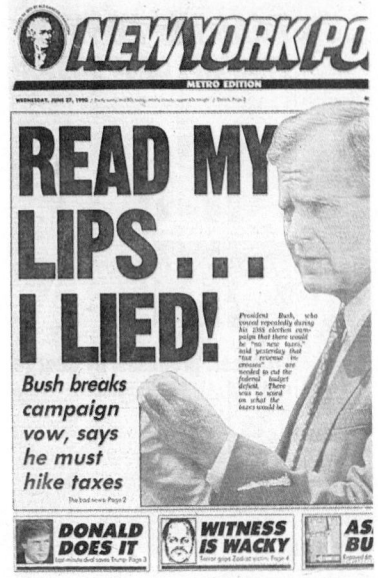

How the New York Post saw it.

June 26. In an embarrassing climb-down, President George Bush has reluctantly admitted that he can no longer stick to the most memorable pledge of his 1988 presidential campaign: "Read my lips: no new taxes!"

In a memo, Bush refers euphemistically to "tax revenue increases" – as if tax takings would somehow mysteriously be made to grow without any citizen paying more – as a key to any attempt to narrow the massive US budget deficit. Republicans and Democrats alike are anxious to cut the deficit, and so far there has been little sniping at Bush's U-turn. Rises are most likely in indirect taxes rather than in income tax (→ 11/7).

June 24. The UK's first Anglican women priests are ordained in Belfast.

IRA explosion rocks Tories' London club

June 26. An IRA bomb ripped through London's Carlton Club, a bastion of the Conservative Party, tonight, seriously injuring one man and hurting a further six, including a peer. A huge pall of smoke rose from the building in St James's Street as diners hurried from the badly-damaged building. Mrs Thatcher is among the club's members. She was at the European summit in Dublin.

The bomb exploded in the club's hallway, severely injuring a commissionaire. Three American tourists were taken to hospital. Police believe that the explosion marks the start of a new IRA campaign against "soft" civilian targets (→ 27).

Clearing up at the wrecked club.

British Aerospace to repay "sweeteners"

June 27. The government today faced opposition accusations of "deception and subterfuge" over its illegal "sweeteners" – financial incentives – to British Aerospace (BAe) when it bought the publicly-owned Rover Group for £150 million in August 1988.

The European Commission has ruled that £33 million in "inducements", paid to BAe as part of the deal negotiated by Lord Young, the then trade and industry secretary, amounted to a state subsidy, in breach of European Community competition laws, and must be repaid. The EC investigators – headed by Sir Leon Brittan – say that BAe must repay the £11.4 million it saved when the government allowed it to defer payment (→28).

Illegal subsidizer: Lord Young.

Nuclear power ills: Parkinson blamed

June 27. Britain's nuclear power industry is in a shambles, and Cecil Parkinson, the former secretary of state for energy, is to blame, says a parliamentary select committee which alleges that the minister ignored warnings and failed to seek adequate advice as he restructured the electricity supply industry. As a result, the government is left with uneconomic and unsaleable nuclear power stations on its hands.

The report adds to the government's embarrassment over its already disastrous attempt to privatize electricity. What is more, the committee which wrote it is dominated by the Tories (→9/7).

British Steel set to close Ravenscraig

June 28. Ravenscraig steel works in Motherwell, Scotland's biggest single employer, is to be shut down by British Steel. The closure plans were made public when a letter from Sir Robert Scholey, the chairman of British Steel, to Malcolm Rifkind, the secretary of state for Scotland, was published today.

Some 11,000 jobs would be lost with Ravenscraig, and independent sources estimate that Scotland stands to lose about £100m in revenue as a result of the closure. Mr Rifkind has demanded an enquiry into the future of steel-making in Scotland, saying that British Steel has not proved that its proposal to close the mill is justified (→29).

In the last minute of extra time, Platt scores the vital goal against Belgium..

ITALIA '90

June 24. Argentina and West Germany defeat Brazil and the Netherlands respectively.
25. Ireland beat Romania 5-4 in a penalty shoot-out after their game ended 0-0 in extra time.
25. Bryan Robson, the England captain, returns home injured.
26. England beat Belgium 1-0 to qualify for a quarter-final place; 246 English fans are deported after violent scenes in Rimini.
28. The Irish team meets Pope John Paul II at the Vatican.
30. Ireland are knocked out in a 1-0 defeat by Italy (→1/7).

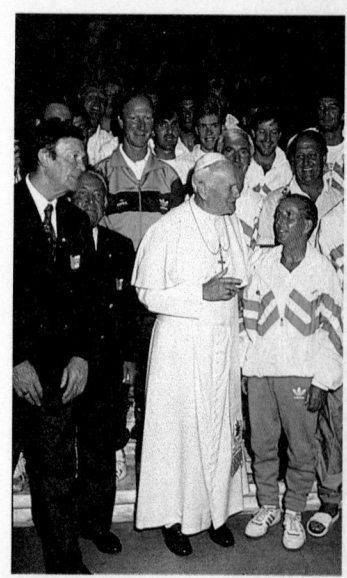

A blessing for the Irish team.

Thatcher stands firm against Delors plan

July 26. Mrs Thatcher, speaking at the end of the European summit in Dublin, made it plain today that she is rock-solid in her opposition to the Delors plan for a single European currency and central bank.

The great differences between the economies of the members of the community, she insisted, would make the Delors plan impossible. The only viable alternative, said the prime minister, was the British proposal for the "hard" Ecu – an alternative that "took us as far as the eye can see at the moment". Chan-cellor Kohl and President Mitterrand disagreed with her strongly-held views on currency reform and national sovereignty.

The new moves towards economic and political union were, said Herr Kohl, "the next step in the direction of a United States of Europe". Mitterrand was tetchy about Mrs Thatcher: "We can always rely on her to ensure the debates are long and that the decisions taken are always retaken – that was confirmed last night and again this morning." (→11/7)

Su	Mo	Tu	We	Th	Fr	Sa
1	2	3	4	5	6	7
8	9	10	11	12	13	14
15	16	17	18	19	20	21
22	23	24	25	26	27	28
29	30	31				

1. Naples: England beat Cameroon 3-2 to win a place in the World Cup semi-finals.→

1. Germany: The *Deutschmark* becomes the official joint currency of both East and West Germany (→ 3/10).

2. UK: Kenneth Clarke, the health secretary, invites NHS hospitals to apply for self-governing status.

2. UK: The Football Association decides to allow Swindon FC to remain in the second division (→ 10).

3. London: Wheelchair users block New Oxford Street in protest at the lack of help given to the handicapped on public transport.

3. Liberia: Samuel Doe, the president, offers to resign as rebels overrun the country (→ 8).

3. UK: House prices have dropped by an average 5.3 per cent since last year (→ 16).

5. UK: A letter in the *Lancet* reveals that the HIV virus has been found in the body of a man who died in 1959 (→ 27).

5. Czechoslovakia: Vaclav Havel is re-elected as president for another two-year term.

6. Somalia: President Mohammed Siad Barre's bodyguard fires on an unruly crowd, killing 62 people and injuring over 200.

6. Bulgaria: Petar Mladenov resigns as president, after admitting that he ordered tanks to crush a riot against the government last December.

6. London: A bomb explodes in a litter bin in the Strand and another is found near an El Al office in Regent Street.

6. UK: Prison officers stage a 72-hour strike, banning the admission of new inmates into already-overcrowded jails.

7. Bari: England lose 2-1 to Italy, to take fourth place in the World Cup (→ 8).

7. Albania: The authorities say that refugees currently seeking asylum in foreign embassies will be permitted to leave (→ 10).

7. Nairobi: Police use tear gas to disperse a violent anti-government demonstration (→ 9).

Nato redefines its role

President Bush, James Baker and Mrs Thatcher enjoy a moment of mirth.

July 6. The leaders of the 16 Nato member countries today agreed to redefine the 40-year-old alliance's military strategy and political goal. At the end of a meeting in London, Nato has cleared the way for a settlement with the Kremlin over a united Germany's defence role and mapped out a new road to pan-European cooperation. President Bush described the outcome of this summit as an historic change. He was confident that it would strengthen the position of President Gorbachev, allowing him to press on with his more liberal Soviet foreign policy. Gorbachev, who also welcomed today's declaration, has been invited to visit Nato headquarters in Brussels for what could be a joint summit of the Nato and Warsaw Pact leaderships.

QC scolds Scargill over "secret accounts"

July 3. A defiant Arthur Scargill tonight declared that he would not resign after a report slammed his financial management of the National Union of Mineworkers. The report, by Gavin Lightman, QC, was commissioned by the NUM after a former top official alleged that Scargill had used union money for himself. Lightman says this is untrue, but criticizes the miners' president for setting up secret accounts during the 1984 pit strike (when official NUM funds were sequestered) and for diverting funds donated by Soviet miners (→ 9).

Ninth Wimbledon win for Navratilova

July 7. Martina Navratilova went into the record books this afternoon after winning her ninth singles championship at Wimbledon, more than any other player. In a one-sided final the Czech-born player beat Zina Garrison of the United States in straight sets, 6-4, 6-1. Navratilova's biggest obstacle to her niche in tennis history could have been Steffi Graf, the defending champion, but the West German, who has been unwell, was beaten in the semi-final by Garrison.

"This tops it all," said a jubilant Navratilova after she punched the air in delight at victory. Now 33 years old, she won her first singles title at Wimbledon in 1976 (→ 8).

Martina gives it everything she's got.

Over a hundred Moslem pilgrims die in Mecca tunnel disaster

Dead and dying pilgrims litter the entrance to Mecca's tunnel of death.

July 2. At least 100 Moslem pilgrims were crushed to death today in a tunnel leading from the *ka'aba* at Mecca to Mount Arafat. In blazing temperatures of up to 43 degrees Celsius (110 degrees Fahrenheit), 5,000 men and women – five times the tunnel's capacity – had poured onto the walkway when panic struck, and over 100 of them were suffocated or stampeded to death. Some 1.5 million pilgrims are in Mecca and Medina for the beginning of the *Eid al-Adha*, the Moslem feast of sacrifice. There is no suggestion that the disaster was caused deliberately.

Mandela accepts Thatcher's policies

July 4. Nelson Mandela, the deputy president of the African National Congress, held a three-hour meeting with Mrs Thatcher at Downing Street today, after which the ANC leader praised her stand against apartheid and racism.

Despite years of criticism of the prime minister's opposition to sanctions against South Africa, Mandela left the meeting saying: "I accept that she is an enemy of apartheid and all kinds of racism. Our differences are in the methods used to dismantle apartheid."

An incident in Dublin two days earlier, when Mandela called for government talks with the IRA, was apparently forgotten (→ 7).

Reconciliation at the door of No 10.

England's agony in World Cup defeat

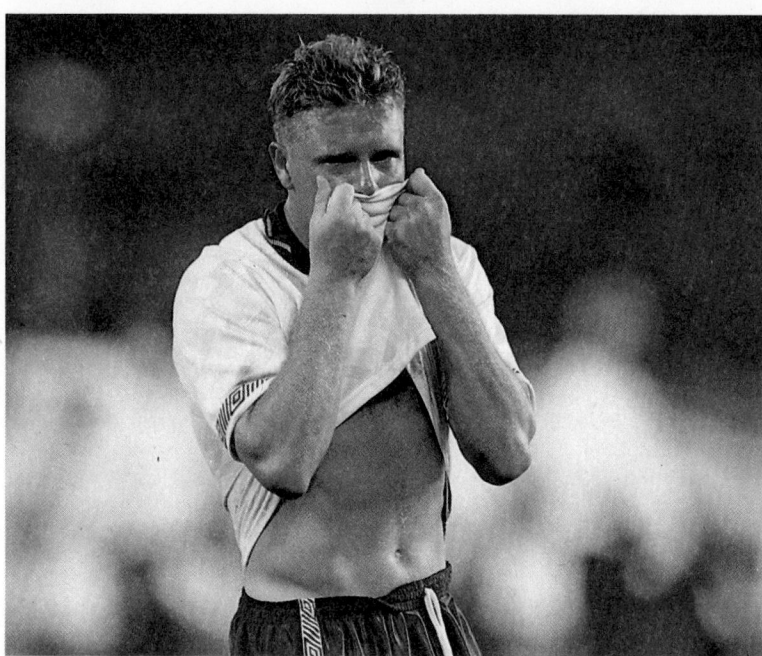

Tears of despair: Paul Gascoigne after his booking and England's defeat.

July 4. There were tears tonight in Turin as English hopes of reaching the World Cup final for the first time for 24 years were dashed by a penalty shoot-out against the West Germans. After their best display in the tournament England had drawn 1-1 after extra time.

Stuart Pearce and Chris Waddle both missed from the spot to send West Germany into next Sunday's final against Argentina. A record television audience back in Britain watched the game as people left work early to see the match.

West Germany scored first, after a cruel ricochet off Paul Parker, before Gary Lineker equalized. Paul Gascoigne was in tears after a booking ensured that he would miss the final even if England won. He was not the only one; but the manager, Bobby Robson, said: "We can go home proud" (→ 7).

Serbs crack down on rebellious Albanians

July 5. The Yugoslav government imposed what amounts to a state of emergency on the district of Kosovo today, following a vote in the province's parliament by rebel ethnic Albanian deputies to declare independence from Serbia, Yugoslavia's biggest republic.

The Belgrade authorities reacted by dissolving the parliament and sacking the provincial government. Police in riot gear moved in to surround the television station and the offices of the Albanian-language newspaper *Rilindja*, whose journalists issued a statement appealing to ethnic Albanians not to repeat the riots in which 50 people have died in the past 18 months.

This is the latest manifestation of the bitter racial quarrel between the 1.7 million ethnic Albanians and 200,000 Serbs who live in Kosovo. The Albanians, accused by the Serbs of wanting to take the province into Albania itself, maintain that all they want is their own republic in Yugoslavia (→ 7).

Bomb injures 27

July 7. Twenty-seven people were injured when a bomb exploded in Johannesburg today, amid rising tension between supporters of the African National Congress and the rival Inkatha movement. The ANC denied responsibility for the bomb, blaming white far-right extremists. Police arrested three members of the ANC who were allegedly planning to kill Inkatha leaders (→ 25).

Chernobyl hero dies of leukaemia in US

July 3. In April 1986, in the hours following the world's worst nuclear disaster, Anatoli Grishchenko made repeated helicopter flights over a blazing nuclear reactor at Chernobyl with loads of sand and concrete. Afterwards he was decorated and credited with helping to limit the massive spread of radiation. Today, aged 53, he died in an American hospital of a lung disease related to leukaemia. Grishchenko made a total of five flights over Number 4 reactor while it spewed radioactive emissions into the sky. He was admitted to hospital on 27 April this year.

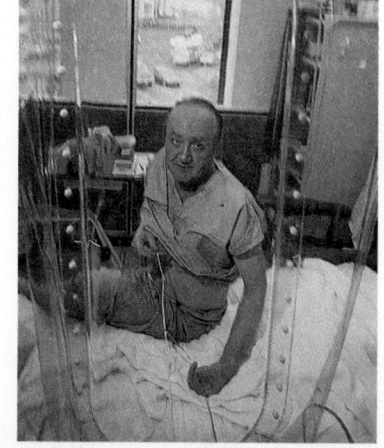

Fighting it: Grischenko in hospital

Air security guards caution flippant MP

July 5. Security men gave a government minister a sharp dressing-down after he had made a flippant remark about a "bomb" in his red dispatch case at Heathrow, it was learnt today. Robert Jackson, the minister for higher education, admitted to a "moment of irritation". Heathrow's security service was in no mood for a joke. Four days ago Jim Swire, the father of a Lockerbie victim, managed to smuggle a "bomb" armed with marzipan onto a Pan Am flight to demonstrate continuing lax security.

Warren Beatty directs and plays the lead in "Dick Tracy", this year's most-hyped film – so far.

July
1990

Su	Mo	Tu	We	Th	Fr	Sa
1	2	3	4	5	6	7
8	9	10	11	12	13	14
15	16	17	18	19	20	21
22	23	24	25	26	27	28
29	30	31				

8. Wimbledon: Stefan Edberg beats Boris Becker 6-2, 6-2, 3-6, 3-6, 6-4, to win the men's singles title.

8. France: Twenty-three Britons are hurt when their holiday coach overturns.

9. Baghdad: Saddam Hussein, the Iraqi president, denies that Iraq possesses a nuclear weapons capability (→ 19).

9. Cumbria: A 15-mile stretch of coast is declared unsafe after items contaminated by the 1983 Sellafield leak are washed ashore (→ 23).

9. London: Melody Radio, a new easy-listening station without any DJs, begins broadcasting.

10. UK: The Advertising Standards Authority accuses British Rail of untruthful advertising.

11. UK: Chris Patten, the environment secretary, warns that wider capping powers will be used next year to reduce poll-tax charges.

11. Havana: Seven Cubans seek political asylum in the Czech embassy, bringing the total taking refuge inside the embassy to 14.

11. Canada: Mohawk Indians and Quebec police fire on each other as a land rights dispute erupts near Montreal.

11. UK: The *Sun* newspaper is censured by the Press Council for publishing "irresponsible" claims that heterosexual sex cannot give you AIDS (→ 27).

11. UK: The home secretary refers the case of the Maguire family, convicted in 1976 of running an IRA bomb factory, to the Court of Appeal.

12. Japan: A magazine describes Melbourne as the sex capital for Japanese tourists visiting Australia.

13. Brindisi: The first 4,500 refugees arrive from Albania.

14. London: The musical "Bernadette" closes after only a month, following scathing reviews.

DEATH

14. Philip Leacock, British film director (*08/10/17).

Ridley quits after "Hitler" outburst

July 14. Nicholas Ridley, the secretary of state for trade and industry, resigned today amid a storm of fury over his anti-German remarks in this week's *Spectator* magazine.

The interview, conducted by Dominic Lawson at Ridley's home after a lunch with which the chain-smoking minister had, readers were reassured, "the smallest glass of wine", began with a skirmish on European monetary union. Ridley called it "a German racket to take over the whole of Europe. It has to be thwarted." An attempt to deflect his fire only made it ricochet onto the European Community, which was run, spat Ridley, by "17 unelected reject politicians" (EC commissioners) and "a supine parliament" whose "arrogance" was "breathtaking". As for handing over sovereignty to "this lot" – "you might just as well give it to Adolf Hitler".

And so on in similar vein. Chancellor Kohl, a spokesman said, was "not amused". Germany's foreign minister claimed Ridley was upset that Germany knocked England out of the World Cup. It was obvious that a trade secretary with such views could hardly negotiate Britain's future in Europe. Ridley did the honourable thing, losing Mrs Thatcher one of her closest comrades and gaining her a fifth cabinet reshuffle in a year (→ 15).

Out: the embarrassing Mr Ridley.

Optimistic ending to Houston summit

July 11. The first post-Cold War summit of the world's seven leading industrial nations ended today with support for Soviet reforms and an uneasy show of unity. The final communique proclaimed the "renaissance of democracy", hiding disagreements between Europe and the US over economic aid for the Soviet Union and farm subsidies.

Nevertheless, the summit in Houston marked a change. Talks on the old themes of inflation, growth and trade were joined by new concerns about the environment and the integration of the Communist bloc into the free market (→ 17).

A quick march-past before the talks.

Albanian refugees reach safety in Prague

Albanian refugees show their passports as they head for freedom.

July 10. The first group of dissident Albanians who stormed into foreign embassies in Tirana last week was flown to Prague this morning on a Czech military aircraft. The arrival of the group, numbering 51, marks the end of long negotiations to extricate the refugees, who occupied embassies to demand the right to leave their country. The Albanian authorities, who are clinging to old-fashioned Stalinist communism, have proved reluctant to embrace the tide of change in Eastern Europe.

The Italian government, meanwhile, is making arrangements to send ships to pick up the 6,000 more Albanians who have taken refuge in the embassies (→ 13).

Israel bombs Hizbollah base in Lebanon

July 9. Israel struck at Hizbollah militia positions in southern Lebanon today with an air raid and a powerful artillery bombardment. Twelve people died when Phantom fighter-bombers fired missiles into the villages of Loweizi and Melita. This attack comes at a sensitive time, just two days after a hint from Iran that another western hostage, possibly the Irishman Brian Keenan, might be released. The Israelis insist that their action was purely military and indignantly reject accusations that it was designed to sabotage any such release (→ 17).

Rebels retreat from centre of Monrovia

Rebel fighters stand guard over a soldier loyal to President Doe.

July 8. The few Monrovians who dared to venture out during a lull in the fighting today found the streets of their capital littered with bodies – including those of children shot and maimed in an orgy of killing. As rebel forces withdrew after a week of fighting and looting, the gravity of Monrovia's situation became clear. The 500,000 population has been without water or electricity for more than a week; and thousands have been reduced to foraging for scraps of food on rubbish dumps as mass starvation looms.

President Samuel Doe took advantage of the lull in fighting to tour the city centre in an open Jeep and announce a six-month ceasefire. Whether his principal opponent – and former friend – the rebel commander, Charles Taylor, agrees is not known. Infighting is reported from behind the rebel lines, with a breakaway faction seeking to oust Taylor (→ 30).

Yeltsin resigns as Gorbachev wins cheers

July 13. President Gorbachev was given a standing ovation today when he made the closing speech at the historic 28th Congress of the Communist Party in the Kremlin. It was a personal triumph for him, because he had forced through his vital reforms of the Central Committee against much opposition.

There were several uncomfortable moments for him during the congress. The worst came yesterday when the radical Boris Yeltsin, the newly-elected president of the Russian republic, announced his resignation from the Communist Party and, to jeers and cheers, marched out of the Kremlin.

Gorbachev also faced trouble from the conservatives in the party, but he brushed them aside, warning them that "no one will be permitted to wreck *perestroika*". To those who accused him of "losing" Eastern Europe he said: "What were we supposed to do? Should we have

Flamboyant Yeltsin makes his point.

used axes and tanks and tried to teach them another lesson in how to live?" He has now secured his position, but his presidency still faces a rocky road ahead (→ 16).

Foul play mars Germany's World Cup win

July 8. West Germany are the champions, but few outside their homeland will remember tonight's lacklustre and ill-tempered World Cup final in Rome with pleasure. A single goal decided the destiny of the competition after a match littered with fouls and during which two players were sent off.

The Argentinians, champions four years ago, could scarcely muster an attack all night. They resorted to negative tactics which kept the Mexican referee busy well before the 68th minute when Monzon became the first player ever to be sent off in a World Cup final. Even so, it took a penalty to break the deadlock before Dezotti became the second Argentinian to be shown the red card (→ 10).

Maradona is shown the yellow card.

Scargill defiant at Durham NUM gala

July 9. Arthur Scargill came out with guns blazing today when he told miners that he had no apologies for his role in the operation of secret NUM accounts during the 1984-5 pit strike. The accounts were the subject of the recent Lightman Report, which, among other things, slammed Scargill for setting up covert funds while the union's official assets had been seized by sequestrators. To an enormous standing ovation at the NUM conference in Durham, the miners' leader said that he was "proud" of what he had done and railed against his "trial by media".

English footballers to return to Europe

July 10. English football teams will be back in European competition next season. The exception will be Liverpool, the team whose supporters were involved in the 1985 riot at the Heysel stadium which led to five years of exile. The decision, agreed unanimously today by UEFA, European football's governing body, follows a relatively peaceful World Cup in which Italian police kept hooliganism under control. Also important was what the British government called the "exemplary behaviour" of the English players who won the "fair play" award in the competition.

Kenya rocked by pro-democracy rioters

July 9. Kenya's capital, Nairobi, closed down early today as rioting broke out for the third day in a row. The violence, which started after a rally to demand multi-party democracy, has spread to six other towns in central Kenya and left eight people dead. President Daniel Arap Moi is facing the worst crisis so far in his troubled presidency. Demonstrators chanting "Down with Moi" have been attacking police with stones and bows and arrows, and the underground Mwakenya organisation has issued a call to "armed insurrection".

President Moi: under fire.

July
1990

Su	Mo	Tu	We	Th	Fr	Sa
1	2	3	4	5	6	7
8	9	10	11	12	13	14
15	16	17	18	19	20	21
22	23	24	25	26	27	28
29	30	31				

15. UK: Peter Lilley succeeds Nicholas Ridley as trade and industry secretary.

15. Oman: Sir Ranulph Fiennes, the British explorer, begins an expedition to find the lost city of Ubar, buried for 2,000 years.

15. Colombo: Tamil Tigers massacre 168 Moslems.

15. Islamabad: A bomb blast in Hyderabad kills 38 people and injures over 100.

15. UK: Cecil Parkinson, the minister of transport, calls for a new inquiry into the sinking of the *Titanic*.

16. USSR: The Ukraine will become a sovereign state (→ 18).

16. Kent: Armed police seize £7 million worth of drugs.

17. UK: Charles Kennedy, with 82 per cent of the vote, is to become the new president of the Liberal Democrats (→20/9).

17. Beirut: Over 30 people die when Hizbollah and Amal militiamen fire on each other.

17. UK: Teacher shortages have increased by 50 per cent in the last year, with south-east England suffering the most (→ 20/8).

18. Washington: The US debates with Vietnam over the fate of Cambodia, in the first talks since 1975 (→ 10/9).

18. Lithuania: The parliament votes to create its own army.

19. Australia: Bob Hawke, the prime minister, withdraws his support from the Victorian premier, John Cain, after the collapse of the Pyramid building society.

20. UK: The NUM executive sues Arthur Scargill for £1.4 million lost during the 1984 miners' strike (→ 25).

21. Berlin: Roger Waters performs "The Wall" in a massive open-air rock concert during which a "Berlin Wall" is built and knocked down.

DEATHS

15. Margaret Lockwood, British film actress (*15/09/16).→

20. Mike Carr, Labour MP for Bootle (*1937).

English girls accused of smuggling heroin

Caught with a massive drugs haul: Patricia Cahill and Karen Smith.

July 19. Two teenage English girls were arrested at Bangkok airport last night as they tried to board a flight to Amsterdam. They were charged with attempting to smuggle a consignment of heroin worth about £4 million out of Thailand, an offence for which they could face life imprisonment.

Patricia Cahill, aged 17, and Karen Smith, aged 19, were carrying 20 kg (44 lb) of heroin hidden in shampoo bottles and coffee and tea containers. They were to fly on from Amsterdam to the Gambia, a major drugs transit point. Both girls' parents thought that their daughters were on holiday in Scotland. Patricia's mother Frances said: "I had no idea she was involved in drugs. She didn't even tell us she was going to Bangkok."

High streets suffer retail sales slump

July 16. Sales in British shops have fallen by the greatest volume for more than ten years, according to official figures released today. Coming hard on last week's figures, which show a rising tide of company bankruptcies, this will be seen by the chancellor, John Major, as the first evidence that high interest rates are finally causing the desired squeeze on consumer spending. Thus the bad news for the high street shops – sales down 2.8 per cent in June – was welcomed as good news in the City where bonds, shares and sterling were all boosted by the figures.

Until now there have been few signs that consumers were cutting spending, despite months of high interest rates – the means by which Major hopes to combat inflation. He also hopes that reduced spending power at home will curb the flow of imports and thus help the balance of payments.

But you cannot please everybody. Some economists and key firms within the Confederation of British Industry, fearing that the medicine may be too harsh and tip the economy into recession, want interest rates to be cut (→ 15/8).

Saddam frees British nurse Daphne Parish after Kaunda plea

July 19. The Iraqi president, Saddam Hussein, has freed the British nurse Daphne Parish from a 15-year jail sentence "for humanitarian reasons". Mrs Parish arrived back in England yesterday after the personal intervention of Zambia's president, Dr Kenneth Kaunda. "Freedom is better than I ever imagined," she said.

She was arrested last autumn, accused of helping her friend, the journalist Farzad Bazoft, to spy on a secret arms plant. Bazoft was executed for spying on 15 March. Mrs Thatcher has expressed her delight, and British diplomats hope that Mrs Parish's release signals an improvement in relations with Iraq, which hit an all-time low with the interception of nuclear triggers and components of an alleged "super-gun" on their way to Baghdad.

Saddam, meanwhile, sent a shiver of fear through the Gulf today

In Iraq, murals acclaim Saddam.

Free: Daphne Parish with daughter.

when he threatened to "cut the necks" of other Arab oil states if they continued to produce more oil than the agreed Opec quotas. His anger is aimed especially at Kuwait, which he accuses of stealing £2.4 billion of oil from a disputed field and of deliberately overproducing to hold down oil prices, damaging Iraq's fragile economy (→ 24).

Bomb fails to halt stock market trade

A city slicker remains unruffled.

July 20. Using an IRA codeword, an Irish voice gave more than eight warnings today before a terrorist bomb blasted the London Stock Exchange. The bomb had been placed overnight in a lavatory at the rear of the visitors' gallery and blew a six-foot gash in the front of the building. Today's bomb marks a shift in direction by IRA bombers. No warnings have been given since the Harrods bombing in 1983: the Stock Exchange is apparently regarded as a "soft" target. In today's attack there were no casualties and little disruption to trading (→ 24).

July 15. Margaret Lockwood, one of Britain's top film actresses, dies, aged 73. She shot to fame in the title role of the highwaywoman in "The Wicked Lady".

Thousands hit in Philippines' quake

July 16. At least 100 people died this afternoon, and many more were injured or missing following the worst earthquake in the Philippines for 14 years. About 800 men, women and children were trapped under a collapsed government building in Baguio, a mountain resort popular with western visitors. At the Philippine Christian College in Cabanatuan 50 students died at their desks while attending the last lecture of the day. The college was at the epicentre of the earthquake – which measured 7.7 on the Richter scale – some 60 miles north of the capital, Manila. President Corazon Aquino said that relief workers had been mobilized and warned that further tremors were expected.

Teams of rescue workers strive to drag shaken survivors from the rubble.

"Rushdie" film banned by British censors

The film distributor Mohammed Fayyaz shows off the poster for the video.

July 21. A Pakistani epic film in which Salman Rushdie, the author of *The Satanic Verses,* is depicted as a sadistic murderer killed by a divine bolt of lightning has been banned by British film censors. The ban is certain to revive the controversy which forced Rushdie to go into hiding. The Iranian death sentence on him still stands. The film's distributor – who expected to sell 5,000 video copies of the film at £20 each – has accused the censor of double standards. Rushdie, still in hiding, is said to be in favour of the film being shown.

Bush has courteous meeting with Kinnock

July 17. In contrast to the cool reception which he received from Ronald Reagan three years ago, the Labour leader Neil Kinnock was given a warm welcome by President Bush in Washington today. According to White House aides, Kinnock appeared to be in tune with Bush on defence policies and the future of Europe. He described the president as "the most courteous man in the western world".

Nigel Mansell pulls in for final pit stop

July 16. Nigel Mansell, the leading British Grand Prix racing driver of the 1980s, today walked off the track at Silverstone and announced that he intends to retire at the end of the season. Mansell, who has won 15 Grand Prix races since his debut in 1980, said he wanted to put his family first. He was speaking after the British Grand Prix had been won by his Ferrari team-mate, Alain Prost. Mansell, who started in pole position, was forced to quit by gear-box problems while in second place. Ferrari hopes he will change his mind (→ 1/10).

Mansell contemplates his future.

July
1990

Su	Mo	Tu	We	Th	Fr	Sa
1	2	3	4	5	6	7
8	9	10	11	12	13	14
15	16	17	18	19	20	21
22	23	24	25	26	27	28
29	30	31				

22. Canberra: For the first time, Asian migration to Australia outnumbers the combined migration from all other areas.

22. Leeds: Riot police raid an "acid house" party and arrest 836 young people.

23. UK: It is announced that PowerGen will be sold not to the small shareholder but to an industrial consortium.→

23. Cumbria: British Nuclear Fuel is fined £1,000 for breaching safety regulations.

24. Iraq: Iraq sends 30,000 troops to the Kuwait border.→

25. UK: The Fraud Squad confirms that it will investigate allegations that Arthur Scargill misled the NUM (→4/9).

25. S Africa: Police arrest Mac Maharaj, a senior ANC member, accused of plotting against the state.→

26. Portugal: The last Citroen 2CV, in production since 1948, rolls off the assembly line.

26. UK: National Power announces the loss of £605 million and 5,000 jobs.

26. UK: Police launch an investigation into 20 missing children, believed to have been murdered in the making of pornographic videos.

27. Geneva: The World Health Organization reports that Aids is the main cause of death for women aged 20-40 (→15/10).

29. Amman: King Hussein of Jordan travels to Baghdad to try to ease the tension between Iraq and Kuwait (→2/8).

30. UK: English legal history is made when a man is jailed for raping his wife; marriage was previously held to be perpetual consent to sex.

30. Liberia: Rebels accuse Samuel Doe, the president, of mass murder (→10/9).

31. Trinidad: Moslems free Arthur Robinson, the prime minister, but continue to hold 40 other hostages (→1/8).

DEATH

24. Alan Clarke, British film director (*28/10/35)

Five die in new wave of IRA violence

Landmine kills nun and three RUC men

July 24. A Catholic nun and three policemen were killed today by an IRA landmine hidden at the side of a road in County Armagh. The bomb was exploded by a command wire run from a bungalow after its occupants had been overpowered and held hostage. The bomb was set off as the officers drove past in their armoured car. Sister Catherine Dunne, who was driving in the opposite direction, was caught in the blast. The IRA expressed its regrets (→30).

The wreckage of Ian Gow's car sits in the driveway where he was killed.

Murdered nun: Catherine Dunne.

MP Ian Gow assassinated by car bomb

July 30. Ian Gow, the Conservative MP for Eastbourne, was murdered by an IRA car bomb at his home in the Sussex village of Hankham today. Police said that the bomb, containing over four pounds (2 kg) of explosive, had been planted overnight under the front seat of his car. He had driven no more than a few feet before it exploded. He died before he could be taken to hospital. A neighbour said that he heard a noise like a door being slammed. The rescue services were called, but they could do nothing for Mr Gow. A forthright opponent of the IRA, Gow knew that he was on its hit list but was determined "not to live in a castle". His opposition to the Anglo-Irish agreement, over which he resigned from the government, made him a target for the bombers, and his refusal to take precautions made him an easy one. He will be greatly missed at Westminster, especially by his friend Margaret Thatcher, for whom he had been a parliamentary secretary (→6/8).

South African communists legalized after 40 years under ground

July 29. South Africa's Communist Party was relaunched today after 40 years under ground. In a speech at a football stadium on the outskirts of Soweto, Nelson Mandela urged the party to support a peaceful transition to democracy and the dismantling of apartheid. He also criticized the government of President de Klerk for alleging that the Communists were manipulating the ANC and planning an armed insurrection.

Mandela has defended the ANC alliance with the Communist Party. He is refusing to drop its leader Joe Slovo from his negotiating team at the next round of talks with the government as he believes it would be damaging for his movement.

Communist Party supporters, wearing ANC uniforms, show their approval.

Chaos follows coup attempt in Trinidad

July 29. Chaos continues to reign in Trinidad after Arthur Robinson, the prime minister, members of his cabinet and 40 other people were seized by Moslem extremists in a coup two days ago. At least 20 people are believed to have died in the arson and looting in the capital, Port-of-Spain. Robinson has been shot in the leg and wired to explosives in an attempt to make him resign and hold new elections.

The leader of the rebels, a former policeman calling himself Imam Yasim Abu Bakr, and an unknown number of followers have taken over the parliament building and television station. Some are armed with AK-47 rifles. Abu Bakr has appeared on television to rail at the government's "oppressive" policies, and says that he will bring drugs charges against Robinson (→ 31).

Scientists puzzled by cornfield circles

July 30. Scientists investigating circular patterns in Wiltshire cornfields were the butt of the British press this week when they fell for circles made by hoaxers. They photographed hovering orange lights, and became ecstatic when dawn revealed new circles in the corn, only to find ouija boards left behind by the jokers. Explanations put forward for the circles included wind patterns, fungus and UFOs.

Mysterious patterns in the cornfields.

New archbishop is a conservative surprise

Caring for his flock: the new Archbishop shows off his grandchildren.

July 25. A moderate conservative who has been a bishop for only two and a half years has defied the tipsters by being named to succeed Dr Robert Runcie as archbishop of Canterbury, the highest ordained position in the Anglican Church.

The new man is Dr George Carey, aged 54, currently the bishop of Bath and Wells. His appointment comes as a surprise to many who tipped Dr John Habgood, the archbishop of York, but he has been welcomed for his vitality and competence. He is regarded as one of the church's evangelicals, who stress the authority of the Bible and are characterized as conservative in their hostile attitude towards, for example, the ordination of homosexuals. This is a change after the relatively liberal Dr Runcie, although Carey is known as a man who listens to many views.

Oil rig crash claims lives of six workers

July 27. Six men drowned in the North Sea today, trapped in the fuselage of a Sikorsky S-61 helicopter. The aircraft crashed on a routine flight for Shell UK Exploration and Production. Seven of the 11 passengers were rescued. The pilot and co-pilot were both among the drowned. In the last 21 years there have been 27 similar incidents in the North Sea with the loss of 110 lives.

Hanson to be paid for PowerGen bid

July 29. Government plans to sell the electricity generating company PowerGen to big business instead of the small investor came under more fire today with the revelation that Hanson Trust could be offered a fee of up to £15 million for opening the bidding. Hanson gives substantial financial aid to the Conservative Party. Labour were quick to accuse the government of "secret deals and privatization sleaze".

OPEC summit pushes up official oil price

July 27. Motorists will face higher petrol prices following today's agreement by Opec, the cartel of oil-producing countries, to put up the official price of oil for the first time for ten years.

The deal, which puts $3 on an $18 barrel and also involves a drop in overall oil production, was made to avert the threat of military action in the Gulf from President Saddam Hussein of Iraq. He wants to rescue his crippled economy by boosting the price of oil – his major export – and has forced the issue in recent weeks in a row with his neighbour, Kuwait, which openly flouts Opec production quotas (→ 29).

Record-breaking week for sports

Faldo and caddy watch the ball.

July 31. British sportsmen have been basking in the sunshine this month. Nick Faldo stormed to a five-shot victory in the Open championship at St Andrew's – his second victory in golf's "major" tournaments this year – to set a new Open record total. England's cricket captain, Graham Gooch, scored 333 in the first innings against India at Lord's. He added 123 in the second innings to help England win a test in which 1,603 runs were scored – the second-highest total ever scored in a test match in England. And Graeme Hick, who qualifies for England next year, scored his 50th first-class century at the age of 24, the youngest person ever to do so.

Gooch: on his way to a record.

August
1990

Su	Mo	Tu	We	Th	Fr	Sa
			1	2	3	4
5	6	7	8	9	10	11
12	13	14	15	16	17	18
19	20	21	22	23	24	25
26	27	28	29	30	31	

1. UK: Neil Kinnock says that the far-left Militant group no longer has any influence in the Labour Party (→ 4/9).

1. UK: Hospital waiting lists are, at 881,000, the highest for six years (→ 8).

1. UK: The government unveils a plan to reduce the over-visiting of tourist attractions such as Bath and the Lake District by promoting new ones such as Wigan and Manchester.

1. Jeddah: Talks to resolve Iraq's claims against Kuwait fail.→

2. London: The Football League announces a return to a 22-club first division, despite opposition from the FA.

2. London: Midland Bank announces the loss of 4,000 jobs after a run of poor results (→ 15).

3. World: Oil prices jump to $26 per barrel (→ 30).

3. Baghdad: Iraq digs its forces in at the Saudi/Kuwait border, but promises to withdraw shortly (→ 4).

3. Cairo: Egypt demands Iraqi withdrawal from Kuwait.→

3. Kuwait: Iraqi forces seize 35 British servicemen.

3. E Germany: Lothar de Maiziere, the prime minister, proposes that unification with West Germany should take place on 13 October (→ 19).

3. North Sea: Oil workers stage a second sit-in to protest against being locked out after a previous strike (→ 9).

4. Tehran: Iran announces that it will seek renewed diplomatic relations with the UK (→ 27/9).

4. Saudi Arabia: Following reports that Iraqi troops have violated the "neutral zone" near the border with Kuwait, Saudi forces are put on full alert (→ 5).

DEATHS

4. Frank Granville Barker, British music critic (*3/6/23).

4. Bernard Falk, British journalist and broadcaster (*1943).

Iraqi forces seize control of Kuwait

Emir flees as battle rages for Gulf state

Aug 2. Iraqi tanks and aircraft stormed across the Kuwaiti border today and, crushing Kuwait's puny defences, have seized control of this tiny oil-rich state on the Gulf of Arabia. Saddam Hussein, Iraq's president, had massed tanks along the border, but few believed that this was more than a bluff. As world leaders universally condemned the invasion, bazooka and machine-gun fire echoed through the streets of Kuwait City. Tanks surrounded government buildings and seized radio and television stations.

Heavy black smoke was seen rising from the area of the Dasman Palace which, according to one eye-witness, was "crawling with Iraqi tanks". The emir, Sheikh Jaber al-Ahmed, has escaped with to Saudi Arabia, but a report from the city suggests that at least one member of the royal family died trying to defend the palace.

One Kuwaiti radio station is still broadcasting desperate appeals for help. "We shall die but Kuwait will live," says the announcer in a shrill voice. "We will make the aggressors taste the chalice of death." Saddam Hussein has threatened to turn Kuwait into a graveyard if any outside power tries to intervene. The 4,500 Britons living in the country have been advised to "keep their heads down".→

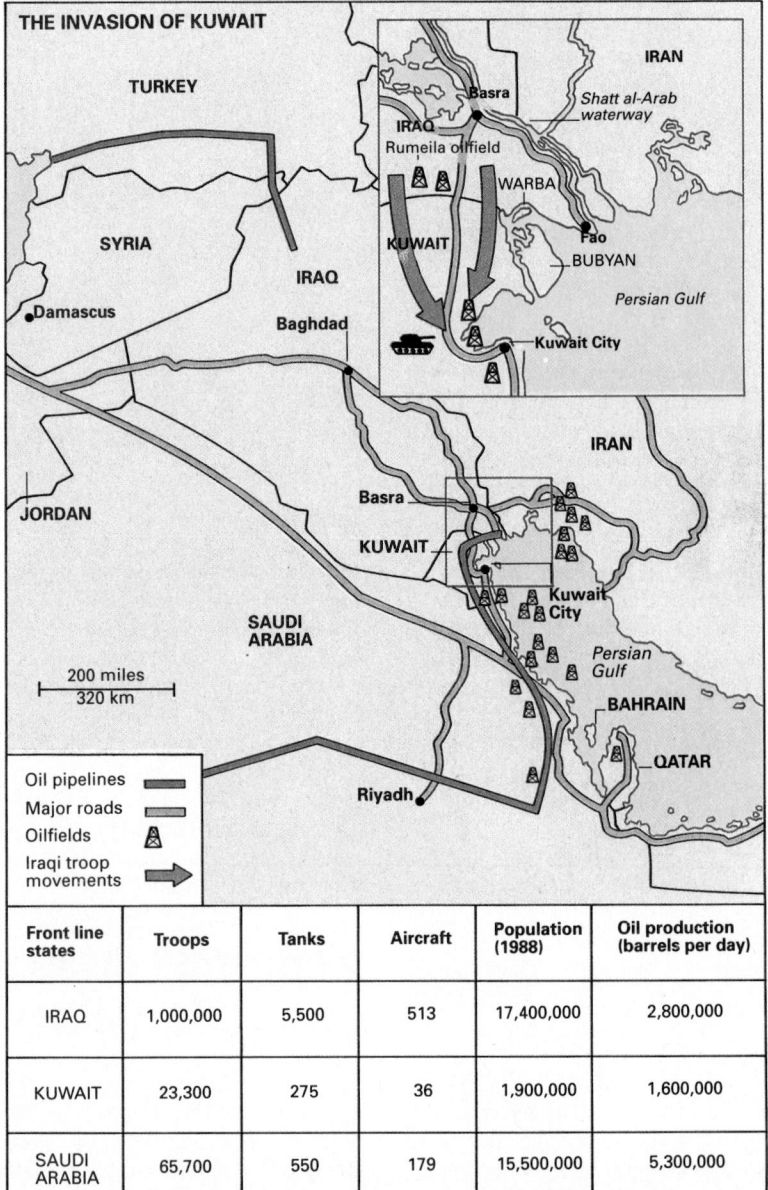

THE INVASION OF KUWAIT

Front line states	Troops	Tanks	Aircraft	Population (1988)	Oil production (barrels per day)
IRAQ	1,000,000	5,500	513	17,400,000	2,800,000
KUWAIT	23,300	275	36	1,900,000	1,600,000
SAUDI ARABIA	65,700	550	179	15,500,000	5,300,000

Drumbeats of war shatter hopes for a more peaceful world

Invading Iraqi armoured personnel carriers blast their way into Kuwait City.

Aug 2. With the end of the "Cold War", the world was hoping for a new era based on the growing harmony between east and west. But now American warships are speeding towards the Gulf as fears grow that Iraq's invasion could trigger war in an area which produces almost one-third of the world's oil supplies. Already oil prices are soaring and Iraqi and Kuwaiti assets frozen. President Bush and Mrs Thatcher, meeting today in Colorado, did not rule out military force to combat what Bush called Iraq's "naked aggression".→

Arab states condemn Saddam Hussein

Aug 3. A majority of Arab nations today called upon Iraq to withdraw its troops from Kuwait. Egypt and Saudi Arabia led a group of smaller states in the Gulf Cooperation Council which denounced President Saddam Hussein for using force against Kuwait. Their declaration came as attempts were made to reconvene an emergency session of the Arab League.

President Mubarak of Egypt wants Arab nations to bury their differences and find an Arab solution to the crisis. The Gulf states, Iran and Egypt are the most hostile to Iraq, with Libya and the Palestine Liberation Organization the most sympathetic. In the middle is Jordan, a volatile kingdom with close links to neighbouring Iraq and acutely vulnerable to any UN-backed trade embargoes (→ 10).

Kuwaitis mourn the brutal conquest.

Iraq isolated by emergency UN resolution

Aug 2. The United Nations has moved swiftly and decisively to condemn Iraq's invasion of Kuwait. The Soviet Union and China were among 14 countries which voted in the UN Security Council for a resolution which also foreshadows sanctions against Iraq. There were no votes against the resolution, and only Yemen abstained.

Security Council members had been roused from their beds by news of the invasion and met through the night. Iraq claimed that its troops were responding to calls for help to form a new government. Kuwait's ambassador said that this was nonsense and unless Iraq was forced to withdraw "no country will be safe". The UN members backed efforts by the Arab League to find a solution, but their resolution allows for a blockade or other military operations should diplomacy or sanctions fail to force Iraq from Kuwait (→ 8).

"New Hitler" casts shadow over Gulf

Aug 4. Saddam Hussein is being branded as another Hitler by the popular newspapers in Britain and the United States this weekend. He is certainly ruthless, using chemical weapons against Kurdish rebels and in the past killing his enemies himself if necessary. He is also unpredictable, surprising the world by his attack on Iran in 1980 as well as by this week's on Kuwait. The love of military uniforms could be seen as another echo of Hitler, as are the fearsome secret police and the cult of a mighty leader seen in vast portraits which now adorn Baghdad.

Saddam: Hitler of the Middle East?

Second rail crash in a week kills driver

Aug 4. Fears that British Rail is still not taking safety seriously have grown, following the second serious railway crash within a week. At Stafford station, a driver was killed – crushed to death in his cab on an empty commuter train which ran into the back of a Manchester to Penzance Inter-City express. The accident occured three days after a collision at Reading station in which a train entered the wrong platform, hitting another train and injuring 29 people. The Labour Party is demanding a national inquiry into rail safety (→ 3/9).

Phew, it's a record-breaking scorcher!

Aug 3. Britain sizzled today as its thermometers recorded the country's hottest day since weather records began. Tempers snapped, forests caught fire, a runway melted at Heathrow and tropical fish were seen in the English Channel. Cheltenham in Gloucestershire recorded the highest temperature – 37.1C (98.8F) – and Londoners were gently grilled as the Weather Centre thermometer hit the 35C mark. Ozone levels rocketed and, with rails starting to buckle, an 80mph speed limit was imposed on high-speed trains.

Attempted Moslem coup in Trinidad fails as hostages are freed

Smiling soldiers arrest one of the Moslem rebels, whose cause is now lost.

Aug 1. Trinidad's Moslem rebels surrendered unconditionally today and released all their 43 hostages. They had kidnapped Arthur Robinson, the prime minister, and seven other government ministers five days ago, demanding Robinson's resignation and fresh elections. But today the coup's leader, Yasin Abu-Bakr, stepped from his headquarters in a television station, holding his rifle above his head. He, and 120 of his followers, are now in custody awaiting trial.

The prime minister, who was released yesterday after earlier promising to resign, is now back in control. The unsuccessful coup attempt is thought to have caused 30 deaths and many more injuries.

Aug 4. Children line up at the gates of Clarence House to wish the Queen Mother – who is 90 today – a very happy birthday.

August
1990

Su	Mo	Tu	We	Th	Fr	Sa
			1	2	3	4
5	6	7	8	9	10	11
12	13	14	15	16	17	18
19	20	21	22	23	24	25
26	27	28	29	30	31	

5. Baghdad: Iraq warns that lives of western nationals here will be in danger if their countries take any military action in the region.→

5. Liberia: Two hundred US Marines arrive to rescue American citizens from the raging civil war (→ 9/9).

5. Pakistan: Opposition parties pass a vote of no confidence in the prime minister, Benazir Bhutto (→ 8).

6. Kuwait: Hundreds of Britons and Americans are transported to Baghdad.

6. London: The foreign office warns Shafiq al-Salihi, the Iraqi ambassador, that his country is responsible for the welfare of all the Britons trapped in Kuwait and Iraq.

6. Pretoria: The African National Congress (ANC) ends its 29-year-old armed struggle against white rule.→

7. Middle East: Saudi Arabia and Turkey shut down Iraqi oil pipelines flowing through their territory.

8. Liverpool: The council, facing a major financial crisis, raises rents by £4 a week.

8. UK: A leaked memo reveals plans to close 2,370 NHS hospital beds in south-east England (→ 9/9).

9. Baghdad: Iraq closes its borders and orders all embassies in Kuwait to move to Baghdad within two weeks (→ 23).

10. Amman: British, Israeli and US flags are burnt at rallies in support of Saddam.

11. Saudi Arabia: As the first squadron of RAF Jaguar fighter-bombers arrives, Saudi guns open fire on Iraqi reconnaissance aircraft (→ 15).

11. Cairo: President Mubarak says that there is no hope of a peaceful solution to the Gulf crisis (→ 16).

11. Sri Lanka: Tamil rebels massacre 144 Moslems in the continuing ethnic violence.

DEATH

9. Joe Mercer, British football manager (*9/8/14).

Benazir Bhutto sacked

Aug 8. Benazir Bhutto was sacked as prime minister of Pakistan today, and her government dissolved, after ruling for just 20 months. She described the action, taken by President Gulam Ishaq Khan, as a "constitutional coup d'etat", but the president accused the government of "wilfully undermining the workings of the constitution" and "scandalous horse-trading for personal interest".

Tonight Miss Bhutto's home is surrounded by soldiers in scenes reminiscent of the arrest of her father on the orders of President Zia. Her father was executed, she was arrested and Zia was murdered by a bomb in his plane. Today's events show the fragility of democracy in Pakistan (→ 12).

Bhutto: dismissed from high office.

IRA bungles attack on Lord Armstrong

Aug 6. The IRA, continuing its campaign of violence in Britain, attempted to kill Lord Armstrong, the former cabinet secretary, with a two-pound (0.9-kg) Semtex car bomb today. It bungled the attempt, however, because its information was out of date and it attached the bomb to a car in the drive of a house from which he moved six years ago.

The car chosen was driven by the present occupant of the house, Miss Cherry Freeman, aged 48, an American computer expert. She had a miraculous escape because the bomb, attached by a magnet and activated by a mercury tilt detonator, fell off and failed to explode as she drove away (→ 13).

Troops are sent in to stop carnage in South African townships

Aug 9. Troops were rushed to the black townships of Port Elizabeth today after violence which has left 33 people dead and 100 injured. Shops, factories and schools have been burnt down and marauding gangs of looters and fire-raisers roam the streets. Ambulances cannot get to the victims and the police are held up by burning barricades.

The trouble began as a political protest against a local increase in rents, but criminal gangs took over the protest. The police retaliated by firing tear gas, and a series of running battles ensued. It is a sad end to a week which began with the signing of an historic peace pact between the government and the African National Congress (→ 15).

Troops move in as a strife-torn Port Elizabeth township goes up in flames.

Thatcher wants European "Magna Carta"

Aug 5. Mrs Thatcher today proposed a new "Magna Carta" to guarantee basic rights for all European citizens. She argued for a stronger United Nations, but compared the European Community to the old Soviet empire. In a speech to the Aspen Institute in Colorado, she said that the new charter should protect the right to "maintain nationhood" and counter "fear of an over-mighty state". And she spoke out against the creation of a centralized European Community (→ 30).

Thatcher makes her views known.

North Sea oil fields again hit by strike

Aug 9. North Sea oil rigs were hit today by the third in a series of unofficial 24-hour strikes, with onshore workers coming out for the first time in support of those working offshore. The strikers are demanding union recognition and the reinstatement of up to 1,000 employees sacked in earlier stoppages. Many contractors in the North Sea refuse to recognize the unions, and more disruption is forecast.

Hussein defies United Nations to annex Kuwait

Aug 8. In an announcement calculated to heighten the tension in the Gulf, President Saddam Hussein of Iraq today defied the United Nations and annexed Kuwait. Baghdad radio repeatedly broadcast news of "an eternal and comprehensive merger" by which "Kuwait should return to the great Iraq, the mother homeland", referring to Iraqi claims to Kuwaiti lands dating from 1961. Saddam claimed yesterday that the invasion of Kuwait was the legitimate outcome of his victory in the Iran-Iraq war.

The move comes just two days after the United Nations Security Council voted to impose some of the toughest sanctions in its history. The council voted by 13 votes to nil (Yemen and Cuba abstained) for a total, mandatory economic blockade of Iraq and occupied Kuwait. The idea is to throttle oil exports, Iraq's main source of income, and prevent Iraq from importing essential supplies or seeking economic support elsewhere.

By invoking Article 51 of the UN Charter, which grants the right of "individual or collective self-defence" if a UN member is attacked, the Security Council has paved the way for military action. President Bush said that it was in the US's national interest to stop Hussein, vowing: "This will not stand. This will not stand, this aggression against Kuwait." Mrs Thatcher has pledged him her full support.→

Saddam calls for holy war against infidel

Victorious: Saddam takes applause.

Aug 10. Saddam Hussein dramatically raised the stakes in the Gulf crisis today by calling for an Arab uprising to topple the Saudi royal family and other Gulf rulers and drive US forces from the region. He called on Arabs everywhere to "rise up and defend Mecca, which has fallen captive to the spears of the Americans and the Zionists ... O Moslems, this is your day to rise up swiftly in defence of the prophet Mohammed. Burn the land under the feet of the aggressive invaders." The tone of the message has raised fears of an Islamic *jihad* [holy war], which could then easily be turned against Israel.→

Arab summit backs Egyptian peace plan

Aug 10. Twelve of the 20 members of the Arab League today demanded that Iraq withdraw from Kuwait. Meeting in Cairo, they voted to endorse UN sanctions against Iraq and send a buffer force to protect Saudi Arabia. The summit also backed the US presence in Saudi. The meeting, convened by President Mubarak of Egypt, failed to find an Arab solution to the crisis. Iraq and Kuwait did sit at the same table for a while, but the Kuwaiti foreign minister fainted during a heated argument with the Iraqis. The emir, clearly shaken, left the summit, and Cairo, before the final session started (→11).

Humiliated: the Emir of Kuwait.

Belligerent Bush draws a line in the sand

President George Bush interrupts his golf game for an important phone call.

Aug 8. President Bush, surrounded by pictures of his family, made a televised address today in which he explained his four objectives in the Gulf: unconditional Iraqi withdrawal from Kuwait, the restoration of Kuwait's legitimate government, a more secure Gulf region and the protection of American lives. With Iraqi troops massing on the Saudi border, President Bush said that the first contingent of US troops, who landed at Dharan today, had drawn a "line in the sand". If Saddam crossed it, there would be war.→

Britain to send troops to back US forces

American soldiers march into camp after their arrival at a Saudi Arabian base.

Aug 8. British air and naval forces will join the multinational effort to defend Saudi Arabia and other Gulf states from Iraq's aggression. The cabinet's overseas and defence committee, chaired by Mrs Thatcher, took the decision today after a one-hour telephone conversation between King Fahd and the prime minister. Labour leaders are backing the move. The foreign secretary, Douglas Hurd, said: "Saddam Hussein now knows that an attack on Saudi Arabia would not be an attack on Saudi Arabia alone" (→11).

August
1990

Su	Mo	Tu	We	Th	Fr	Sa
			1	2	3	4
5	6	7	8	9	10	11
12	13	14	15	16	17	18
19	20	21	22	23	24	25
26	27	28	29	30	31	

12. Bridport: Gemma Lawrence, aged seven, is snatched from a holiday caravan.→

12. Pakistan: Benazir Bhutto is offered an amnesty from charges of corruption, provided that she withdraws from politics (→ 27/10).

13. Oxfordshire: A suspected IRA bomb is discovered in the garden of General Sir Anthony Farrar-Hockley, a former Nato commander (→ 19/9).

13. Kuwait: Iraqi soldiers prevent a British consul from recovering the body of Douglas Croskery.

14. Iran: Ahmad Khomeini, the son of the late Ayatollah, calls Saddam "the modern replica of Hitler".→

14. UK: The audit commission warns that one person in five is evading paying the poll tax (→ 18/9).

15. Washington: "No one should doubt our staying power and determination," President Bush tells Pentagon staff (→ 16).

16. Baghdad: Saddam says that he will send US soldiers home in their coffins, and orders Britons and Americans in Kuwait city to report to two hotels.→

16. Washington: The US warns that it is prepared to use chemical weapons in the Gulf, and sends at least 20 Stealth fighters to Saudi Arabia.→

17. UK: The ban placed on the video "International Guerrillas" is lifted.

17. UK: Manual workers at the Vauxhall car plant win a 12.4 per cent pay rise (→ 14/9).

17. Yugoslavia: Armed Serbian nationalists seize Croatian territory near the town of Knin.

18. Wellington: The All-Blacks lose for the first time in four years, beaten by Australia's rugby team 21-9.

DEATHS

18. Pearl Bailey, US singer and entertainer (*29/3/18).

18. Burrhus Frederick Skinner, US psychologist (*20/3/04).

Crisis grows despite diplomatic effort

George Bush rules out Jordanian plan

Aug 17. The Gulf crisis worsened today as, hours after King Hussein of Jordan's peace mission to the United States had collapsed, Iraqi authorities ordered 4,000 Britons and 2,500 Americans trapped in Kuwait to assemble at hotels. William Waldegrave, a foreign office minister, called this a "grave and sinister development". Fears are growing that the westerners will be held hostage by President Saddam Hussein who yesterday warned that thousands of American soldiers might return home in coffins.

Hopes that the momentum towards war might be halted were further dashed by a frosty meeting between President Bush and King Hussein. The king has been actively seeking a diplomatic solution and last Monday met Saddam Hussein. But western leaders insist that Iraq must leave Kuwait unconditionally and are resisting any linkage between the Gulf crisis and the perennial problems of Palestinians and Israel.

King Hussein described his meeting with President Bush as "very frank, open and candid" – diplomatic euphemisms for disagreements. And, contrary to earlier reports, the king carried no new proposals from Iraq. Talks focused upon Jordan's problems in enforcing UN sanctions (→ 19).

Jordanian demonstrators unleash their anger by burning the Stars and Stripes.

Disappointed: King Hussein has no good news after his meeting with Bush.

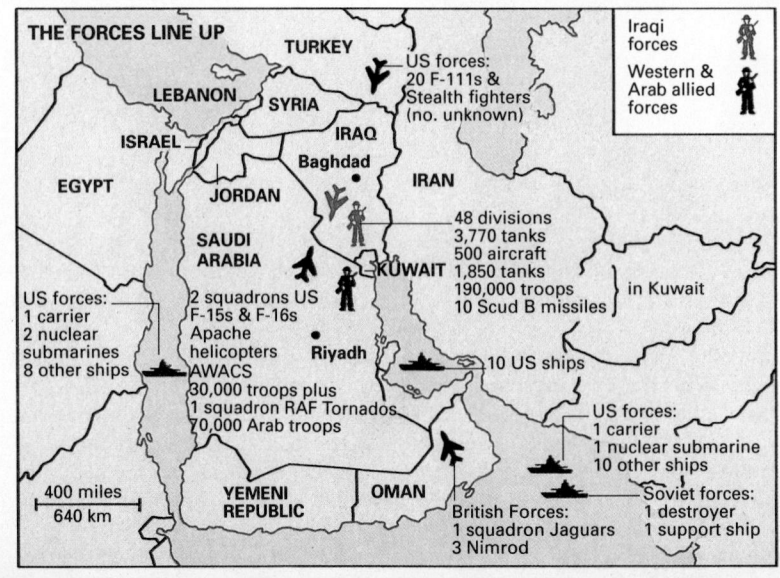

THE FORCES LINE UP

TURKEY

LEBANON   SYRIA

ISRAEL

EGYPT

JORDAN

IRAQ
Baghdad

IRAN

SAUDI ARABIA

KUWAIT

Riyadh

US forces:
20 F-111s & Stealth fighters (no. unknown)

48 divisions
3,770 tanks
500 aircraft
1,850 tanks
190,000 troops
10 Scud B missiles
in Kuwait

2 squadrons US F-15s & F-16s
Apache helicopters
AWACS

US forces:
1 carrier
2 nuclear submarines
8 other ships

30,000 troops plus
1 squadron RAF Tornados
70,000 Arab troops

10 US ships

US forces:
1 carrier
1 nuclear submarine
10 other ships

Iraqi forces

Western & Arab allied forces

400 miles
640 km

YEMENI REPUBLIC

OMAN

British Forces:
1 squadron Jaguars
3 Nimrod

Soviet forces:
1 destroyer
1 support ship

Build-up continues

Aug 18. Troops from 12 nations are involved in the "Desert Shield" force now being assembled in the Gulf. Already in Saudi Arabia are 30,000 US soldiers plus aircraft and anti-tank weapons. Also in Saudi Arabia are ground forces from Morocco, Syria, Egypt and Saudi Arabia itself, plus an RAF squadron from Britain. The US, Britain and – to a much smaller extent – the Soviet Union have ships in the region. Reinforcements are coming from Australia, Belgium, Canada, France and West Germany, but so far the only western ground forces are American.

Saddam frees forces by bowing to Iran

Iranian soldiers arrive back home after their long stay in Iraqi prison camps.

Aug 16. President Saddam Hussein of Iraq today offered to end ten years of conflict with Iran, buying peace with one arch-enemy in order to concentrate Iraq's forces against the international army now being mustered in Saudi Arabia following the invasion of Kuwait.

A truce was reached in 1988, after eight years of war between the countries in which a million people are thought to have died. Today Saddam Hussein offered a formal peace treaty which accepts all of Iran's key demands. It was hailed by Ali Akbar Velayati, the foreign minister in Tehran, as the "biggest victory" in his country's history.

Iraq's territorial claims along the border and the Shatt al-Arab waterway, which were the ostensible cause of its invasion of Iran in 1980, will now be abandoned. Up to 24 divisions – about 300,000 men – could be redeployed along its southern borders (→ 12/9).

Gulf conflict claims first British casualty

Aug 12. The Gulf crisis claimed its first British victim today when Iraqi soldiers shot dead a businessman trying to flee Kuwait. Douglas Croskery, the manager of a printing company, was apparently helping to dig out Kuwaiti families whose cars had become stuck in the sand on the Saudi Arabian border when the soldiers opened fire on the group. Two other Britons and an American who were in other cars in the convoy said that Mr Croskery was left bleeding in the sand.

"This tragic death is a direct result of the Iraqi occupation of Kuwait," said the foreign office. "We are mobilizing the international community to bring renewed pressure on Iraq to let foreigners leave both Kuwait and Iraq" (→ 13).

British casualty: Douglas Croskery.

Rampaging Zulus bring township deaths

The ugly face of township violence.

Aug 15. Running battles between Zulu workers of the *Inkatha* movement and rival Xhosa tribesmen raged out of control in three black townships outside Johannesburg today. At least 150 people have been killed. "It is a battlefield. There are corpses all over the place," said one policeman.

The trouble started after a weekend rally by the African National Congress. The Zulus, claiming they had been attacked by ANC supporters, went on the rampage. Armed with *pangas* and spears they roared through the streets. Some residents claim that policemen accompanied the Zulus on house-to-house raids, but the police deny this and insist they are trying to impose order "without showing favour" (→ 22).

Missing girl found

Safe and well: Gemma Lawrence.

Aug 14. Gemma Lawrence, the missing seven-year-old girl, was found unhurt today after police surrounded a house near Bridport, in Dorset. A man aged 23 was charged with having snatched her two days ago as she slept in her parents' caravan on a site just 300 yards away.

Denning speaks out and raises hackles

Aug 16. Lord Denning, the former master of the rolls, has stunned his admirers with an outrageous interview in *The Spectator*, out today, in which he says that if the Birmingham Six (whose conviction on terrorist offences is under review) had been hanged, they "would have been forgotten" and "we shouldn't have had all these campaigns to get them released". The Guildford Four, released because they were wrongly convicted, were probably guilty and should also have been hanged, he said.

He went on to attack the supremacy of European law over British law, describing Sir Leon Brittan, the European commissioner, as a "German Jew telling us what to do with our law". Sir Leon was, in fact, born in London and is of Lithuanian extraction.

Carpets-to-furniture giant bites the dust

Aug 15. Lowndes Queensway, Britain's largest furniture and carpet retailer, today closed down its 270 stores and sent 4,000 employees home. Faced with debts of almost £300 million, the group has called in the receivers. The events have served to underline Britain's retail slump. Customers who turned up at the stores today – many of them to collect goods for which they have paid in full – found the doors locked and a bemused staff unwilling to talk (→ 10/9).

Showdown at a Queensway store.

August
1990

Su	Mo	Tu	We	Th	Fr	Sa
			1	2	3	4
5	6	7	8	9	10	11
12	13	14	15	16	17	18
19	20	21	22	23	24	25
26	27	28	29	30	31	

19. E Germany: Social Democrats quit the government, leaving the prime minister, Lothar de Maiziere, without a parliamentary majority.→

19. New York: The UN Security Council demands that Iraq free all foreigners held against their will, and sends two envoys to Baghdad.→

19. Islamabad: Pakistan denounces Iraq and sends 5,000 troops to aid Saudi defence forces (→ 20).

20. Kuwait: Eighty-two Britons are rounded up by Iraqi troops (→ 25).

21. Washington: The US rejects an Iraqi offer of talks to resolve the Gulf crisis.

21. Paris: Nations of the Western European Union meet, and agree a unified response to events in the Gulf.

21. Kuwait: Saddam moves Scud-B missiles, capable of delivering chemical and nerve-gas weapons, into place near the Saudi border.

21. Australia: The government promises to abolish unemployment benefit.

22. Washington: President Bush calls up the reserves.

22. UK: The City is disappointed by news that in July the trade deficit increased to £1,400 million (→ 14/9).

23. Kuwait: Many western embassies defy Iraqi orders to close by midnight tonight (→ 24).

23. USSR: The republic of Armenia declares independence from Moscow (→ 27).

23. UK: The government rules out the sale of Powergen to a private company, reinstating the plan to float the generating company on the stock market.

24. S Africa: A state of emergency is imposed on 27 townships as the death toll reaches 500 (→ 31).

24. Kuwait: Iraqi soldiers ring the British, US and 20 other embassies which have ignored orders to close (→ 9/9).

25. UK: Government figures show that Britain's teachers are among the worst-qualified in Europe.

Brian Keenan is set free

Aug 24. An ordeal of 1,597 days in captivity ended yesterday for the Irish hostage Brian Keenan when the mysterious Islamic Dawn organization handed him over to Syrian officers in Beirut. The 39-year-old teacher looked pale and haggard as he was greeted by the Irish ambassador in Damascus. Mr Keenan will be flown back to Dublin as soon as possible. His two sisters, who have campaigned continually for his release, are on their way to fly home with him. His release has inevitably raised hopes that Terry Waite, John McCarthy and other western hostages will soon be freed as well (→ 30).

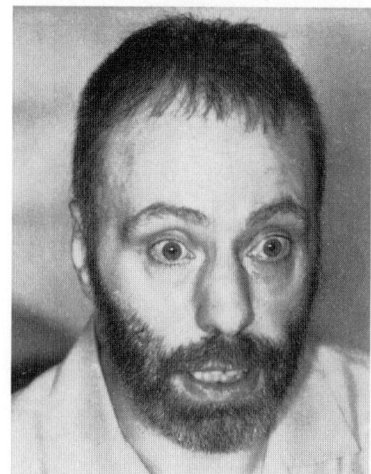
Still dazed: Keenan, free once more.

East Germans agree date for reunification

East German president De Maiziere.

Aug 23. In the early hours of this morning, the East German *Volkskammer* [parliament] chose 3 October as the date on which the two halves of Germany will be reunited. Spokesmen from east and west greeted the decision with joy and relief, for it has taken months of fierce argument to agree on a date. The West German chancellor, Helmut Kohl, said: "3 October will be a great day in the history of our people." Hans-Jochen Vogel, the leader of the Social Democrats, said it was a cause for celebration that "the Germans will once again live together in a single state" (→ 12/9).

British children are ill-taught, says don

Aug 20. Britain is selling its schoolchildren short, according to Sir Claus Moser, the warden of Wadham College, Oxford and vice-president of the British Association for the Advancement of Science. In a speech to the British Association, Sir Claus today warned that "hundreds of thousands of children have educational experiences not worthy of a civilized nation". The problems of a demoralized and underskilled teaching profession and the fact that only one child in three stays on at school after the age of 16 are compounded, he said, by ten years of government cuts in education spending. He called for a royal commission to assess the country's ailing education system.

Moser: critical of schooling.

Violence still tears townships apart: corpses litter the streets

Aug 22. Corpses littered the dusty streets of South African townships this morning after a night of terror in which nearly 100 people died, bringing the death toll in the past ten days of inter-communal fighting to over 500. Migrant Zulu workers of Chief Buthelezi's *Inkatha* movement and supporters of the African National Congress have been pursuing a bitter struggle which has brought only suffering to the blacks and satisfaction to those who wish to preserve apartheid.

Much of the fighting has taken place in Johannesburg suburbs, with black mobs attacking the security forces trying to separate them. Inkatha and the ANC have issued a joint plea for peace (→ 24).

Residents of Kagiso township cremate the body of a dead Inkatha Zulu.

Western hostages are dragged to centre stage

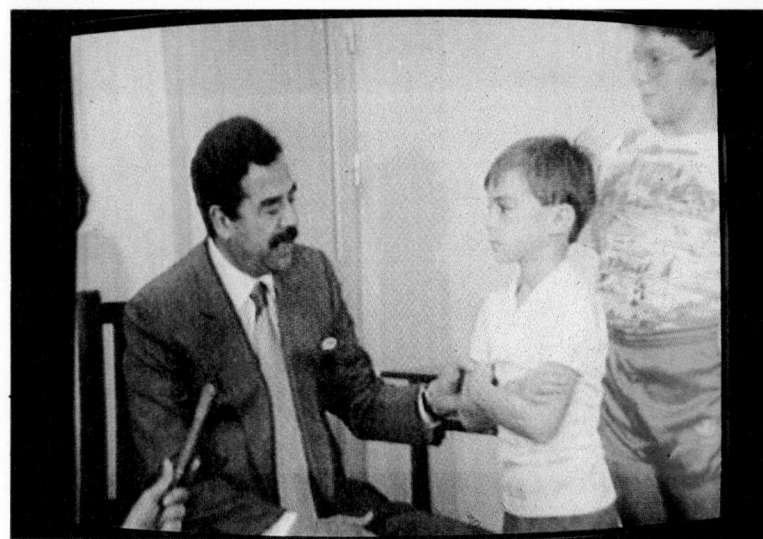

Stuart Lockwood shrinks away from the Iraqi president, Saddam Hussein.

Desperate conditions at the Marj al-Hamman camp, near Amman in Jordan.

Broadcast stars Saddam with "guests"

Aug 23. In a bizarre broadcast that has stunned the west, Saddam Hussein has appeared on TV to meet a selection of his "guests". The Iraqi president assured about 15 British hostages that they were "heroes of the peace" who by their presence would prevent a Gulf war.

Dressed in a grey casual suit, he was apparently trying to cultivate a new peaceful image, smiling as he reached out to ruffle the hair of a six-year-old British boy, Stuart Lockwood, asking him if he was getting enough cornflakes. The boy squirmed nervously. After a brief question and answer session Saddam's bodyguards lined them up for a collective photograph.

Saddam seems to have believed that the broadcast would allay fears about the welfare of hostages. But their obvious discomfort, and his handling of a frightened little boy, served only to underline the real danger in which he has placed them. As the broadcast took place, Iraq announced plans to use six Baghdad warehouses to detain 3,000 foreign "guests" (→ 24).

Jordan moves to stem flood of refugees

Aug 22. Jordan tonight sealed its border with Iraq, desperate to stop the flow of foreigners fleeing Iraq and occupied Kuwait. Over 40,000 people, mainly from Egypt, the Far East and the Indian subcontinent, have crossed the border today, bringing the total number of refugees in Jordan to 140,000.

The area around the Ruweishid border post has become a vast transit camp, and relief organizations are hurriedly setting up refugee camps outside Amman. The new arrivals need to be fed, watered and housed while arrangements are made to get them home.

The refugees are exhausted by their long journeys to Jordan, and often distressed by their losses in Kuwait. Iraqi troops are accused of looting their businesses and stealing their goods; the invasion has wiped out their savings and destroyed their businesses. Most of the Indians, Bangladeshis and Thais sent much of their earnings back home to support their dependent families. Now they will have to find other ways of supporting them.

Sabre-rattling Bush speaks of hostages

Aug 20. President Bush made it clear today that he was prepared to take the US to war in defence of national interests and international stability. Speaking at a war veterans' rally, he described American citizens detained in Iraq and Kuwait as "hostages" for the first time and stressed that he expects Saddam Hussein to ensure their safety.

He also warned the American people that the conflict ahead would need "planning, patience, and yes, personal sacrifice, a sacrifice that we must and will meet if we are to stop aggression". It sounds as if he believes that war in the Gulf is now inevitable (→ 22).

Lucky escapers: the Maine family.

Westerners brave Iraqi soldiers in search of desert escape route

Aug 25. Many of the western hostages in Iraq and occupied Kuwait are ignoring the official advice from their embassies to stay put and keep a low profile, choosing to make a risky dash for freedom across the desert. They say that they would rather risk the Iraqi patrols and the dangers of the desert than wait for events to unfold in the Gulf.

Typical among them are the power station workers (seven Britons and one Australian) who drove for 43 hours in a truck to get from Baghdad to the Syrian border. They said that they spotted no Iraqi troops and were amazed when they realised they had made it into Syria. "I wanted to go home. If I had to walk I would have walked," said Martin Watts, an engineer. The usual escape route from Kuwait, where British and US citizens are now being rounded up on the streets, is via Saudi Arabia. Convoys of jeeps – anything else gets stuck in the sand – leave at nightfall. Bedouins, said to know every grain of sand in the desert, act as guides. Greg and Patricia Maine and their children (from Bristol), for example, reached Bahrain after driving out of Kuwait.

Most westerners still prefer to stay where they are, hoping for a diplomatic breakthrough to ensure their release. The pressure on the families left behind at home is agonizing, as reports of Iraq's "human shield" trickle through (→ 28).

August
1990

Su	Mo	Tu	We	Th	Fr	Sa
			1	2	3	4
5	6	7	8	9	10	11
12	13	14	15	16	17	18
19	20	21	22	23	24	25
26	27	28	29	30	31	

26. Washington: The US says that it will give sanctions time to bite before mounting a military attack on Iraq.→

26. Iraq: Saddam Hussein allows 50 dependents of US diplomats to leave.

26. Yugoslavia: A gas fireball rips through a coal mine, killing 178 miners.

27. Gulf: Qatar invites foreign forces onto its territory to defend it against a possible attack.

27. Baghdad: Iraqi captains are ordered to stop and allow their ships to be searched if challenged by US patrols in the Gulf.→

27. Sofia: Anti-communist demonstrators ransack the headquarters of the Bulgarian Socialist Party.

28. Baghdad: Saddam Hussein formally erases Kuwait by making it the 19th province of Iraq. He gives Kuwait City a new name: Kadimah.

28. London: Police Constable Lawrence Brown is shot dead while investigating a suspected car theft in Hackney.

28. London: England win the England v India Test series (→1/9).

29. Washington: The US announces a $6,000 million arms deal with Saudi Arabia.

29. Vienna: Oil-exporting countries agree to boost production to make up the deficiency caused by the embargo on Iraqi oil.→

30. Helsinki: Mrs Thatcher upsets many EC foreign ministers by accusing them of a hesitant and inadequate response to the Gulf crisis (→2/9).

30. UK: Two days after their conviction, the three guilty Guinness businessmen are moved to an open prison; most prisoners must wait for an average of eight weeks for a transfer (→25/9).

31. Moscow: President Gorbachev calls for a political settlement in the Gulf (→5/9).

31. S Africa: President de Klerk opens his National Party to all races (→9/9).

Captive women and children set free

Aug 28. Women and children held in Iraq and Kuwait can go home. This was announced last night by the Iraqi government after President Saddam Hussein had met a group of westerners – "guests" as he called them, but hostages since the invasion of Kuwait.

Some two million foreigners, no fewer than 800,000 of whom were Egyptians, were in Iraq and Kuwait at the time of the invasion. Huge problems have been caused as this migrant army trekked home, notably along the Jordanian border. But at least the Iraqis have not blocked the exit of Africans, Asians (apart from Japanese), Latin Americans and East Europeans. Others have not been so lucky, and many American and European men have been taken to potential military targets to act as human shields in the hope of deterring attack.

Saddam hopes that by allowing the women and children home he will increase the pressure on western governments to start talks. US and British officials have welcomed the news, but have said that all foreigners who wanted to leave should be allowed to do so (→2/9).

Saddam walks with his henchmen.

West tightens blockade as troops pour in

Helicopters come down to land on the French aircraft carrier "Clemenceau".

Aug 31. The relentless build-up of US military forces in the Gulf continues. More tanks and helicopters are on their way from West Germany and F-16 fighter planes from Spain. More than 60,000 US troops are now in Saudi Arabia to back up a formidable array of high-tech military equipment now patrolling the Gulf. Dick Cheney, the US defense secretary, insists that the force is there to deter attacks and to enforce the blockade – not to take offensive action against Iraq. President Bush knows that such action would jeopardize the international alliance which he has formed against Saddam Hussein, especially when he wants more countries to help to finance the costly operation (→4/9).

Soaring fuel prices squeeze motorists

Aug 30. Petrol prices in Britain jumped again from midnight when Esso added 8.2p to a gallon, taking the price of a gallon of four-star to 225.9p – 30 per cent higher than before tension over Kuwait sparked the first price rise in July. Other oil companies are expected to follow Esso's lead, fuelling inflationary fears and prompting accusations that they are cashing in on the crisis. Crude oil prices have eased back from $30 a barrel to around $25.60 this week, but oil companies say that they are still 50 per cent above levels last month (→24/9).

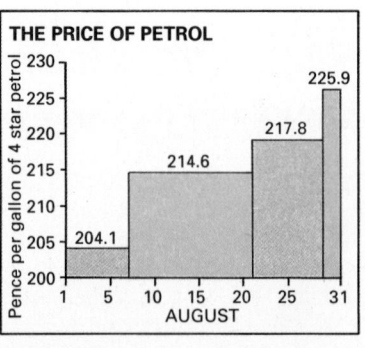

THE PRICE OF PETROL

Pence per gallon of 4 star petrol

August	Price
1	204.1
10	214.6
20	217.8
31	225.9

UN chief finds no easy answers in search for diplomatic solution

Aug 31. Javier Perez de Cuellar, the UN secretary-general, spent five hours today in Baghdad locked in talks with Iraqi leaders in a bid to find a diplomatic solution to the Gulf crisis. Further talks with Tariq Aziz, Iraq's foreign minister, will be held today, but there are no signs of a breakthrough. Senor Perez de Cuellar, who described his talks as "constructive", welcomed the promise to release women and children, but said that all foreigners should be allowed to leave. Mr Aziz sought to link the Gulf crisis, which he blamed on western forces, to peace talks on the Palestinian problem. For the UN, though, this is secondary to its unanimous call for Iraq's withdrawal from Kuwait. President Bush wished the UN leader well, but said he was not optimistic that the peace mission would succeed.

Corrupt Guinness city men sent to prison

Ernest Saunders: five years prison.

Gerald Ronson: £5 million fine.

Parnes (here, with wife): 18 months.

Aug 28. Large fines and prison sentences were imposed on three men at the centre of the Guinness scandal today. Yesterday, a jury had found them guilty of theft, false accounting and conspiracy in an operation to support the price of shares during Guinness's takeover of Distillers four years ago.

Tony Parnes, a stockbroker, collapsed in the dock just as Mr Justice Henry was preparing to pass sentence. But the court was later reconvened and Parnes was sentenced to 18 months' imprisonment. Gerald Ronson, the garage and property tycoon, was fined £5 million and jailed for a year. The judge said that Ronson's charitable work had persuaded him to award a shorter prison sentence. Ernest Saunders's daughter was in tears as her father, the former Guinness chairman, was sentenced to five years' imprisonment for "dishonesty on a massive scale". Sir Jack Lyons, also found guilty, is too ill to be sentenced today (→ 30).

Lamb dispute turns into ugly violence

Aug 31. Baton-wielding French riot police clashed with farmers demonstrating against imported British meat today. About 100 farmers had lain down in front of lorries carrying sheep and cattle as they tried to leave a ferry in Calais.

At Sisteron, in southern France, farmers searched all British lorries until one carrying lamb was found. Sixty-five carcasses were burnt on the spot, and 85 were dumped at government offices. Britain has protested at the lack of protection for British lorry drivers (→ 7/9).

"Birmingham Six" case is reopened

Aug 29. The home secretary, David Waddington, today announced that the case of the "Birmingham Six" – sentenced in 1975 to life imprisonment for bombing two Birmingham pubs in which 21 people died – is to be sent back to the court of appeal. New forensic evidence suggests that police may have fabricated a key statement on which two of the men were convicted. Supporters of the Six hope that their case will end like that of the Guildford Four – in their names being cleared and their being released from prison.

Canadian Mohawks' land protest over

A militant Mohawk keeps watch.

Aug 29. Armed troops in full battle order watched today as Mohawk warriors began to dismantle barricades which have blocked a major bridge across the St Lawrence river near Montreal. The Mohawks had been told that, unless they came out from behind the barricades and surrendered their weapons, soldiers would be prepared to use whatever force was necessary to overwhelm them. Troops were ordered in when police failed to stop fighting between the Mohawks, who are claiming an ancient right to the land, and angry local residents.

Returned hostage evokes "crucifying aloneness" of Beirut hell

Keenan is flanked by his sisters and the Irish premier, Charles Haughey.

Aug 30. Brian Keenan today spoke of his four years and four months as a hostage in Beirut – and confirmed that at least one British hostage, John McCarthy, is alive. After a joyous reception from his fellow Irishmen, Keenan faced the press in Dublin and gave a moving description of the ordeal that he shared with other hostages.

"Hostage is a crucifying aloneness ... it is a silent, screaming slide into the bowels of ultimate despair. Hostage is a man hanging by his fingernails over the edge of chaos, feeling his fingers slowly straightening," he said, going on to pay tribute to the men he left behind, especially McCarthy, whose sense of humour played a major part in keeping them all sane.

International aid starts to flow as refugees from Iraq and Kuwait continue to stream into Jordan.

September
1990

Su	Mo	Tu	We	Th	Fr	Sa
						1
2	3	4	5	6	7	8
9	10	11	12	13	14	15
16	17	18	19	20	21	22
23	24	25	26	27	28	29
30						

1. Nottingham: Prince Charles has a hip-bone graft on his arm, broken in a polo match in July.

1. London: Lancashire beat Northamptonshire to win the NatWest trophy, becoming the first side to win both the NatWest and the Benson & Hedges cups in the same summer (→ 20).

2. Baghdad: Iraqi newspapers say that Mrs Thatcher is a "circus buffoon ... vomiting poison like a spotted serpent".

3. New Zealand: Just weeks before a general election, Geoffrey Palmer, the prime minister, resigns.

3. London: Robert Morgan, the driver of a train which crashed at Purley in March 1989, killing five passengers, receives six months' jail for manslaughter (→ 13).

4. Gulf: US Marines take over an Iraqi freighter which was on its way to deliver tea to Basra.→

4. Baghdad: Over 300 British women and children arrive from Kuwait in a fleet of chartered buses.

4. Devon: A fire destroys the historic town centre of Totnes.

5. Cambodia: The US agrees to take part in talks with the government in Phnomh Penh (→ 10).

5. Moscow: President Gorbachev holds fruitless talks with the Iraqi foreign minister, Tariq Aziz (→ 9).

7. Saudi Arabia: The exiled Emir of Kuwait pledges $5,000 million to help fund military operations against Iraq.

7. UK: Mrs Thatcher sacks Michael Forsyth as chairman of the Scottish Conservative Party, promoting him to minister of state at the Scottish office.

DEATHS

2. Robert Holmes a Court, Australian entrepreneur (*27/7/37).→

6. Sir Leonard Hutton, English cricketer (*23/6/16).→

7. Alan John Percival Taylor, British historian (*25/3/06).→

Gulf conflict hardens into stalemate

Iraqis are prepared for a lengthy siege

Sept 6. Sanctions, now in their fifth week, are starting to bite in Iraq. But it is far from certain that they will succeed in forcing Saddam Hussein out of Kuwait. Analysts say that Iraq has stockpiled enough spare parts to ensure that industry, and the colossal war machine, can keep going for a long time.

Saddam's propaganda machine is working hard to prove that sanctions are hurting only the old, the young and the sick. He has claimed that the US is taking milk away from Iraq's children, and doctors have testified to desperate shortages of medical supplies. Meanwhile, matters are confused by the many countries – including India and Pakistan – who are anxious to get food and drugs to their nationals still stranded in Iraq or Kuwait.

Food stocks remain high, with up to 18 months' supply of rice and wheat stored away, and fresh vegetables are still reaching the shops. Rationing of basic foodstuffs has been in force for four days, but there are said to be no shortages. The only difference is that the Iraqi people have to go to designated shops for various foodstuffs. In any case, they are used to the hardship of war. "Bread and dates," said one old man in Baghdad, "bread and dates. That's all you need" (→ 14).

Where east and west meet: Saudis offer shade and water to the US military.

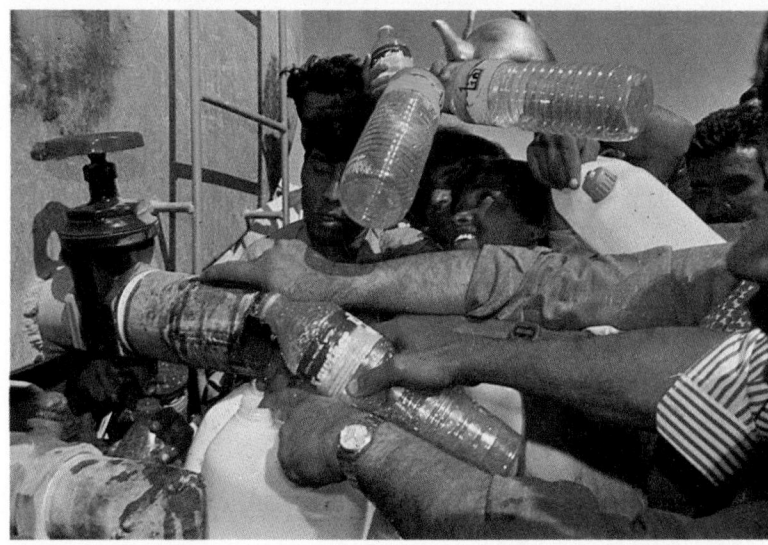

Refugees fight for water at a refugee camp near the Jordanian/Iraqi border.

Britons fly home in a blaze of publicity

Sept 2. Just before first light today, an Iraqi Airways jumbo jet touched down at Heathrow, bringing 199 British women, children and teenagers – who until yesterday were the unwilling "guests" of President Saddam Hussein – to freedom. Under the glare of television lights, the first families to be released since their detention in Baghdad emerged from the aircraft to be greeted by a mob of relatives, journalists and politicians.

For most of the women it was a joyful homecoming – always tempered by the knowledge that many of their husbands were still being used as human shields by the Iraqi dictator. Everyone was pleased to see little Stuart Lockwood, whose hair the dictator had ruffled in a chilling broadcast, come off the plane – even if it was in the arms of the Rev Jesse Jackson, who brought his own TV crew to film the event. It looked for a moment as if the poor boy was being used for political capital yet again.

All were exhausted. It is five days since they were told that they could go, but there was never certainty that they would actually leave Iraq until they took off. There were few complaints about their treatment. "They gave us everything – except our freedom," said one woman.

Entrepreneur dies of a heart attack

Sept 2. Robert Holmes a Court, the Perth businessman who came within an ace of acquiring Australia's largest company, BHP, died today of a heart attack. He was 53. Australia's second-richest man (after Kerry Packer), Holmes a Court controlled an estimated A$800 million of assets, mostly in Australia and Britain. He was recognized as a master of business strategy and a shrewd investor who out-thought his business opponents and forced leading companies to become more efficient by exposing them to the threat of takeover.

Hutton bats for the umpire in the sky

Striking out: England's first professional cricket captain in his prime.

Sept 6. Sir Leonard Hutton, one of the century's greatest cricketers and the first professional to captain England, died today, aged 74, after suffering a stroke. An elegant opening batsman with an exemplary technique, he made his debut for Yorkshire at the age of 18 and was only 22 when he set a test record score of 364 against Australia in 1938. In 1953 he became captain of England, winning back the Ashes that summer and retaining them in Australia two years later. Despite losing six years of his career to the war, he scored over 40,000 runs at an average of 55, including 129 centuries of which 19 were in tests.

Scargill deserted by Labour leadership

Sept 4. Arthur Scargill sat stony-faced among his fellow TUC delegates in Blackpool today as Neil Kinnock accused him of demanding "special favours" from a future Labour government. Although he did not mention the controversial miners' leader by name, the Labour leader pulled no punches.

Two days ago Scargill called for concessions to the miners, just as Mrs Thatcher had granted concessions to her class. Kinnock told the conference: "The purpose of what we do is not favours – it's justice." Referring to Scargill's style of leadership, he said it was a peculiar set of principles that "produces martyrdom for the followers and never sacrifice for the leaders". He was given a standing ovation (→ 15).

Scargill: increasingly isolated.

British athletes strike gold in Europe

Sept 1. British athletes today completed their best-ever haul of gold medals in the European athletics championships at Split, in Yugoslavia. Their victory in the final event of the championships – the men's 4 x 400 metres relay – gave them nine gold medals alongside five silvers and four bronzes. Only East Germany fared better.

Hopes of a clean sweep of the men's short and middle-distance track events were dashed in an event which was once a British preserve. Injury-hit Steve Cram and Peter Elliott failed to get any medals in the 1,500 metres. But Christie (100m), Regis (200m), Black (800m), Jackson (110m hurdles), Akabusi (400m hurdles) and Backley (javelin) all struck gold, as did Yvonne Murray (3,000m) the lone female British champion.

Linford Christie wins the 100 metres.

Koreans talk at last

Sept 7. After 45 years of mutual hostility, the divisions between North and South Korea may finally be coming to an end. Delegates from both sides – which are still technically at war – met at the border today and parted smiling, with promises to meet again. Delegates agreed to discuss economic cooperation and more cross-border travel when they next meet. A meeting between the president of South Korea, Roh Tae Woo, and Kim Il Sung, his northern counterpart, was also discussed.

TV historian dies

Sept 7. The historian A J P Taylor, who died today aged 84, was a television star and journalist as well as an academic. His unscripted TV lectures became unexpectedly popular and Taylor relished the role of bringing history to the people. He was also in the public eye as a newspaper columnist and as one of the founders of CND. But his enduring fame will be as an Oxford historian, the author of many closely-argued, always-readable and often controversial books such as *The Origins of the Second World War* (1961).

Violence stepped up as Anglo-French "lamb war" rumbles on

Unsavoury hotpot: British lamb, intercepted by French farmers, is burnt.

Sept 7. A French lorry driver was attacked and savagely beaten this morning on the M2 in Kent. Police have said that the assault may be linked with recent attacks by French farmers on British meat and livestock. Eric Gunther, aged 28, who was carrying pharmaceutical goods, was forced over at 3.30am by a white Ford Fiesta before being dragged from his cab and attacked by three men armed with a bat and a wooden stave. He was left bleeding. Feelings in Britain are running high over the French farmers' actions. Yesterday alone, 400 British lambs were hijacked and burnt as the "lamb war" intensified.

Sept 5. Forbidden by law to embrace in public, gay activists stage a defiant "kiss-in" in London.

September
1990

Su	Mo	Tu	We	Th	Fr	Sa
						1
2	3	4	5	6	7	8
9	10	11	12	13	14	15
16	17	18	19	20	21	22
23	24	25	26	27	28	29
30						

9. S Africa: Thirty-five people die in a new wave of township violence.→

9. UK: A survey shows that one in five dentists will stop doing NHS treatment when the new contract comes into force.

10. Baghdad: Iraq offers free oil to the Third World countries, provided that they come and collect it.

10. Pakistan: The government files two charges of abuse of power against Benazir Bhutto.

10. UK: Pegasus, one of the country's largest travel operators, goes bust.

11. Moscow: The Russian Federation parliament votes to adopt the "fast track" economic reforms of its premier, Boris Yeltsin.

11. UK: The official report into the 1988 Lockerbie air crash is published; it recommends reinforcing civil aircraft.

12. Iran: Ayatollah Khamenei denounces the presence of American troops in Saudi, and calls the struggle against the US a "holy war".

12. UK: The Liberal Democrats unveil their new logo, a "bird of freedom" (→ 20).

12. UK: The government launches an £18 million advertising campaign to sell off the twelve regional electricity boards of England and Wales.

13. London: An inquest jury finds that the 35 people who died in the December 1988 Clapham train crash were unlawfully killed.

14. New York: The UN agrees to allow humanitarian supplies of food and medical equipment through to Iraq and Kuwait.

14. London: Tom King, the defence secretary, announces the sending of the "Desert Rats" – the 7th Armoured Brigade – to the Gulf.

15. UK: A "poll of polls" conducted between June and August shows that Labour, with 46 per cent support, has a nine-point lead over the Conservatives.

Embassy raid stirs France to send troops

French troops undergo a gas drill.

Sept 9. France has reacted swiftly to an Iraqi raid on its Kuwait embassy in which four Frenchmen were detained and the building was looted. President Mitterrand has ordered an extra 4,000 men to the Gulf, with three army air regiments, 48 tanks, 48 anti-tank helicopters and 30 fighters, including Mirage F1s and Jaguars. The total of French forces there will now be 14 warships, nearly 100 anti-tank helicopters and 13,000 men. At a cabinet meeting yesterday, Mitterrand described Iraq as a "bellicose state which seems to estimate the risks poorly". He is now pressing for an air embargo (→ 16).

Up and up: inflation hits eight-year peak

Sept 14. Inflation in Britain has soared to 10.6 per cent, according to figures for August released today. This is the highest rate for eight years and worse than the 10.3 per cent which Mrs Thatcher inherited when she came to power.

The jump into double figures had been expected, after the annual rate had hit 9.8 per cent a month ago. But the August figure is higher than City analysts had predicted – and only a third of last month's increase can be blamed on higher petrol prices caused by the Gulf crisis. "Bad and disappointing" was the treasury's verdict, and the figures cast a shadow over hopes of an early cut in interest rates (→ 26).

Rural values under threat, says church

Sept 11. More low-cost housing is urgently needed in Britain's rural areas, according to a Church of England report published today. Living conditions in the countryside are suffering because many farmers are in difficulty and public transport systems have declined.

Faith in the Countryside also draws attention to growing tensions between traditional village dwellers and wealthy new arrivals from the cities. Newcomers often resist changes to the rural way of life which are essential if small country communities are to survive. More government money would help rural areas, it says, but the church has a major role to play.

Sept 10. The pope consecrates the biggest Christian church in the world – the Our Lady of Peace basilica at Yamoussoukro, in the Ivory Coast.

Iraq opens Kuwaiti border for a day

A short rest after fleeing Kuwait.

Sept 15. Thousands of Kuwaitis fled into Saudi Arabia today after the Iraqis unexpectedly opened the border for the first time since they invaded what they now describe as the 19th province of Iraq. Refugees arriving at Khafji told of looting, pillaging, shooting and other atrocities by Iraqi soldiers. Saudi authorities fear that Iraqi agents may be among 3,000 refugees who arrived today, stripped of all passports and identity papers.

Liberian president is beaten to death

Tortured, then killed: Samuel Doe.

Sept 9. Samuel Doe, the former sergeant who shot his way to power in Liberia ten years ago, has been beaten to death by rebel troops of his arch-enemy, Prince Johnson. Doe and his bodyguards were ambushed as they made their way to the West African peace-keeping army, apparently seeking a safe passage out of the country.

Superpowers show unity

Sept 9. The two superpower presidents, George Bush and Mikhail Gorbachev, agreed at a one-day snap summit in Helsinki today that they they would stand united in opposition to Iraq's occupation of Kuwait and its seizure of "human shield" hostages.

In a joint statement, issued at the end of a sombre day's work, they affirmed their determination to make Saddam Hussein comply with the United Nations resolutions ordering him to withdraw unconditionally from Kuwait and to free the hostages.

The two leaders were not, however, in complete accord. Gorbachev did not give Bush the clear endorsement that he wanted for the use of force against Saddam Hussein if sanctions fail, and Bush did not give Gorbachev the aid package which he sought (→ 25).

Talking over, presidents Bush and Gorbachev laugh at a cartoon of themselves.

Wartime allies surrender to new Germany

Sept 12. The Second World War was finally laid to rest in Moscow today when the four allied powers signed the treaty which handed back full sovereignty to a soon-to-be-united Germany. More than 45 years of division, occupation and the dangers of the "Cold War" were wiped away with a few strokes of the pen. "We are thinking of all nations in the war and the agony they suffered, especially the Jewish people," said the West German foreign minister, Hans-Dietrich Genscher. It must never happen again, he added (→ 20).

Foreign ministers raise their glasses for a toast to Germany's new autonomy.

Commuters murdered on a crowded train

Sept 13. Two armed gangs boarded a Johannesburg commuter train tonight and, in a carefully-planned attack, ran through the train, shooting, knifing and hacking the terrified black commuters returning to their township homes after working in the city.

The first gang boarded the train in Johannesburg and started its killing a few minutes after it pulled out. The gangsters ran through the coaches leaving a trail of slaughter. They pushed some of their victims off the train, while others jumped.

The second gang was waiting for the train as it pulled into its first stop in the suburb of Denver, and cut down the people who fled as the train halted. The killers then ran away, leaving behind 26 dead and more than 100 wounded.

A tragic victim of township violence.

Jakarta deal brings peace to Cambodia

Khieu Samphan, political leader of the Khmer Rouge, talks to newsmen.

Sept 10. After two years of negotiation, the four Cambodian factions have agreed a peace formula aimed at ending the civil war and preparing the ground for free elections. A supreme national council will be formed, and United Nations troops will be stationed in the country.

Whether a call for a cease-fire will succeed remains to be seen. Hun Sen, the prime minister of the Phnom Penh government, makes no secret of his hatred for the Khmer Rouge delegate, Khieu Samphan, and vice versa. Today's agreement came after a week of drawn-out talks which nearly broke down midway. The two non-communist delegations were delighted with the agreement, but clearly worried about its implementation. "Now all the Khmer parties are in one car," said Prince Ranariddh, representing Prince Sihanouk's party. "But we don't have the instructions to drive it."

The reason for the sudden breakthrough was the fear by the superpowers that the growing strength of the Khmer Rouge could lead to the return of Pol Pot. Pressure was applied on all sides by Moscow, Beijing and Washington – each with different motives.

September
1990

Su	Mo	Tu	We	Th	Fr	Sa
						1
2	3	4	5	6	7	8
9	10	11	12	13	14	15
16	17	18	19	20	21	22
23	24	25	26	27	28	29
30						

16. New York: The UN Security Council condemns Iraqi moves against diplomats in Kuwait.→

16. N Ireland: The IRA says that it has kidnapped and shot dead RUC Constable Louis Robertson.→

16. Australia: Wayne Gardner wins the Phillip Island motorcycle Grand Prix for the second year in a row.

17. London: The IRA shoots, and badly injures, a forces recruitment officer.→

18. London: The High Court backs Lambeth council's decision to set its poll tax at £521, flouting government orders to charge £493 (→27).

18. UK: The department of health orders an inquiry into reports of a child-abuse ring in Rochdale.

19. Moscow: The Russian parliament gives a vote of no confidence to the Soviet prime minister, Nikolai Ryzhkov (→24).

20. Hove: Middlesex beat Sussex to pip Essex for the county cricket championship.

20. Germany: The East German *Volkskammer* and the West German *Bundestag* ratify the unification treaty (→3/10).

20. London: Shares in the Polly Peck group dive after the serious fraud squad raids the offices of the chairman, Asil Nadir, on suspicion that he organized a share-rigging operation (→25/10).

21. Baghdad: Iraq expels 40 diplomats in a tit-for-tat move.

21. Birmingham: Chris Patten, the environment secretary, tells car manufacturers to stop producing "gas guzzlers" (→25).

22. Perth: Alex Salmond is elected leader of the Scottish Nationalist Party.

22. Riyadh: Saudi Arabia cuts off oil supplies to Jordan and expels 20 Jordanian diplomats.

22. Iraq: Ron Campbell, Dennis Canavan and Bob Parry, the Labour MPs who are in Baghdad on a peace mission, give up hope of meeting Saddam Hussein.→

IRA attacks former governor of Gibraltar

Sept 19. An IRA gunman severely wounded Air Chief Marshal Sir Peter Terry at his home near Stafford today. The gunman opened fire with an automatic weapon on Sir Peter as he sat in the lounge of his home. Two bullets hit him above the left eye and stopped just short of his brain; another shattered his jaw. Lady Terry was slightly hurt by a bullet which passed through an inside wall.

Sir Peter, who is expected to survive, was a marked target, for, as governor of Gibraltar, he authorized the SAS operation which led to the killing of three IRA terrorists which became notorious as "Death on the Rock" (→23).

Lady Terry: injured in the attack.

Ashdown pillories Thatcher in key speech

Ashdown spells out the message.

Sept 20. The Liberal Democrat leader, Paddy Ashdown, set the seal on his party's revival with a fiery speech to its annual conference at Blackpool today. He turned his venom above all on Mrs Thatcher, noting wryly that if you were a friend of the Tories, you could buy a pint of beer and three cemeteries and still have change from a pound. A Liberal Democrat government would, he said, increase income tax to pay for an improved education service. Petrol and electricity charges would also go up to tackle the greenhouse effect. Despite these possible electoral liabilities, the leader received a four-minute ovation.

Best scores TV foul

Sept 19. George Best scored a dramatic own goal before television millions tonight. Appearing on BBC1's "Wogan" to promote his autobiography, the one-time football genius, swearing and clearly very drunk, spoke repetitively (and luridly) of his sex life and love of the drink. Best was widely considered to be the greatest European footballer of the 1960s. A hero of the legendary Manchester United team and a Northern Ireland international, he was idolized like a pop star. But Georgie was not on his best form tonight. And Terry Wogan, his chat-show host, was obviously highly uncomfortable.

Atlanta wins battle to host Olympics

Sept 18. Six cities had battled for the honour of hosting the 1996 Olympic Games. Manchester, Melbourne and Toronto were early casualties of the voting today, along with Belgrade. That left Athens, the sentimental favourite and birthplace of the modern Olympics in 1896, or Atlanta, the birthplace of Coca-Cola. By 51 votes to 35 the International Olympic Committee meeting in Tokyo awarded the Games to Atlanta.

The carefully-costed plans put forward by the Georgian capital, plus the certainty of lucrative television contracts, won the day. Manchester vowed to fight again, but may face a challenge from London for the summer games of 2000.

Atlantans celebrate their good luck.

Which comes first – the cartoon character or the merchandising opportunity? Perhaps only the Teenage Mutant Hero Turtles themselves can answer.

Iraq invasion might lead to home terror

Terrorist leader: George Habash.

Sept 18. A leading Palestinian today warned that an attack on Iraq would provoke retaliation within the United States and other western countries. The spectre of a terrorist backlash was raised by George Habash, the leader of the Popular Front for the Liberation of Palestine (PFLP). "At this moment our fingers are touching the trigger," he said. "We will shoot the moment Iraq suffers aggression."

Dr Habash's followers were responsible for several hijackings in the 1970s, and he was expelled from Jordan. But today he was back in Amman where King Hussein is under strong pressure to link the Gulf crisis with demands for Israel to withdraw from the West Bank.

The Asian Games open in Beijing in a flurry of lavish choreography.

Chief of US air force is sacked for "bomb Baghdad" comments

Sept 18. General Michael Dugan, the US Air Force chief of staff, was sacked today for speaking too publicly about contingency plans to bomb Baghdad, and the targeting of Saddam Hussein and his family. The Pentagon said the dismissal, which had the backing of President Bush, was because the 53-year-old USAF general had shown "poor judgement at a sensitive time".

Dick Cheney, the US defense secretary, implied that the general's remarks had jeopardized the "very fragile, very important international coalition" assembled to combat Iraqi aggression. General Dugan was quoted yesterday about contingency plans to bomb "downtown Baghdad" and "the best way to hurt Saddam". Nobody doubts that such plans exist; the general's mistake was to make them public.

General Dugan, who spoke out of turn, dines with troops in Saudi Arabia.

Iraqi diplomats are expelled from Europe

French guards escort an Iraqi military attache out of the country.

Sept 17. Iraq's military attaches are to be expelled from all 12 nations in the European Community. Other Iraqi diplomats will face curbs on their movements, it was agreed today by EC foreign ministers meeting in the wake of last Friday's raids on the embassy residences of France, Belgium and the Netherlands in Kuwait.

The violation of the French compound has already led to the dispatch of 4,000 French soldiers to the Gulf, including one regiment of the Foreign Legion. Today's meeting in Brussels saw the Community

united in protest against what it described as Iraq's "suicidal" behaviour towards the international community and united, too, in its determination to strengthen the UN trade embargo against Iraq.

In London, the home office said that 23 Iraqis, in addition to the two military attaches, had been told that they must leave by next Tuesday. The expulsions were condemned by Dr Azmi Shafiq Al-Salihi, the Iraqi ambassador to Britain, who hinted that the authorities in Baghdad may initiate "tit-for-tat" expulsions (→ 21).

Saddam plans to fall back on second front

Sept 22. Iraqi soldiers are preparing a second line of defence along the Iraqi/Kuwaiti frontier to which they could withdraw if the US and other forces attacked Kuwait. The front line for Iraq remains Kuwait's border with Saudi Arabia, with an estimated 360,000 Iraqi troops now in Kuwait itself. Iraqi leaders say that they have annexed Kuwait "for ever", and US strategists fear that the capital would be a bloody battleground. But Iraq's military chiefs also fear that their forces could be easily encircled unless they can withdraw within the first few days of any conflict. This would also extend the US lines of supply and make them more vulnerable to an Iraqi counter-attack.

Saddam contemplates his next move.

23. Wentworth: Ian Woosnam wins the Suntory World Matchplay golf championship.

23. Co Armagh: Terrorists kill Colin McCullough, a part-time UDR soldier, in front of his girlfriend (→ 27).

23. Hemel Hempstead: A major search begins after Simon Jones, aged four, goes missing (→ 18/11).

24. World: Oil prices reach $40 a barrel for the first time since 1980 (→ 28).

25. London: Former world heavyweight boxing champion George Foreman continues his comeback by knocking out Terry Anderson.

25. Australia: A tourist coach falls down a ravine in the Gold Coast, killing 11 people.

26. UK: Mrs Thatcher tells businessmen and journalists to "stop talking us into a crisis".→

27. London: An IRA bomb is discovered at a conference on terrorism.

28. Spain: The British racing driver Martin Donnelly is flung from his Lotus at 160mph, but walks away, only slightly hurt.

28. USSR: Kazakhstan declares a disaster zone, following a huge leakage of beryllium gas from a nuclear-fuel plant.

28. UK: A government inquiry clears oil firms of profiteering in the Gulf crisis.

30. Moscow: The USSR agrees to reopen diplomatic relations with Israel, cut off in 1967.

30. New York: World leaders, meeting for the Unicef summit for children, commit themselves to measures to improve the lives of the world's poor children.

DEATHS

23. Lord (Michael Meredith) Swann, British academic and administrator (*1/3/20).

26. Alberto Moravia (Alberto Pincherle), Italian author (*28/11/07).

30. Patrick Victor Martindale White, Australian author (*28/5/12).→

Government claims green credentials, but critics unimpressed

Environment secretary Chris Patten.

Sept 25. Chris Patten, the environment secretary, launched the government's latest plans for the environment today in a long-awaited and much-vaunted White Paper – 291 pages of recycled paper entitled *This Common Inheritance*.

Notable proposals included the "greening" of Whitehall. Every government department will have a minister to monitor the impact of its policies on the environment, and a ministerial committee on energy efficiency is to be set up. Other plans include a new MoT test on emissions from cars, and heavier fines for water pollution. But there was no action to make the polluter pay – believed by many to be the only way to make industrialists clean up their act. Nor were there any new initiatives on the urgent need to cut carbon emissions and control CFCs. There is no commitment to improving public transport, and much of the document was taken up with promises to undertake vague studies.

Opposition parties and environmental pressure groups criticized the white paper as a missed chance. Greenpeace called it a "woolly wish-list", while the Labour Party said that it was "long on waffle and short on policy". Friends of the Earth claimed that it did nothing to encourage recycling, adding that it consisted largely of recycled ideas.

Australian novelist Patrick White is dead

White: a masterly imagination.

Sept 30. The novelist Patrick White might well have chosen to have kept the news of his death this morning out of the newspapers, for he enjoyed a difficult and sometimes antagonistic relationship with the Australian establishment.

But this is big news. When White won the Nobel Prize for literature in 1973, it was regarded as a cultural turning point in Australia. Raised in Australia but largely educated in England, he initially set out as a writer in London, but after the war he settled in Sydney with his lifelong Greek companion Manoly Lascaris. Here he began writing the finely-wrought novels, such as *Voss* (1957) and *Riders in the Chariot* (1961), which won him wide acclaim.

Army shoots joyriding Belfast teenagers

Sept 30. Two teenage joyriders were shot dead tonight as they drove a stolen car through an army checkpoint in west Belfast. Martin Peake, aged 17, and Karen Reilly, aged 18, were killed, and a third teenager was injured, after their Vauxhall Astra knocked down a soldier at the checkpoint on Glen Road.

Peake had been in court three times before on joyriding charges. Earlier this year, the IRA broke his arm and his ankle to try to stop him taking cars. But it seems that, like many Belfast teenagers, he was addicted to the excitement of stealing cars and the bravado of daring the police, the army and the IRA all at the same time.

Nationalist politicians were quick to condemn the incident. Gerry Adams, the president of *Sinn Fein*, accused the army of carrying out a "shoot-to-kill" policy and called the deaths summary executions. The government has promised that a full report will be sent to the director of public prosecutions. This tragic incident has served to highlight the tremendous difficulties of trying to keep law and order in Northern Ireland (→ 10/10).

Threat of recession looms over economy

Major: looking for the right policy.

Sept 26. Margaret Thatcher tonight dismissed the "voices of gloom" who were claiming that Britain was heading into recession. A monthly trends survey published this week by the Confederation of British Industry showed manufacturers expecting their biggest drop in output for eight years and a growing number of bankruptcies. The CBI called for interest rates to be cut in order to avert a full-scale recession. John Major, the chancellor of the exchequer, has said difficult times are necessary to squeeze inflation out of the economy. The prime minister simply argued that inflation was easing and urged a tough line on pay settlements (→ 5/10).

Gorbachev gains powers

Gorbachev: assuming new powers.

Sept 24. With the Soviet people bracing themselves for a winter of food shortage, industrial discontent and increasing crime, President Gorbachev was handed sweeping power to rule by decree today. The Soviet parliament voted by 305 to 36 to give the president authority to handle every aspect of reform – and to introduce measures that will lay the basis of decentralization.

After weeks of argument, the Supreme Soviet has agreed a compromise plan for the economy which combines the "fast track" plan for a move to a free market system in 500 days with the more gradual approach favoured by the government. Gorbachev has been instructed to come up with a final version by mid-October (→ 8/10).

Court thwarts transsexual marriage plea

Sept 27. Caroline Cossey, who started her life as a man, failed today to overturn the British law which bars her from marrying or having her birth certificate changed. Cossey, who had a sex-change operation in 1974 and then began a highly successful career as a model under the name "Tula", had brought a case before the European court in Strasbourg claiming that the law violated the European Convention of Human Rights. But the court ruled that Article 12 of the convention, which guarantees men and women the right to marry and have families, concerned "traditional" marriage only.

Sex-change model Caroline Cossey.

Fourth Guinness defendant escapes jail because of ill health

Sir Jack Lyons is saying nothing as he leaves Southwark Crown Court.

Religious freedom for Soviet citizens

The last czar's portrait is paraded.

Sept 26. The Soviet parliament tonight voted to put aside 70 years of religious suppression, and agreed a draft law which will allow full freedom of belief. Laws introduced by Stalin in 1929, which equated religious proselytizing with undermining the communist revolution, have been reversed.

Under Mr Gorbachev, religious freedom has grown and thousands of places of worship have been reopened. Bibles and prayerbooks are no longer contraband. Now the USSR's religious revival is official. The new law bans the church from involvement in politics, but similarly prevents the state from interfering in the church. Education is to remain strictly atheist for fear of reinforcing ethnic divisions.

Sept 25. Sir Jack Lyons, the fourth main defendant in the Guinness shares fraud trial, was today fined £3 million and ordered to pay £440,000 costs. The judge told the 74-year-old millionaire, found guilty of conspiracy, false accounting and theft, that he avoided prison only because of his ill health. Mr Justice Henry added that Sir Jack had put in a "shabby and undignified perfomance" by telling "cock-and-bull stories" to try to conceal "dishonesty on a major scale". Sir Jack, once a close friend of the prime minister, just smiled.

London and Tehran renew diplomacy

Sept 27. Britain and Iran today announced that they are to restore diplomatic relations, broken off 18 months ago amid controversy over Salman Rushdie's book *The Satanic Verses*. The agreement was sealed in talks at the United Nations between Douglas Hurd, the British foreign secretary, and his Iranian counterpart, Ali Akbar Velayati. Both governments say they will use their influence to win the freedom of British hostages in Lebanon.

Diplomatic links were broken off when Ayatollah Khomeini issued a *fatwa* calling for the death of Rushdie for his alleged blasphemy. His successors now state that this should not be carried out on behalf of Iran's government.

Soviets make firm statement backing UN Gulf policies

Sept 25. The Soviet Union has thrown its weight behind an unprecedentedly tough stand by the United Nations against Iraq. With Eduard Shevardnadze, the Soviet foreign minister, in the chair, the UN Security Council tonight voted to add an air embargo to the naval blockade with which it plans to enforce sanctions against Iraq.

Mr Shevardnadze was unequivocal in his denunciation of Iraq and his support, if necessary, for military action to end the crisis. He told the UN General Assembly that Iraq's invasion of Kuwait was an "affront to mankind", and warned that the UN had the power and will to suppress acts of aggression by taking military force "if the illegal occupation of Kuwait continues".

He said that Moscow was willing to contribute military forces to any action under the UN umbrella. Soviet leaders still hope for a peaceful settlement, a plea echoed by the UN secretary-general, Javier Perez de Cuellar. But the Security Council, meeting at foreign-minister level for only the third time in its 45-year history, voted by 14 votes to one to warn Iraq of "potentially severe consequences" if it did not withdraw from Kuwait (→ 3/10).

October
1990

Su	Mo	Tu	We	Th	Fr	Sa
	1	2	3	4	5	6
7	8	9	10	11	12	13
14	15	16	17	18	19	20
21	22	23	24	25	26	27
28	29	30	31			

1. UK: An offer worth £7 million tempts Nigel Mansell to reverse his decision to retire from Grand Prix racing.

1. UK: The health minister Kenneth Clarke vows to fight on to stop haemophiliacs infected with HIV by contaminated blood products winning compensation.

1. New York: Bush tells the UN that the Kuwait issue is a test of its unity which must not be seen to fail.

2. Johannesburg: Chief Buthelezi, the *Inkatha* leader, declines an invitation to meet Nelson Mandela.

3. Kuwait: Saddam Hussein visits his troops (→ 6).

3. London: The Telecom Tower is 25 years old today.

3. UK: Arthur Scargill is taken to hospital with suspected pneumonia.

4. Blackpool: Against the wishes of the leadership, Labour delegates vote to examine proposals for proportional representation.

4. UK: British Rail announce that rail fares will go up by 9.5 per cent in January.

4. Birmingham: Wayne Greening, a bar manager who served spiked cocktails to a youth who died, is cleared of manslaughter.

5. Yugoslavia: Federal forces move in to halt Slovenian separatist movements.

5. London: Council tenants reject government proposals for a "housing action trust", in effect killing off the scheme.

6. Baghdad: Mohammed Abu Abbas, the leader of the Palestine Liberation Front, threatens to destroy US aircraft if Iraqi ones are shot down.

6. Washington: Public buildings close as the government goes temporarily bankrupt (→ 11).

DEATHS

1. Curtis Emerson LeMay, US air force officer (*15/11/06).

4. Jill Bennett, British actress (*24/12/31).

Sterling to join exchange mechanism

Oct 5. Margaret Thatcher's government today surprised the City of London (and its political opponents) by applying for membership of Europe's Exchange Rate Mechanism (ERM). John Major, the chancellor of the exchequer, delighted Tory MPs by coupling the move with a one-per-cent cut in interest rates. Share prices and sterling soared after the unexpected announcements came shortly after 4pm, just hours after Labour had concluded what was generally regarded to have been a succesful party conference.

Mr Major denied, however, that the timing was political, although the cut in interest rates especially will hearten his party as it trails Labour in the opinion polls. As opposition leaders had wanted Britain to join the ERM and to cut interest rates, they had no alternative but to welcome the moves, although Neil Kinnock argued that it was "the action of a cornered government". Mrs Thatcher, speaking in Downing Street, insisted that the timing was dictated solely on economic grounds because Conservative policies "were seen to be working".

Britain's inflation rate, for so long cited as the reason for staying out of the ERM, would fall closer to the European average in the coming months, she said. Sterling will enter the ERM at a central rate of 2.95 *Deutschmark*, with fluctuations allowed to a six-per-cent margin either way – wider than that for most other currencies (→ 8).

Major: the surprising chancellor.

Labour makes education its "big idea"

Kinnock and Hattersley look forward to heading a future government.

Oct 2. Neil Kinnock declared that Labour was ready for government in a rousing speech to his party conference in Blackpool today which singled out education as "the most fundamental requirement of future success". Labour sees education as the long-sought "big idea" to help win the next general election.

"We have got to raise the standards of training and education to the levels that at least compare with those of our competitors," said Mr Kinnock, who attacked what he called Tory "experimentation" in schools. He added: "The greatest adventure people can have is still through education and the fulfilment of their desires." Although the Labour leader did promise improvements in the supply of teachers and equipment, he was careful to avoid specific commitments on spending. This reflects the party's desire to use the party conference as a shop-window for its new "realism" in economic policy. This was hammered home yesterday by John Smith, the shadow chancellor, and endorsed by union leaders who promised to moderate inflationary pay demands.

Mr Kinnock strove to strike a positive note, avoiding personal attacks on Mrs Thatcher and seeing in the Gulf crisis not only dangers but also hopes for improved world security through the UN.

Melodious end to a superlative career

Oct 2. A career in opera that lasted for 40 years is a long time, but the thunderous ovation which greeted Dame Joan Sutherland after her last, wondrous performance in the Sydney Opera House tonight seemed to go on for even longer.

After the final curtain call on Meyerbeer's *Les Huguenots*, the curtain rose once more – to Dame Joan alone. Balloons, streamers and even fireworks filled the air. She smiled, waved and bowed before a tremendous homage to greatness.

Joan Sutherland, the supreme diva.

German dream of unity becomes reality

Oct 3. Germany is one nation again. Its rebirth was ushered in at midnight with a triumphant peal from the Freedom Bell at Schoneberg city hall. A roar went up from the thousands of cheering, weeping people who hugged each other with joy and waved a forest of black, red and gold flags. Germany, 45 years after the war, was free and united in liberty.

As fireworks exploded like flak in the Berlin sky the people found it hard to believe that it was only eleven months since the hated Wall began to collapse and the Russians loosened their iron grip. They know that the future holds many difficulties but that is for tomorrow. Tonight there is only joy.

The flag of unity flies in Berlin.

Hijacker crash jet in China: 127 die

Oct 2. At least 127 people were killed and some 53 injured in a horrific collision this morning at White Cloud Airport, Canton. A Boeing 737, which had been hijacked on an internal Chinese flight, went out of control on landing and smashed into two airliners waiting on the runway – one empty, and one containing 150 passengers due to fly to Shanghai. Survivors on the 737 said there was a scuffle in the cockpit as the plane came into land.

Suspected hit-men held at Stonehenge

Oct 2. Two Irishmen were seized by armed police in a swoop on a car parked at Stonehenge this afternoon. They are now being questioned by detectives investigating the murder of the Tory MP Ian Gow. The two men were in a blue Ford Sierra, a type of car hunted by the police for the past two weeks after armed men were frightened away by police guarding the Hampshire home of Sir Charles Tidbury, who is on the IRA "hit list".

High-caste Indians march to save jobs

Oct 2. Upper-caste Hindus continued their violent demonstrations today against plans by the Indian prime minister, V P Singh, to rid the country of its traditional discrimination against the lower castes. The plans, to make more government jobs available to the "untouchables", seem modest enough to western minds, but they have roused the higher castes to such a pitch of fury and despair that dozens of students have burnt themselves to death in protest. In Hoshiarpur 2,000 went on the rampage after a 17-year-old student poisoned herself to death and in her suicide note blamed Mr Singh for her death (→9).

Police prepare to fire on protesters.

Soviet optimism for Gulf peace doomed to be disappointed

Oct 6. Yevgeny Primakov, the Soviet Union's special envoy to Iraq, emerged from talks with President Saddam Hussein today to say that he was more hopeful of a peaceful resolution of the Gulf crisis. However, he was unable to give details to clarify the reason for his sudden optimism which runs contrary to the opinion of most diplomats who take a gloomy view of the aggressive speech made by an Iraqi representative at the UN last night.

The feeling is that Mr Primakov's optimism is the result of Saddam Hussein's promise to allow the 5,000 Russians being held in Iraq to leave the country rather than of any glimmer of light in the overall situation. He may also be reflecting Mr Gorbachev's known desire for a political rather than a military solution to the crisis and acting in the belief that optimism could have its own dynamic for peace.

It is not a belief shared by most western nations involved, many of whom now feel that war is inevitable. This view has been strengthened by the arrest in Egypt of a group of Palestinians and Iraqis suspected of being Iraqi saboteurs. Ominously, four of them belong to a Palestinian terrorist group (→9).

Noble attempt but Philippines coup is stopped without difficulty

Oct 6. An attempted coup against President Aquino's government in the Philippines ended today after just 48 hours. Colonel Alexander Noble surrendered unconditionally at the captured army camp at Cagayan de Oro, on the southern island of Mindanao, after he had told journalists that, if all else failed "I will die with my boots on."

Noble had been in jungle hiding since a previous coup in which he had taken part – in Manila – had failed in December 1987. Two days ago he emerged to occupy two army camps without violence. Mrs Aquino ordered the army to recapture the camps at any cost, and her emissary accepted Noble's surrender this morning. Just one person died in the uprising.

Government troops in Manila dance to celebrate the rebels' surrender.

Oct 3. Princess Caroline of Monaco is distraught at the news of the death of her husband, Stefano Casiraghi. He was killed when his powerboat overturned during an offshore racing competition.

October

1990

Su	Mo	Tu	We	Th	Fr	Sa
	1	2	3	4	5	6
7	8	9	10	11	12	13
14	15	16	17	18	19	20
21	22	23	24	25	26	27
28	29	30	31			

7. UK: John Major denies he is trying to create a mini-boom before the next election (→ 12).

7. Sydney: Kerry Packer, the entrepreneur, collapses with a heart attack.

8. Moscow: President Gorbachev warns that separatism, if unchecked, would turn the USSR into a "new Lebanon" (→ 28).

8. UK: Britain formally joins the European Monetary System.

9. Washington: The US, determined to hold together the fragile coalition against Iraq, condemns Israel for the Temple Mount killings (→ 13).

9. Bournemouth: Cecil Parkinson is booed and heckled when he claims there is a transport "revolution".→

10. UK: Kenneth Clarke, the health secretary, is embarrassed when a document in which he offers further cuts in spending is leaked.

10. London: Dennis Andries retains the world light-heavyweight boxing championship after he breaks Sergio Merani's jaw.

11. Oslo: Octavio Paz, the Mexican poet, is awarded the Nobel prize for literature.

11. UK: Edward Heath announces that he will go to Iraq to plead for the release of British hostages (→ 21).

12. Moscow: Courts sentence a leading anti-Semite to two years' hard labour.

12. Germany: Wolfgang Schauble, the interior minister, is wounded in a gun attack.

12. UK: Inflation reaches 10.9 per cent, the highest for over eight years.

13. New York: The UN votes to condemn Israel for the deaths of 20 Palestinians in the Temple Mount massacre (→ 17).

13. Belfast: The IRA murders two RUC dog handlers (→ 24).

DEATHS

9. Richard Bernard Murdoch, British actor and radio comedy star (*1907).

13. Le Duc Tho, Vietnamese statesman (*1910).

Debate on Europe splits Tory conference

Oct 12. Margaret Thatcher mocked Labour's new moderate image as a "masquerade" when she sought to raise Tory spirits at the close of a lacklustre conference in Bournemouth. Cecil Parkinson being heckled, Ted Heath announcing his trip to Iraq and a junior minister arrested for drinking and driving were not the headlines wanted by a party lagging in the polls; but more ominous are divisions over Europe.

Hopes that the decision to enter the Exchange Rate Mechanism (ERM) might defuse the tensions were as short-lived as the euphoria ERM entry had induced on the stock market. On Tuesday two former cabinet ministers, Nicholas Ridley and Michael Heseltine, spoke for the anti- and pro-European wings, but potentially the most damaging intervention came yesterday from Sir Geoffrey Howe, the deputy prime minister. He said that Britain should take a leading part in talks about moves towards a single European currency and monetary union. Undaunted, Mrs

Thatcher: party is split on Europe.

Thatcher today reiterated her opposition to "unacceptable" plans for a single currency and the notion of a federal Europe, attacking "socialism" in Brussels (→ 28).

Drink-driving MP resigns in disgrace

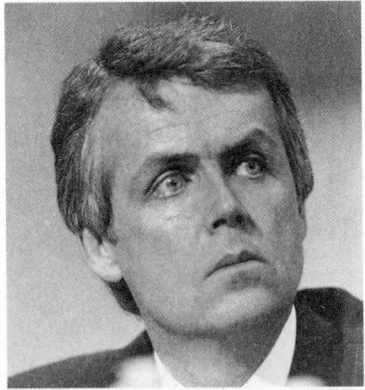
Drunk in charge: Patrick Nicholls.

Oct 11. Patrick Nicholls, the government minister behind an official campaign against drinking at work, has resigned this morning after being arrested for drunken driving. Mr Nicholls, who was attending the Conservative Party conference in Bournemouth, was stopped at about 1.30am after local police were alerted by a cab driver who had dropped the minister off at his car. His ministerial career ended in that instant.

Gazza is a mystery to operatic judge

Oct 12. The soccer star Paul Gascoigne was today refused an injunction to halt publication of an unauthorized biography, *Gazza*, so called after his nickname. Gascoigne's lawyers had argued that this nickname was so well-known that people would think he had authorized the book. But Mr Justice Harman said the England player was not famous enough to justify an injunction, adding: "Isn't there an operetta called *La Gazza Ladra?*"

Decidedly a footballer, not an opera.

Lester Piggott back in the saddle at 54

Oct 11. Lester Piggott, the greatest British jockey since the Second World War, is to make a comeback at the age of 54. Piggott, who rode a record 29 Classic winners, retired five years ago after a glittering career in which he was champion jockey 11 times. Three years ago he made less happy headlines, being sentenced to three years' imprisonment for tax evasion. He has since acted as assistant to his wife, Susan, at their training stables in Newmarket. Piggott was awarded his licence today by the Jockey Club, and is expected to ride his first race on Monday.

Syria flexes muscle to make Christian ruler quit Lebanon

Aoun, pictured before his surrender.

Oct 13. General Michel Aoun, the Iraqi-backed Christian warlord, has been forced to surrender to the Lebanese president, Elias Hrawi, and, fleeing from his concrete bunker beneath the ruins of the presidential palace, has sought sanctuary in the French embassy.

Aoun had promised to fight to the death to maintain his claim to be the legitimate leader of Lebanon, but it took just one raid by the Syrian air force to convince him that his days of power were over. His flight is seen in Beirut as the first defeat for his principal armourer, Saddam Hussein.

Arabs killed in Jerusalem bloodbath

Israelis stand guard over Palestinians near the mosque on Temple Mount.

An Israeli soldier pins down a youth.

Oct 8. Israeli border police shot dead 21 Arabs during rioting around the Western Wall and the Dome of the Rock, holy places to Jews and Moslems, in Jerusalem today. The rioting started when Palestinians gathered to fight off an attempt by a small Jewish sect, the Temple Mount Faithful, to lay a cornerstone for a new Jewish temple on the ancient site. The police turned back the members of the sect, but the enraged Palestinians, who had collected supplies of stones, threw them down on Jews praying at the Wall to mark the festival of Tabernacles.

The police opened fire with tear gas, rubber bullets and live ammunition. "It was a massacre, a bloodbath," said one young Palestinian. Dead and wounded fell in the open courtyard of the Mount. Tonight the Israeli authorities are insisting that the police opened fire only when their lives were "in grave danger", and that the affair had been deliberately provoked by Palestinian "extremist factions".

The Arabs point to their martyrs as proof of Israeli perfidy. There has been instant international condemnation of the killings amidst fears that Saddam Hussein will use the incident to weaken Arab opposition to him in the Gulf ($\rightarrow$9).

Saddam seizes on massacre to attack western presence

Oct 9. Saddam Hussein attempted today to link the shooting of 21 Palestinians by Israeli police with the crisis in the Gulf. Broadcasting from Baghdad, he told the Israelis: "You have no choice but to leave the lands of Palestine and Moslem shrines." He said that he had a new long-range missile that could strike at targets hundreds of miles away and, linking the rocket with the stone-throwers of the Temple Mount, said that it was called *al Hijara,* the Stone.

The rocket would serve, he said, like the Palestinian rocks, and was able "from somewhere in Iraq to reach the targets of evil". He claimed that, like the Israelis who must leave Palestine, "the armies of America and its allies have no choice but to leave the holy sites of Arabs and Moslems".

Western diplomats fear that if he continues to play the Israeli card he could harm the fragile alliance of western and Arab nations ranged against him ($\rightarrow$16).

Bush makes his mind up on tax increases

Oct 11. Leading Republicans are worried that their chances in congressional and state elections due next month have been scuppered by their own leader. President Bush seems today to have changed his mind for the fourth time in two days as to whether he would support increased income taxes on America's rich. Today's proposal is the one originally put forward two days ago, but then withdrawn: a rise in top-rate income tax balanced by a cut in capital gains tax.

Scandal: Vita Sackville-West and Violet Trefusis's affair still shocks in a television adaptation of Nigel Nicolson's "Portrait of a Marriage".

IRA men shot dead as Loyalists go free

Oct 10. Two leading members of the IRA were shot dead yesterday by an army undercover team. The dead men, Desmond Grew and Martin McCaughey, were seen carrying AK-47 rifles at a farm near the small town of Loughall, where eight IRA men died in an SAS ambush three years ago.

Grew was wanted by the German police for the murder of an RAF corporal and his six-month-old daughter at Wildenrath a year ago. McCaughey had only just recovered after being wounded in a shootout with the police last March.

In Belfast today five leading loyalists walked free after charges of illegally possessing documents were withdrawn. The charges had been brought following the investigation by John Stevens, the deputy chief constable of Cambridgeshire, of links between loyalist paramilitary groups and members of the security forces ($\rightarrow$13).

Caste row turns to murderous terror

Oct 9. Violence over the government's attempts to improve the lot of India's lower castes continued in the most horrific fashion today. Youths demonstrating in favour of the reforms boarded a train in the southern state of Andhra Pradesh, handed out pamphlets, then poured kerosene over the floor of a packed compartment and set fire to it.

They jumped off as the train slowed at a railway crossing, but the panic-stricken passengers found that most of the doors were locked. Forty-seven of them died.

"They said don't worry, no harm would come to us. Then the fire started. It was all over in a few minutes," said one of the badly-burnt survivors. Nobody seems to know the identity of the attackers, but some Indian newspapers say that they were Naxalites, a group of Maoist terrorists whose organization was thought to have been destroyed by Indira Gandhi ($\rightarrow$23).

October
1990

Su	Mo	Tu	We	Th	Fr	Sa
	1	2	3	4	5	6
7	8	9	10	11	12	13
14	15	16	17	18	19	20
21	22	23	24	25	26	27
28	29	30	31			

14. London: An 11-year-old girl is raped in the children's ward of a Carshalton hospital.

14. St Andrew's: Ireland beat England in the Dunhill Cup golf competition.

15. UK: Figures show that the rate of increase of heterosexual Aids cases is now higher than that of homosexual men or intravenous drug users.

15. Oslo: Mikhail Gorbachev wins the Nobel Peace Prize.

16. London: A S Byatt wins the Booker prize with her novel *Possession*.

17. Washington: James Baker, the US secretary of state, warns that there can be no partial solution to the Gulf crisis – Saddam must leave Kuwait unconditionally (→ 19).

17. Westminster: John MacGregor, the education minister, secures extra funds for schools at an emergency meeting with Mrs Thatcher.

17. UK: Shell cuts petrol prices by 9.6p per gallon, heralding a fall in fuel prices.

18. Israel: Serious rioting breaks out in the Gaza strip, and soldiers wound at least 55 Palestinians (→ 21).

18. Florida: Howard Marks, the notorious British cannabis smuggler, is jailed for 25 years and fined £100,000 for narcotics offences.

18. Warsaw: The Polish health ministry admits that it withheld West German monies intended to compensate victims of Nazi medical experiments.

19. Moscow: The Supreme Soviet endorses the introduction of the market economy, and adopts Gorbachev's plan to introduce it over two years.

20. Australia: Ornithologists discovery the body of a dead night parrot, a species hitherto thought extinct.

DEATHS

14. Leonard (Louis) Bernstein, US composer and conductor (*25/8/18).→

14. Clifton Pugh, Australian artist (*17/12/24)

The "dead parrot" bites back as Liberals win safe Tory seat

David Bellotti and comrades celebrate their surprise by-election triumph.

Oct 19. The Conservatives crashed to a shock defeat in the early hours of this morning when the Liberal Democrats overturned a majority of nearly 17,000 to win the by-election at Eastbourne. One of the safest Tory seats in the country now has a Liberal Democrat MP in David Bellotti, with a majority of 4,550. The by-election was caused by the murder of the former MP Ian Gow, and the Tory candidate, Richard Hickmet, was criticized for exploiting anti-IRA feeling.

The Eastbourne result will be hailed by the party leader, Paddy Ashdown, as proof of a centre-party revival. Only a week ago the prime minister ridiculed the new symbol of the Liberal Democrats, comparing it to the "dead parrot" of a "Monty Python" sketch. Yesterday the parrot bit back (→ 24).

Poll-tax protesters battle with police

Oct 20. Demonstrators carrying the red and black flags of anarchism clashed with police outside Brixton prison in south London this evening following an anti-poll-tax meeting. The meeting, addressed by four Labour MPs, went off peacefully, except for scuffles between Class War anarchists and members of the left-wing Militant Tendency. Later, however, about half the 5,000-strong crowd marched on the prison and demanded the release of demonstrators being held on remand there following the anti-tax riot in Trafalgar Square last March. Violence erupted, and 18 people were arrested.

Police pin down a Brixton protester.

Kegworth report blames over-hasty crew

Flashback to the scene of destruction after the aircraft crashed onto the M1.

Oct 18. The official report into the Kegworth air disaster, in which 47 people died when a British Midland Boeing 737 crashed on the M1 last year, has laid the blame firmly on the pilots. The report of the CAA air accidents investigation branch published today says that the pilots of the twin-engined 737 mistakenly turned off the plane's right-hand engine after the left-hand one had failed. They acted too hastily and without looking closely enough at the bank of engine instruments in the cockpit, it said. Other members of the crew are criticized for not taking action when they could see which engine had failed.

The report recommends improvements to cockpit instruments and to pilot training. And, in a very rare attack on the US federal aviation administration it criticizes the fact that tests should have failed to detect inbuilt weaknesses in the new engines for the uprated Boeing 737.

A separate report says that better design of aircraft cabins and advice to passengers on how to brace themselves for impact would vastly reduce the number of serious injuries caused by such crashes.

Zeebrugge disaster hearing is stopped

Oct 19. The trial for manslaughter of P&O European Ferries and seven former employees collapsed dramatically today when Mr Justice Turner directed the jury to acquit. He said that the prosecution did not have enough evidence to convict the company.

The trial related to the sinking of the P&O ship *Herald of Free Enterprise* at Zeebrugge in March 1987, in which 192 people died. It was a vital test case on the principle of corporate criminal liability. In the event, a sample charge of unlawful killing has failed at the first hurdle. Angry relatives of those who were drowned now say that the law must be changed to ensure that companies which wantonly disregard safety do not go unpunished.

Sanctions hit Iraqi oil refineries hard

Oct 19. Iraq, the world's second-largest producer of oil, is to ration petrol. This is because the sanctions imposed by the United Nations and enforced by a multinational fleet of warships are preventing chemicals essential for refining crude oil into petrol from reaching Iraq. This is the first effect of the sanctions to hit the man in street. Iraqis have always enjoyed a supply of cheap oil, and grumbles are being heard even before rationing comes into force in four days' time (→ 21).

A small Iraqi shows his support.

America's flamboyant musical genius dies

The lion of American conductors.

Oct 14. Just five days after announcing his retirement through ill health, Leonard Bernstein is dead. Well known for his impassioned conducting style and brilliant communication skills, he was a towering musical talent.

Best known for the outstanding scores which he wrote for three mould-breaking Broadway musicals – *On the Town, West Side Story* and *Candide* – he blended a love of jazz and popular music with a solid classical training. For many years he conducted the New York Philharmonic Orchestra, and he has left a great legacy of recorded music, including his own classical works such as the *Jeremiah* and *Kaddish* symphonies and the *Chichester Psalms*.

Peers puzzle over rock music problem

Oct 16. The House of Lords today frowned over the tricky question: when is pop rock? In a debate on an amendment to the Broadcasting Bill, Earl Ferrers sought to defend government policy that pop includes rock, being music "characterized by a strong rhythmic element and a reliance on electronic amplification". Viscount Falkland could not agree. "There is a world of difference between rock and pop," he said. The latter was recorded mainly for the teenage market; the former – whose practitioners include one Bruce Springsteen, "known also as the Boss" – was ... well ... *different*. The bemused peers simply scratched their grey heads.

Palestinian snub supplies final touch to disastrous Hurd trip

Oct 17. Douglas Hurd's crumbling visit to Israel fell into ruins today when 28 leading Palestinians, furious at remarks attributed to the British foreign secretary by the Israeli press, cancelled a meeting designed to "build bridges".

The visit started badly when the Israelis, angry that he had described their policy towards the Palestinians as "misguided", gave him a distinctly chilly welcome. The trouble with the Palestinians started last night when Mr Hurd met a group of Israeli MPs and one of them leaked a story saying that he had told them that Britain strongly opposed the idea of a Palestinian state.

British officials failed to pick up this story when it was first broadcast and, despite later denials, the damage was done. A disappointed Mr Hurd commented: "I am too well-trained to be angry about it, but it is an opportunity lost" (→ 18).

Hurd holds up a letter from the Palestinians who refused to meet him.

Desert Rats rumble into Saudi, but they're not dressed for it

Oct 16. The Desert Rats, in the form of an advance guard of 247 men and one woman of Britain's 7th Armoured Brigade, returned to the desert today for the first time since they drove Rommel out of North Africa. Landing at an airbase in eastern Saudi Arabia, they are to pave the way for the arrival of 5,500 men with 120 Challenger tanks and their supporting arms to take up their positions alongside the Americans.

The brigade is made up of some of the proudest regiments in the British army: Royal Horse Artillery, Queen's Dragoon Guards, Royal Scots Dragoon Guards, Queen's Royal Irish Hussars and infantrymen from the Staffordshire Regiment. The sole woman, Corporal Mandy Fisher, will be responsible for seeing that the men get their letters from home. As yet they have no desert camouflage uniforms; the ministry of defence sold all its stocks to the Iraqis (→ 17).

Su	Mo	Tu	We	Th	Fr	Sa
	1	2	3	4	5	6
7	8	9	10	11	12	13
14	15	16	17	18	19	20
21	22	23	24	25	26	27
28	29	30	31			

21. Gulf: Allied warships go onto the alert after the USS *O'Brien* fires shots across the bows of a sanctions-busting Iraqi tanker.→

21. Jerusalem: A Palestinian youth stabs three Jews to death (→ 24).

21. Baghdad: Edward Heath meets Saddam Hussein, who promises to release some hostages.→

22. Stow-on-the-Wold: Princess Anne is banned from driving for speeding.

22. UK: The Football Association charges Arsenal and Manchester United with bringing the game into disrepute after Saturday's on-pitch brawl (→ 12/11).

23. Chepstow: Pat Eddery becomes the first jockey since 1952 to ride 200 winners in a flat-racing season.

23. India: V P Singh, the premier, orders the arrest of the Hindu party leader (→ 25).

24. UK: The government announces a £1 rise in child benefit – but only for the eldest child.

24. Israel: Palestinians are ordered to stay in the occupied territories.→

25. India: Sixty-three people are feared dead in the second day of religious riots (→ 27).

26. Las Vegas: Evander Hollyfield downs James "Buster" Douglas to become the new world heavyweight boxing champion.

26. Washington: Mayor Marion Barry is sentenced to six months' jail for possession of cocaine.

27. India: Troops and police seal off the mosque at Ayodhya to protect it against Hindu militants who wish to demolish it (→ 31).

27. Rome: Mrs Thatcher forces discussions on farm prices after talks in Brussels fail to agree on withdrawing subsidies.

DEATH

27. Xavier Cugat, Spanish-born US bandleader (*1/1/1900).

Heath's rescue mission returns home

Freed hostages drink a happy toast to their rescuer, Edward Heath (centre).

But US warns: war clouds are looming

Oct 23. President Bush, reacting to suggestions that Saudi Arabia might be softening its attitude towards Iraq, today rejected the possibility of a compromise peace in the Gulf. "There can never be a compromise, any compromise," he said, " with this kind of aggression." The US president, speaking in Washington, once again compared Saddam Hussein to Hitler. He was supported by the Saudi ambassador to the US, Prince Bandar bin Sultan, who added: "We are determined not to let aggression pay" (→ 28).

Oct 23. Edward Heath, the former British prime minister, took off from Baghdad tonight with 33 Britons and two pet dogs whose release he had won from Saddam Hussein in 48 hours of often tense negotiations. The Iraqi president also promised Mr Heath that a further 30 Britons would be freed.

Mr Heath's mission has been much criticized because it was feared that Saddam Hussein would use it to make propaganda, and it has not achieved Mr Heath's aim of bringing home 200 hostages. Nevertheless, the 27 sick and elderly men,

five wives and one single woman who are flying home on a Virgin Atlantic jumbo jet equipped with life-support machines and a medical team are extremely happy to be going home and have nothing but praise for Mr Heath.

One of the freed hostages, Jim Thomson, revealed that some westerners being held as human shields at an arms factory rioted after being mistreated by bullying guards and fed starvation rations. "We tore down fences," he said, "broke all the windows and daubed anti-Saddam slogans on the walls" (→ 28).

Holding firm against the tide of world opinion: Saddam Hussein.

Jewish immigrants snatch jobs from banned Palestinian Arabs

Oct 27. When thousands of Palestinians returned to work in Israel today after a four-day ban imposed following the stabbing to death of three Israelis, as many as 600 from the West Bank and the Gaza strip found that they had been sacked. The Israeli authorities have used the fear caused by Palestinians' revenge attacks following the killing of some 21 rioters at the Temple Mount to give their poorly-paid jobs to Jewish immigrants flooding in from the Soviet Union.

Something like 120,000 Palestinians rely on their jobs in Israel and cross the "Green Line" every day to work on building sites and at other menial jobs. "Arik" Sharon, the hard-nosed housing minister, says: "We need to cut back on their numbers."

An Israeli soldier stands guard over Moslem women on their way to prayer.

IRA reveals new weapon: a human bomb

Oct 24. The IRA used human bombs today to attack two border checkpoints and an army camp, killing six soldiers and a civilian. Three Catholic civilians – called "collaborators" by the IRA because they worked for the security forces – were strapped into cars loaded with explosives and ordered to drive to the targets while their families were held hostage. They were told that they would have time to get out of the cars before they ex-

ploded, but it seems that the bombs were set off by radio command as soon as they were in position.

Patsy Gillespie, a married man with three children, stood no chance. He was blown to pieces at a checkpoint near Derry. Five soldiers of the King's Regiment died with him. At Newry another driver miraculously suffered only a broken leg, but a soldier of the Irish Rangers died in the blast. The third bomb failed to go off.

A soldier surveys the scene of devastation at one of the border checkpoints.

Fraud squad arrests Liverpool bigwigs

Oct 26. Derek Hatton, the former deputy leader of Liverpool city council, was among 22 people arrested in north-west England today in connection with allegedly corrupt land deals. The arrests were made in a series of coordinated raids involving 280 police led by the Merseyside police fraud squad.

Mr Hatton, who was released on police bail after being questioned for nine hours, became nationally known as a flamboyant champion of the left-wing Militant organization. After frequent clashes with the Labour leadership, he was expelled from the party. His solicitor, David Phillips, said tonight that Mr Hatton had not been charged and denies all offences. A number of other city councillors were among the 22 people arrested by police.

City miracle Polly Peck goes bankrupt

Oct 25. Polly Peck International, one of Britain's top 100 companies, now with debts of more than £1.3 billion, today called in administrators. The man who created the company, Asil Nadir, faces a bankruptcy petition after the collapse of Polly Peck, whose interests include fruit, hotels and electronics in the United States, Japan and Turkey.

Mr Nadir's business empire had grown from a small rag-trade company in the East End of London to a multinational concern valued three months ago at £1.92 million. Share prices collapsed last month, however, after the serious fraud squad raided the premises of another company linked to Mr Nadir as part of an inquiry into illegal share dealings. Attempts to secure a rescue have so far failed.

Bhutto claims fraud after election defeat

Oct 27. More than 30 people were killed and 100 injured in violent clashes today as Benazir Bhutto's Pakistan People's Party (PPP) suffered its second crushing electoral defeat in a week. Three days ago, the PPP was swept aside in Pakistan's general election by the Islamic Democratic Alliance (IDA), a coalition of nine parties. Today, in elections to the country's four provincial assemblies, the PPP lost out in three of the provinces – Punjab, Sind and North West Frontier Province – while in Baluchistan there was no clear majority.

PPP support seems to have been transferred to regional and ethnic parties, although PPP officials claim that voting has been rigged.

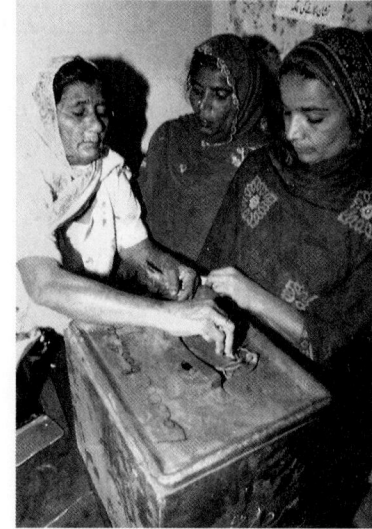

Women cast their vote in Karachi.

Senna crashes to a Grand Prix victory

Oct 21. Ayrton Senna spent just seven seconds on the racetrack at Suzuka in Japan today, but it was enough to become world motor-racing champion for the second time. He clashed with the only man who could have beaten him, Alain Prost, with both cars ending up off the track at the very first corner.

"He did it on purpose," claimed Prost. "He knew he had no chance of winning the race if I got ahead, so he pushed me off." Not so, said Senna: it was Prost's fault for moving in front of him. Either way, both cars were out of the Japanese Grand Prix, and for Prost out, too, of the world championship. He had to win today to beat Senna. Last year Prost won the title after a crash with Senna, also at Suzuka.

Senna (l.) and Prost walk to the pit.

Child benefit boost

Oct 24. An extra £1 a week in child benefit for the oldest child was announced today by Tony Newton, the social security secretary, following an intervention by the prime minister. The increase ends a three-year freeze on child benefit at £7.25 a week which had dismayed many Tory MPs, who are already worried about the party's image in the wake of the Eastbourne election defeat. A statement due on Monday was delayed to enable Mrs Thatcher to approve this compromise between a continued freeze and the all-round increase backed by opposition parties.

FBI Special Agent Dale Cooper investigates murder, and enjoys coffee, in TV's "Twin Peaks".

October

1990

Su	Mo	Tu	We	Th	Fr	Sa
	1	2	3	4	5	6
7	8	9	10	11	12	13
14	15	16	17	18	19	20
21	22	23	24	25	26	27
28	29	30	31			

28. UK: As Sir Geoffrey Howe adopts a softer line towards European monetary union than Mrs Thatcher, opinion polls put Labour 16 points ahead of the Tories.→

28. USSR: Troops intervene in Moldavia to keep Gaugaz Turks and ethnic Moldavians apart.

28. London: Families of men detained in Iraq and occupied Kuwait march to Downing Street to demand more action to free them.

28. Baghdad: Yevgeny Primakov, the Soviet envoy, meets Saddam Hussein for talks but makes no progress.

28. US: General Norman Schwarzkopf, the commander of the US task force in Saudi Arabia, warns that the Gulf conflict could be "as bloody as Vietnam".→

29. New York: The UN votes to gather information on Iraqi brutality in Kuwait in order to mount a war-crimes trial against Iraqi leaders.

29. Luxembourg: The EC, excluding Britain, agrees to set 2000 as the target date to stabilize carbon dioxide emissions.

29. UK: The Consumers' Association says that it will take legal action to try to give travellers the right to claim compensation for poor service from British Rail.

30. Westminster: Mrs Thatcher reaffirms her opposition to a single European currency and maintains that it would be an intolerable loss of national sovereignty (→ 1/11).

30. Westminster: The government defeats a Lords amendment calling for compulsory dog registration by just three votes.

30. Nottingham: The police force is found guilty of racial discrimination for failing to promote an Asian constable, Surinder Singh, and others.

31. Westminster: The government lays down strict new guidelines for capping local councils to keep poll tax levels below £400.→

Taoiseach sacks his deputy to save skin

Lenihan puts a brave face on it all.

Oct 31. Charles Haughey, the Irish prime minister or *Taoiseach*, today lost his deputy but saved his government. He sacked Brian Lenihan just an hour before a vote of confidence, which was forced by opposition parties following revelations that Lenihan had made calls to the Irish president in 1982 to try to delay a general election. Lenihan is due to be *Fianna Fail* candidate for president next week.

The junior party in Ireland's coalition government, the Progressive Democrats, threatened to withdraw its support so long as Lenihan stayed in the cabinet. Today Haughey reluctantly acquiesced, sacking his closest ally and winning the crucial vote in the *Dail* by 83 votes to 80 (→9/11).

Former premier to face perjury charge

Oct 29. Sir Johannes Bjelke-Petersen, the former premier of Queensland, has been charged with corruptly receiving $100,000 from an Asian businessman in 1986. He will also face two charges that he committed perjury while giving evidence to the 1988 Fitzgerald Inquiry into massive police corruption in Queensland. Sir Joh, who is 80, was premier for 19 years before his forced resignation. He is the seventh former National Party minister, and the most senior, to face criminal charges arising from the Fitzgerald Inquiry.

Thatcher alone in Rome

Oct 28. European leaders moved with unexpected speed today to set deadlines for the next stages of economic monetary union, sweeping aside objections from Margaret Thatcher who was left isolated in her opposition. "Cloud cuckoo land" was the prime minister's angry response, and she warned that Britain would veto moves to a single European currency.

Decisions about the next stages of monetary union had not been expected before December. Instead, European leaders meeting in Rome agreed to set 1 January 1994 for the creation of a European central bank to control monetary policy, and cleared the way for a single currency by the end of the century.

Mrs Thatcher said that the British parliament would never agree to abolish the pound. She scorned her counterparts for failing to tackle short-term disagreements over farm subsidies, accusing them

Mitterrand and Thatcher step out.

of taking refuge in "grandiose" words to avoid discussions of substance. Her isolation (and tough words) will alarm the City – and some of cabinet colleagues (→30).

Holy site sparks off religious war in India

Hindu fanatics attack the 16th-century mosque at the disputed site.

Oct 31. Hindu fundamentalists made a fresh attempt today to storm the mosque at Ayodhya, the focus of a bitter conflict between India's Hindus and Moslems. Paramilitary troops were called in to defend the 460-year-old mosque, targeted by Hindus because they claim that the site is the birthplace of one of their principal gods, the Lord Rama. Over the past eight days at least 170 people have been killed throughout the country in clashes over the temple.

It is a dispute which threatens to bring the government down, for the coalition of the prime minister, V P Singh, is in crisis after the Hindu fundamentalist Bharatiya Janata Party deserted earlier this month in protest over his policy on the mosque (→7/11).

Furious president warns he's "had it" with Iraqi intransigence

Oct 31. President Bush's frustration with Saddam Hussein boiled over today at a political campaign breakfast in Virginia. Speaking off-the-cuff to reporters, he said that he had "had it" with the Iraqis' treatment of Americans in Kuwait.

"The embassy is being starved," he said. "The American flag is flying over the embassy and our people inside are being starved by a brutal dictator. Do you think I am concerned about it? You're darned right I am.

"And what am I going to do about it? Let's just wait and see, because I've had it with that kind of treatment of Americans."

When he was asked if the hostages had become more important to his Gulf strategy, he replied: "I would not say more, but I am very concerned about it." Mr Bush's anger stems from intelligence reports of hostages being shuttled between potential bombing targets in appalling conditions.

Showing signs of strain, President Bush tells pressmen of his frustration.

Small hole signals new era for Britain

Oct 30. Crews deep beneath the sea-bed at work on the Channel Tunnel met up tonight for the first time, when French workers drilled a five-centimetre (two-inch) pilot hole through to the British side of a service tunnel. But the workers will not meet face to face until early December, when it is expected that they will be able to walk through a final hand-dug section of the tunnel and shake hands. Meanwhile, labourers on the running tunnels, through which trains will travel, are scheduled to meet next autumn.

At the other end of this hole: France.

Georgians flock to first multi-party polls

Oct 28. The people of the Soviet republic of Georgia turned out in huge numbers today to enjoy the novelty of voting in the first free multi-party election for 70 years. The Communists, discredited by the killing of 20 peaceful demonstrators in Tbilisi, are struggling to maintain control of this nation of free spirits. They are hoping to capitalize on Georgian nationalism, promising the voters a form of independence and a move towards a market economy.

Moldavian women protest in silence.

Poll-tax guidance

Oct 31. Tough new rules for next year's poll tax were outlined today by Chris Patten, the environment secretary. He claimed that they will ensure that the average poll-tax (or community-charge) bill will be no more than £380 – and capping will be imposed to keep costs down. Council leaders say that as the projected rise is below the current rate of inflation widespread cuts in services will be necessary to achieve the government target. Local authority finance officers thought the average would be nearer £420.

Left ousted in NZ

Oct 28. New Zealand's weekend general election has resulted in a landslide of unprecedented proportions for Jim Bolger and his National Party. Eight Labour cabinet ministers lost their seats in the poll which gave the Nationals 68 out of the 97 seats in parliament. The Labour government's decision only eight weeks ago to dump Geoffrey Palmer, the prime minister, in favour of Mike Moore helped to precipitate the government defeat. The Green Party polled a record 8.9 per cent, but did not win any seats.

Australia lurches into a recession

Oct 31. The opposition leader, John Hewson, says that Australia is in its worst recession since World War II. Most people believe him. Bob Hawke, the prime minister, and Paul Keating, the treasurer, say that they have now successfully cooled down the economy and found the right macro-economic mix for the return of the good times. But the battling wage-earners and small businessmen are no longer listening to theory.

The corporate high-flyers are either in court (Bond, Skase, Connell) or reorganizing their empires to reduce debt (Murdoch, Elliott, Spalvins). Bankruptcy is rife, and the gleaming skyscrapers of the boom years contain acres of space to let.

Rupert Murdoch has made one of his classic lightning strikes to overcome mounting losses at his Melbourne flagship, the 150-year-old *Herald*. Casting aside any sentiment over his father's long stewardship of the paper, he has merged it with the morning *Sun* to make the hybrid *Herald-Sun*, a so-called 24-hour paper. The same rationale has produced the *Telegraph-Mirror* in Sydney.

The government is also reeling under the strain of a series of financial body-blows. In Victoria, the State Bank lost A$1,500 million, and the Victorian economic development corporation is accused of wanton lending. The premier, deputy premier and treasurer have all resigned. The state government has now charged an extra three cents per litre of petrol (on top of increases due to the Gulf crisis) in order to recoup some of its voluntary indemnity to investors in the collapsed Pyramid Building Society.

Stock-exchange trading is slow and jittery. Wool is down, and 40 million sheep face the bullet to get flocks back to economically rational levels. Wheat, too, is at rock-bottom prices and debtors like Iraq, the USSR and Romania do little to instil confidence.

Su	Mo	Tu	We	Th	Fr	Sa
				1	2	3
4	5	6	7	8	9	10
11	12	13	14	15	16	17
18	19	20	21	22	23	24
25	26	27	28	29	30	

1. UK: The Liberal Democrats make the adoption of proportional representation the precondition of any future government pacts.

2. UK: Neil Kinnock backs the adoption of a single European currency (→ 5).

2. South Africa: The government agrees to free all political prisoners.

3. London: Facing a severe cash crisis, the Royal Shakespeare Company is forced to close both of its Barbican theatres.

4. Baghdad: Saddam Hussein invites relatives of hostages to come and spend Christmas with their loved ones (→ 5).

5. UK: Sir John Stokes, a Tory MP, says that families of hostages in the Gulf should keep stiff upper lips and stop "mewling and puking".

6. Tel Aviv: Having apparently received a warning from his constituency party, Michael Heseltine says that he will not force a Tory leadership election (→ 11).

7. US: The Democrats make gains in mid-term elections.

7. Hollywood: Fire destroys historic film sets at the Universal Studios.

8. Poland: Germany and Poland agree to sign a friendship treaty in which the Germans recognize the Oder-Neisse line as the border.

8. UK: In the autumn budget statement, John Major admits that Britain is in a recession and announces tight public spending plans (→ 9).

9. UK: The Tories are driven into third place at the Bradford & Bootle by-election (→ 11).

10. India: Chandra Shekhar is sworn in as prime minister.

DEATHS

4. Mary Martin, US actress (*1/12/13).

4. Sir David Archibald Stirling, founder of the SAS (*15/11/15).

7. Lawrence George Durrell, British author (*27/2/12).

Howe resignation shatters Tory unity

No compromise on sovereignty issue.

Maggie denies split on European policy

Nov 7. Margaret Thatcher showed no signs of bowing to demands for a softer line towards European monetary union when she spoke in the Commons today. The prime minister claimed that there were no significant differences over policy with Sir Geoffrey Howe, who resigned last week. But she repeated the fears about loss of sovereignty which Douglas Hurd, the foreign secretary, had sought to dismiss as "ogres" this week. Her task, she insisted, was "to preserve our national currency" (→ 9).

Nov 1. Sir Geoffrey Howe, the deputy prime minister and Margaret Thatcher's most loyal servant, left the cabinet tonight and plunged the beleaguered prime minister into the greatest crisis of her 11-year tenure of Downing Street. "I believe I can no longer serve with honour," declared Sir Geoffrey in his resignation letter [*see below right*]. He was the last surviving member of Mrs Thatcher's original 1979 administration, and as her first chancellor of the exchequer was the architect of Thatcherite economics.

The resignation, coming hours after Sir Geoffrey, who was also leader of the House, had attended this morning's cabinet meeting, stunned his colleagues. It has again exposed Tory differences over Europe, rekindled by Mrs Thatcher's unbending opposition to monetary union at the Rome summit.

The split has been highlighted by three ministerial resignations in barely a year: Sir Geoffrey and Nigel Lawson wanted closer integration with the European Community, Nicholas Ridley wanted less. Mrs Thatcher said tonight that she did not believe the differences to which Sir Geoffrey referred are "nearly as great as you suggest". But his departure increases the risk that she will be challenged for the leadership, possibly by Michael Heseltine who himself left over European policy four years ago (→ 5).

Sir Geoffrey: lost faith in Thatcher.

Deputy spells out a basic disagreement

Nov 1. In his letter of resignation Sir Geoffrey Howe said: "The risks of being left behind on economic and monetary union are severe. All too much of our energy during the last decade has been devoted to correcting the consequences of our late start in Europe. I am deeply anxious that the mood you have struck ... will make it more difficult for Britain to hold and retain a position of influence in this vital debate ... I now find myself unable to share your view of the right approach to this question" (→ 13).

Heseltine weighs in with criticism of Thatcher stance on Europe

The Heseltines at the airport today.

Nov 3. Michael Heseltine today fanned the flames of Tory turmoil by accusing Margaret Thatcher of putting the party's future at risk by her attitude to Europe. It was his most direct, and fiercest, attack on the prime minister since he walked out of the cabinet in 1986.

Downing Street sources are furious tonight over what they see as a blatant attempt by Mr Heseltine to exploit the divisions caused by Sir Geoffrey Howe's resignation two days ago. Nonsense, say the Heseltine supporters: it was the prime minister's attitude to Europe which led Sir Geoffrey to quit and caused what Mr Heseltine called today a "crisis of confidence".

Michael Heseltine's attack – in an open letter to the chairman of his Henley constituency – has fuelled speculation that he will challenge the prime minister for the leadership of the Conservartive Party later this month. So far he has always insisted that there were no foreseeable circumstances in which he would oppose her. That is still his position, urging the cabinet to impose its "collective wisdom" to achieve greater party unity.

Mr Heseltine, who left Heathrow today on a visit to the Middle East, warned that divisions over Europe would condemn the Tories to a decade in the political wilderness. An opinion poll released tonight showed him to be more popular than the prime minister (→ 9).

Ireland chooses a surprising president

Mary Robinson: a mould-breaking election win for an independent activist.

Nov 9. Mary Robinson was tonight confirmed as the first woman president of the Republic of Ireland. In one of the greatest political upsets in Ireland's history, a young (46-year-old) liberal feminist lawyer will occupy a post traditionally filled by elderly conservative men.

Robinson, standing as an independent, beat her nearest rival, *Fianna Fail*'s Brian Lenihan, by 86,566 votes days after he had been sacked as deputy to Charles Haughey, the premier. Second-preference votes, mainly from Austin Currie, the *Fine Gael* candidate, secured her victory in the second count. Leaders of the two main parties are in a state of shock, and Alan Dukes, the leader of *Fine Gael*, now faces a vote of no confidence.

Mrs Robinson has spent the years since 1985 – when she resigned from the Labour Party – campaigning for civil and women's rights. She says that she will use the office of president, which brings few powers but immense prestige and authority, to speak up for the disadvantaged in society (→ 13).

Boxer is cleared of attempted murder

Nov 7. Terry Marsh, a former world light-welterweight boxing champion, was today cleared at the Old Bailey of attempting to murder Frank Warren, his former manager and one of the sport's leading promoters. Cheers from the galleries greeted the jury's majority verdict after a 12-day trial.

A masked gunman had shot Mr Warren as he entered a London club. Mr Marsh's lawyers claimed that there was no evidence against him except the testimony of a prisoner to whom Marsh allegedly confessed. The former champ spent his first hours of freedom auctioning his story to newspapers.

Indian government loses confidence vote

Nov 7. India's prime minister of 11 months, V P Singh, has resigned today after losing a vote of no confidence. In a parliamentary debate marked by fisticuffs and shouting, Singh failed to persuade MPs that he could stop the tide of violence sweeping the country.

Angry MPs heard that Singh had given his personal backing to fundamentalist Hindu plans to demolish the mosque at Ayodhya, only to change his mind and arrest the Hindus' leader. Since then, battles around the mosque site have cost over 200 lives. Singh's plans to reform the caste system have brought a series of bloody protests, while in Kashmir guerrillas have started a war of independence (→ 10).

Singh: a disastrous prime minister?

Gun protest spoils Red Square parade

Protesters want Yeltsin, not Lenin.

Nov 7. The traditional Revolution Day parade in Moscow's Red Square was disrupted today by a lone gunman who fired two shots in the air. KGB men quickly bundled the man, from Leningrad, away from the scene. It is not known whether his shots were meant for President Gorbachev.

Soviet dissidents marked the day in their own way. Two "alternative" marches, whose purpose was to celebrate democracy rather than the 1917 Bolshevik revolution, took place in Moscow. In Kiev, Ukrainian separatists shouted "Ivan go home". But Mr Gorbachev is perhaps breathing a sigh of relief tonight as a rumoured military coup failed to materialize (→ 17).

Some hostages out but more troops in

Nov 10. The US secretary of state, James Baker, has spent a busy week firming up his country's allies in the Middle East and Europe. At the end of his diplomatic rounds today, he said that the allies were completely united on the goal of pushing Iraq out of Kuwait, by force if need be. The US has announced a virtual doubling of its ground forces in the Gulf, with 1,000 more tanks and 200,000 more men to be deployed. The world's elder statesmen, meanwhile, are still courting Saddam Hussein. Germany's Willy Brandt and Japan's Yasuhiro Nakasone both left Baghdad with their quotas of hostages (→ 12).

Sky absorbs BSB in satellite TV merger

Nov 2. Britain's two satellite television companies are to merge. The announcement tonight ends a rivalry which had left both Sky Television and British Satellite Broadcasting (BSB) with huge losses. Sky, owned by Rupert Murdoch's News International, is the victor of this TV war. Although the new company will be jointly owned, the Sky satellite system will eventually be the sole source of transmissions and Sky staff will run the renamed British Sky Broadcasting. The Independent Broadcasting Authority was caught unawares by the move, and plans to investigate it.

Nov 6. Cahal Daly, the bishop of Down and Connor, is to be the new Catholic primate of All Ireland.

November
1990

Su	Mo	Tu	We	Th	Fr	Sa
				1	2	3
4	5	6	7	8	9	10
11	12	13	14	15	16	17
18	19	20	21	22	23	24
25	26	27	28	29	30	

11. UK: Michael Heseltine's constituents deny that they intended to discourage him from standing for the Tory leadership.→

11. London: Steve Hill, aged 29, sets himself on fire at the Remembrance Sunday parade at the Cenotaph.

11. London: Police seize an IRA arms cache in Kilburn and arrest two men.

12. UK: Government scientists warn that clingfilm can be carcinogenic.

12. Kuwait: Iraq gives Kuwaitis until 25 November to take up Iraqi identity cards.→

13. Dublin: Alan Dukes, the leader of the opposition *Fine Gael* party, resigns.

13. Morocco: An Iraqi official arrives to discuss a proposed new Arab summit.→

14. Moscow: Soviet MPs force an emergency debate on the state of the nation.

14. Dublin: In a European soccer championship match, England and Ireland draw 1-1.

14. Coventry: The city observes the 50th anniversary of the *Luftwaffe* bombing raid in which hundreds died.

15. Vienna: Nato and the Warsaw Pact agree on the terms of the Conventional Forces in Europe treaty to slash their armed forces.

15. UK: Mrs Thatcher's aides confirm that she will fight Mr Heseltine to the end (→ 17).

16. Washington: President Bush admits that he is losing the battle for American public opinion on the Gulf crisis.→

17. UK: Polls in early editions of Sunday papers show that under Michael Heseltine the Tories would beat Labour in a general election.

17. Thailand: A mass grave, believed to contain the bodies of hundreds of PoWs, is uncovered at the bridge over the river Kwai.

DEATH

14. Malcolm Muggeridge, British writer and broadcaster (*24/3/03).

Student marches rock French government

Nov 14. The French government today offered an extra £450 million for education, after scenes of street violence reminiscent of the student riots of 1968. Michel Rocard, the prime minister, is still reeling from Monday's rally of over 200,000 secondary-school pupils demanding better education, which degenerated into fighting. The Alma district of Paris found itself at the centre of looting and rioting. Shop windows were smashed, 190 cars were damaged, 234 policemen injured and 83 youths arrested.

The police had turned on the marchers with tear gas and water cannon to prevent them from reaching their destination in the Champs Elysees; ordered to avoid confrontation with the rioters, however, they could only watch from behind their riot shields as the destruction unfolded. President Mitterrand is accused of stoking up violence by publicly backing the students.

Rock-throwing French school students take the law into their own hands.

FA punishes teams for on-pitch battle

Nov 12. Two top English football clubs today forfeited league points as an unprecedented punishment for an on-pitch brawl involving 21 players last Saturday. Arsenal lost two points and Manchester United one point following a Football Association disciplinary commission hearing which also imposed £50,000 fines on both clubs. Arsenal are now eight points behind the league leaders, Liverpool.

"The commission, in reaching its decision, wished to emphasize their determination to eliminate mass confrontations between players," said Graham Kelly, the chief executive of the FA. "Financial penalties have not succeeded in the past, so the only way to get the message across was to take the action of deducting points."

Gorbachev wins in emergency debate

Nov 17. The Soviet parliament has agreed to change the country's constitution in a desperate attempt to stave off total collapse. President Gorbachev has won increased powers and the assistance of a vice-president. While the republics are to have more say in central government, so too are the police, the KGB and the army.

The vote comes at the end of a turbulent week. MPs scrapped the parliamentary agenda and demanded that Mr Gorbachev appear before them to answer questions on the breakdown of the economy and the desperate "war of laws" between Moscow and the 15 Soviet republics. Boris Yeltsin, the Russian president, led calls for food rationing and a "crisis committee". But Mr Gorbachev has survived.

Arab peace summit plan is torpedoed

US fighter planes over Saudi Arabia.

Nov 17. Proposals for a new Arab summit to discuss the crisis, floated this week by Morocco's King Hassan, were torpedoed first by Iraq (which said that it would not attend) and then by Saudi Arabia. Any meeting, said the Saudis, would be a waste of time unless Iraq left Kuwait first.

President Bush today reminded a Czech audience of the appeasement of Hitler which led to the Second World War. The moral was that you "cannot turn a blind eye to aggression" – a message aimed squarely at Saddam Hussein.

Nov 12. Emperor Akihito of Japan wears court dress for his official enthronement ceremony today.

94

Howe speech opens door for challenge to Thatcher

Nov 13. Sir Geoffrey Howe today delivered a devastating indictment of the prime minister, and almost certainly triggered a challenge for the Tory leadership from Michael Heseltine. MPs were startled by the vehemence of Sir Geoffrey's resignation speech to the House of Commons. He accused Mrs Thatcher of conjuring up a "nightmare" vision of a Europe "positively teeming with ill-intentioned people scheming, in her words, to extinguish democracy". It was a tragedy, he said, that the prime minister's "perceived attitude towards Europe is running increasingly serious risks for the future of our nation".

It was also tragic, he said, that Britain had not joined the exchange rate mechanism at least five years ago, and, asserting that Mrs Thatcher's attitude was undermining colleagues such as the chancellor, he turned the prime minister's cricketing metaphor [*see below*] against her: "It's rather like sending your opening batsmen to the crease only for them to find, the moment the first balls are bowled, that their bats have been broken before the game by the team captain."→

Heseltine announces his intention.

Challenger swoops on wounded leader

Nov 14. Michael Heseltine today announced his candidature for the leadership of the Conservative Party – and he fired the first shots by demanding an urgent review of the poll tax. With the prime minister already marshalling her campaign team to fight him, it seems likely to be a two-horse race. Douglas Hurd, the foreign secretary, is seen as a unity candidate, able to heal party wounds, but neither he nor John Major, the chancellor,

> ## 'I have a better prospect ... of a fourth poll victory'

will oppose Mrs Thatcher. Mr Heseltine resigned as defence secretary in January 1986 after a losing a row over the future of the Westland helicopter company in which he backed a European solution.

He now cites attitudes towards Europe and cabinet disunity as reasons for his challenge. "I am now persuaded that I would have a better prospect than Mrs Thatcher of leading the Conservatives to a fourth electoral victory and preventing the ultimate calamity of a Labour government" (→ 15).

Thatcher warns she will put up a fight

Nov 12. Margaret Thatcher tonight vowed to fight hard to retain the leadership of the Tory party. In a combative speech at the Lord Mayor's banquet in London, she coupled claims that her government had broken the post-war mould of bureaucracy and decline with a warning to any potential challengers for the Tory crown.

"I am still at the crease, though the bowling has been pretty hostile of late. And in case any of you

> ## 'I am still at the crease, though the bowling is hostile'

doubted it, can I assure you there will be no ducking the bouncers, no stone-walling, no playing for time. The bowling is going to get hit all round the ground," she said.

On the thorny question of Europe, Mrs Thatcher reiterated her suspicions of "grand designs and blueprints" in more muted tones than those which so upset Sir Geoffrey Howe. "Surely it's more sensible to see that every country fulfils its existing obligations before moving on to set new targets," she insisted gently (→ 13).

Thatcher arrives at the Guildhall.

Oil rigs are not safe enough, says report

Nov 12. Virtually every aspect of offshore safety came under sharp criticism today with the publication of Lord Cullen's official report into the explosion on the Piper Alpha oil platform in July 1988, in which 167 men died. Occidental, the operator, had a "superficial attitude" to the assessment of potential major hazards. The department of energy's inspections of the platform were "little use as a test of safety", and the regulations governing the industry are "unduly restrictive" and "out of date". Responsibility for North Sea oil rigs is now likely to be transferred to a division of the health and safety executive.

Gunman runs wild in New Zealand village

Nov 14. A gunman was shot dead by police this evening after killing 11 of the 50 inhabitants of the tiny seaside village of Aramoana, near Dunedin. A six-year-old boy and a local police sergeant were among the dead in New Zealand's worst-ever mass killing. It all started yesterday evening when David Gray, aged 33, set fire to his neighbour's house and then started shooting. Today police flushed him out of another house with tear gas. Gray, described as a loner who loved guns and liked to wear military uniforms, is thought to have used an AK-47 automatic rifle in his purposeless killing spree.

November
1990

Su	Mo	Tu	We	Th	Fr	Sa
				1	2	3
4	5	6	7	8	9	10
11	12	13	14	15	16	17
18	19	20	21	22	23	24
25	26	27	28	29	30	

18. Hemel Hempstead: Simon Jones, the four-year-old boy missing for eight weeks, is found safe in a hostel for homeless men.

18. UK: Mrs Thatcher proposes a referendum to decide the issue of a single European currency (→ 19).

18. Birmingham: Chris Eubank beats Nigel Benn to become the WBO middle-weight boxing champion.

19. UK: Mrs Thatcher says that Michael Heseltine's economic policies are like those of the Labour Party.→

20. UK: Paris: The Soviet foreign minister says that the USSR will back a new UN resolution against Iraq.→

21. Lebanon: The Christian militia, led by Samir Geagea, agrees to withdraw from Beirut.

21. UK: The opening share price of the privatized electricity companies is announced as 240p each.

21. New York: Michael Milken, who made a fortune on Wall Street in the 1980s, is jailed for ten years for violating tax laws.

22. Bulgaria: Over 20,000 protesters march to demand the resignation of the government (→ 29).

22. North Sea: Four fishermen are believed drowned after the nuclear submarine HMS *Trenchant* sinks their vessel.

22. UK: It is announced that 15,000 more British troops are to be sent to the Gulf.

23. Northern Ireland: An enormous IRA proxy bomb fails to detonate at an army checkpoint at Roslea (→ 30).

24. South Africa: Right-wing white extremists attack 300 black children picnicking in a park in Louis Trichardt.

24. Saudi Arabia: Travellers report that Kuwaiti resistants, bent on revenge, have murdered eight girls in a Baghdad school (→ 30).

DEATH

23. Roald Dahl, British author (*13/9/16).

Tories force Mrs Thatcher from office

Time to go? Mrs Thatcher checks her watch as Tory MPs vote in Westminster.

Tuesday: Maggie fails to win first ballot

Nov 20. Margaret Thatcher tonight vowed to fight on as prime minister after falling just four votes short of outright victory against Michael Heseltine. She sought to quell talk of a cabinet revolt by announcing her determination to contest the second round next week within minutes of the ballot result.

Ministers were dismayed by the inconclusive vote by Tory MPs – 204 votes for Mrs Thatcher, against 152 for Mr Heseltine with 16 abstentions. Under the complex Tory rules, she fell just short of the margin required. Some ministers met privately tonight to discuss how the Heseltine bandwagon can be stopped, as MPs switch to the man who opinion polls say is more likely to lead the Conservatives to victory than Mrs Thatcher.

Potential new candidates such as Douglas Hurd and John Major were sidelined, however, by the prime minister's pre-emptive statement in Paris where she is attending an international conference. Both have said that they will not stand against her.→

Wednesday: feisty premier to fight on

Nov 21. The prime minister is tonight locked in a struggle for survival as she prepares for the second round of the Tory leadership election. Publicly, she remains defiant. "I fight on. I fight to win," she said as she left Downing Street for parliament. Behind the scenes, however, Margaret Thatcher is thought to be under intense pressure to step down and allow other candidates to enter the fray.

A succession of party chiefs made their way to Downing Street after the prime minister returned early from the Paris summit. Westminster was abuzz with rumours that senior party figures – the so-called "men in grey suits" – were advising Mrs Thatcher that, with votes steadily haemorrhaging to Mr Heseltine, she was unlikely to win a second round. It is also being said that the party can never unite again under her. But her supporters, such as the former party chairman Norman Tebbit and the right-wing "No Turning Back" group of MPs, urged her to stand firm.

Mrs Thatcher has replaced her campaign manager, George Younger, with the more vigorous John Wakeham. Tonight she is canvassing her ministers individually for their opinions.→

Thursday: end of an era as Thatcher opts for dignified exit

Nov 22. The Thatcher era ended shortly after nine o'clock this morning when the prime minister told her cabinet that she would not fight on for the Tory leadership. "It's a funny old world," she is said to have commented when, with eyes moistening, she reflected on the end of the record-breaking premiership she had never lost at the polls.

Mrs Thatcher made up her mind to quit less than 24 hours after publicly declaring her intention to fight on against Michael Heseltine. A series of meetings yesterday evening had made it clear that a majority of her cabinet colleagues felt she could no longer beat her former defence secretary. After sleeping on her decision, she told close colleagues at 7.30 this morning and prepared to visit Buckingham Palace.

"I have concluded that the unity of the party and the prospect of victory would be better served if I stood down," she said. And as her cabinet colleagues Douglas Hurd and John Major announced their candidacies [*see report on page 97*] the retiring prime minister was off to Westminster for a bravura performance during a censure debate. Tory MPs greeted her with cheers, mingled with some nostalgia and not a little guilt about the nature of the coup which had ended the 11-year reign of Britain's first woman prime minister.

One woman's reaction to the news.

Three-horse race is setback for Heseltine

The Hurd family feeds the ducks, while John and Norma Major take a stroll.

Nov 24. Michael Heseltine today won heavyweight Tory backing – from Sir Geoffrey Howe, Nigel Lawson and Lord Carrington – but John Major is emerging as the new front-runner in the race to succeed Margaret Thatcher as the next prime minister. "It's a two-horse race," said aides of Mr Major, the chancellor of the exchequer, as the third candidate, Douglas Hurd, lagged in early estimates of support amongst Tory MPs.

No candidate appears likely to win an overall majority in the second-round voting next Tuesday, making a third ballot apparently inevitable. Supporters of Douglas Hurd, the foreign secretary, say

that he will then emerge as the "unity candidate" most likely to heal the wounds of a party which this week toppled Mrs Thatcher.

Michael Heseltine's backers have acknowledged that their man has lost some momentum since the prime minister's dramatic withdrawal two days ago. They have seen both Mr Hurd and Mr Major promise similar reviews of the poll tax and tonight opinion polls have also shown John Major to be even more popular than Mr Heseltine as a potential vote-winner. The latter is also suffering a backlash from a Thatcher camp seething over the cabinet revolt which forced the prime minister to quit (→ 27).

European arms slashed

Nov 19. The Cold War officially ended today when 22 heads of state agreed to start dismantling Europe's massive armouries. The Treaty on Conventional Armed Forces in Europe (called the CFE treaty for short) slashes the amount of conventional weaponry held by the Nato and Warsaw Pact countries to 20,000 battle tanks, 20,000 heavy artillery pieces, 30,000 armoured combat vehicles, 2,000 attack helicopters and 6,800 combat aircraft each – a low level of armament which should make sudden attacks impossible. Complicated arrangements, which cover Europe from the Atlantic to the Urals, provide for the parties to shed over 100,000 pieces of military hardware and to check each others' future holdings.

Although the treaty heralds a new and more peaceful Europe, the delegates were in a sombre mood. Instability and ethnic strife in eastern Europe, looming famine in the USSR, and above all, the threat of imminent war in the Gulf mean that potentially catastrophic new problems have stepped into the shoes of the old familiar ones.

A chance for peace: Nato and Warsaw Pact leaders agree to limit weaponry.

Freeing of hostages confuses war plans

Nov 18. President Saddam Hussein of Iraq tonight promised to release all his hostages in a slow trickle, starting on Christmas Day and ending on 25 March next year. The offer, which is open provided that "nothing comes to disturb the climate of peace", could affect western plans for an offensive in early January if Saddam fails to withdraw from Kuwait voluntarily.

Allied commanders would prefer the fighting to be over by the end of March, when temperatures soar. And the Saudis would like the Americans to leave before the festival of Ramadan (starting on 17 March) brings pious Moslems flocking to Mecca. They fear that the presence of westerners could provoke a fundamentalist backlash.→

President spends Thanksgiving Day with troops in Saudi Arabia

Surrounded by sand, Bush addresses the soldiers of Operation Desert Shield.

Nov 22. President Bush, with his wife Barbara, spent today in the eastern desert of Saudi Arabia, eating Thanksgiving Day turkey with the marines in whom he has staked so much. His visit to the frontline troops of Operation Desert Shield left them in no doubt that they might see action. "We won't pull our punches. We're not here on some exercise. This is a real-world situation," he told them.

Mr Bush warned Saddam Hussein that he should not confuse US restraint with a lack of resolve. Nevertheless, opinion polls suggest that less than 50 per cent of Americans think the Gulf is worth a war. Memories of the disastrous US engagement in Vietnam in the 1960s have resurfaced, and Mr Bush seems to have more support in the UN than in the US Congress (→ 24).

November
1990

Su	Mo	Tu	We	Th	Fr	Sa
				1	2	3
4	5	6	7	8	9	10
11	12	13	14	15	16	17
18	19	20	21	22	23	24
25	26	27	28	29	30	

25. Ivory Coast: In their first ever multi-party parliamentary elections, Ivorians vote to keep the president, Felix Houphouet-Boigny, in power.

25. India: A man is killed when a bomb explodes at a meeting addressed by V P Singh, the former prime minister.

26. Singapore: Lee Kuan Yew, who has been prime minister for the last 31 years, resigns.

26. London: The Duke of Westminster wins a court battle to stop Westminster council selling off housing leased by his estate for rent to the working classes.

26. UK: Jerry Hall, the model, reveals that she has married her boyfriend, Mick Jagger in a secret ceremony.

27. Lebanon: Five Israeli soldiers and two Palestinian gunmen are killed in a clash in Israel's "security zone".

27. London: The *Sunday Correspondent* newspaper closes down.

28. UK: Diplomatic relations with Syria, broken off in October 1986, are reopened.

28. Baghdad: Tony Benn, the Labour MP, meets Saddam Hussein for talks.→

29. Paisley: Labour wins two by-elections, but loses ground to the SNP.

29. Bulgaria: Popular pressure, including street protests and a general strike, forces Andrei Lukanov to resign as prime minister.

29. Poland: Lech Walesa warns there will be civil war unless he is elected president.

30. Northern Ireland: Five hundred extra troops are sent in amid fears that the IRA will mount a major Christmas bombing campaign.

30. UK: British Aerospace announces the loss of 5,000 jobs in the military aircraft division and Rover announces the closure of two assembly lines at Cowley.

DEATH

26. Dodie Smith, British author (*3/5/1896).

John Major to be new prime minister

Nov 27. John Major has crowned his meteoric career by becoming, at 47, Britain's youngest prime minister this century. His succession was warmly welcomed by Margaret Thatcher, who joined the chancellor of the exchequer and his wife, Norma, in celebrations at 11 Downing Street after Major's election rivals had conceded defeat.

Mr Major was two votes short of outright victory in the second ballot for the Tory leadership. He won 185 votes, against 131 for Michael Heseltine and 56 for Douglas Hurd. But immediately after the vote was announced, Mr Heseltine said that, for the sake of party unity, he would withdraw from the third and final ballot due on Thursday. Minutes later Douglas Hurd, the foreign secretary, also withdrew.

It is an astonishing rise for John Major, who joined the cabinet only three years ago [*see below*] and it was achieved despite claims that the deposed Mrs Thatcher would remain as "back-seat driver". Certainly, the outgoing premier backed

John Major, with his campaign team behind him, beams from ear to ear.

Mr Major, telephoning wavering MPs to lobby for support. She said she was "thrilled" by his victory.

Speaking in Downing Street tonight, Major said: "We are going to unite totally and absolutely and win the next election." The opposition parties were predictably dismissive. "The face may have changed, but the policies remain the same," said Paddy Ashdown, the leader of the Liberal Democrats.→

Heseltine secures Thatcher's downfall

Heseltine announces his withdrawal.

Nov 27. Who dares does not always win. Michael Heseltine dared to challenge Margaret Thatcher and, although he scored fewer votes than the prime minister, forced her to quit. But now his hopes of being prime minister himself are dashed – and at 57, ten years older than John Major, the best he can hope for is a return to the cabinet.→

Emotional Thatcher says her goodbyes

A quick word before leaving No. 10.

Nov 28. The Iron Lady fought back the tears as she left Downing Street this morning. "Now it is time for a new chapter to open," she said. And then, as her last act as Her Majesty's First Lord of the Treasury, she was off to see the Queen and resign formally before heading, as the MP for Finchley, to her new home in south London.

Humble origins of Britain's new PM

Nov 27. John Major will be the youngest prime minister since Lord Rosebery formed a cabinet in 1894 at the age of 46. He is little known in the country, having entered the cabinet for the first time only three years ago as its most junior member in charge of public spending at the treasury. An uneasy three months as foreign secretary followed, before he became chancellor after Nigel Lawson resigned last year.

His father had lived a colourful life, which included stints in music halls and as a trapeze artist. John left school at 16 and spent some time out of work before, after a variety of labouring jobs, he joined the Standard Chartered Bank. Cricket was his greatest passion outside work, until he discovered politics. He became a local councillor in south London and through politics met his wife Norma; they now have two children, Elizabeth, aged 19, and James, aged 15. They live in Huntingdon, for which he has been MP since 1979.

UN backs use of force to free Kuwait

Nov 30. The Gulf crisis has moved forward a couple of steps, with President Bush today seeking high-level talks with Iraq in the wake of a crucial UN resolution. The UN security council yesterday authorized the alliance ranged against Iraq to use force to liberate Kuwait and "restore international peace and security" if Saddam Hussein fails to withdraw by 15 January.

Military analysts say that the resolution blunts the tactic of surprise – the Iraqis can rest safe in the knowledge that there will be no attack for six weeks – but note that in any case, 214,000 British and US reinforcements intended to bring the force up to full strength will only arrive in mid-January.

Today's surprise invitation to the negotiating table is a complete U-turn by President Bush, who has so far refused to countenance discussions with Iraq until after it leaves Kuwait. Mr Bush wants Tariq Aziz, the Iraqi foreign minister, to come to Washington while James Baker, the US secretary of state, flies to Baghdad to meet Saddam Hussein. At the same time he has made it clear that the UN resolutions demanding Iraqi withdrawal from Kuwait and the freeing of all hostages are not negotiable. It looks as though he is keen to show that he is giving peace yet another chance, and, by doing so, he hopes to prepare the American people for war.

Men-only cabinet draws Labour fire

Nov 29. John Major made his bow as prime minister today, with only criticisms of his all-male cabinet to cloud the Tory euphoria over his emergence as leader. "I am my own man," he said, in a somewhat nervous debut at question time, enthusiastically cheered by Conservative MPs despite some misgivings (and Labour attacks) about the complete exclusion of women from the cabinet for the first time since 1964.

Among the men, Michael Heseltine returns as environment secretary, Norman Lamont becomes the new chancellor and Chris Patten takes over as party chairman from Kenneth Baker who becomes home secretary. Cecil Parkinson has left the cabinet and there are changes, too, in Scotland and the Lords.

Poles force premier to resign after vote

Walesa: front-runner in round two.

Nov 26. Tadeusz Mazowiecki has resigned as prime minister after a humiliating defeat in the Polish presidential elections. He polled just 18 per cent of the vote, coming a poor third behind the Solidarity leader Lech Walesa and Stanislaw Tyminski, a Polish emigre who returned from Canada just six weeks ago to win a surprising 23 per cent of the vote. Walesa – condemned recently for alleged anti-Semitism – is ahead, but must now go a second round with Mr Tyminski, who has promised to make all Poles rich, arm Poland with nuclear weapons, and investigate what he says is an international conspiracy against the country (→ 29).

Food crisis puts Soviets on the breadline

A shopper despairs as a Moscow fishmonger's displays its sad lack of fish.

Nov 29. Germany today started to airlift desperately-needed food supplies to Moscow as Soviet cities face the threat of a winter famine and the prospect of rationing. One of the side-effects of *perestroika* has been the collapse of the state agricultural and distribution system; nothing has replaced it. As a result, food is left rotting in the fields. Lack of transport, bad handling, poor storage facilities, corruption and theft all conspire to prevent three-quarters of the harvest from reaching city stores. While the state shops are empty, Mr Gorbachev's free farmers' markets are groaning with produce – at unaffordable prices. The problem is compounded by hoarding and a flourishing black market in goods diverted from the state network.

Plastic surgeons murdered in Wakefield

Nov 26. In an apparently motiveless attack, two surgeons have been stabbed to death at Pinderfields hospital, near Wakefield. A 24-year-old man was arrested after armed police sealed off and searched the hospital area. Michael Masser and Kenneth Patton, who were found dead in their offices by a secretary, were highly-respected plastic surgeons at Pinderfield's world-renowned burns unit.

The murders come in the wake of three serious hospital assaults around the country, including the rape of both an 11-year-old girl and a 77-year-old woman. Doctors and health unions tonight renewed their calls for improved security in hospital premises.

Arab attacks rattle nervous Israelis

Nov 25. Tension heightened along the Israeli-Egyptian border today after an Egyptian border guard crossed it and ambushed a succession of vehicles with a Kalashnikov assault rifle. He shot dead four Israelis, and injured 26 others, before being wounded by an Israeli security guard and fleeing back across the border where he was arrested by Egyptian police. The fundamentalist Moslem terrorist group Islamic Jihad has claimed reponsibility.

Two other, apparently unconnected, incidents today have served to underline Israel's vulnerability. An Israeli gunboat intercepted five Arab gunmen heading for the northern coast, killing them all, and a young woman blew herself up at an Israeli army post in the south Lebanese security zone, killing herself and injuring two soldiers (→ 27).

A bereaved Israeli weeps bitterly.

December
1990

Su	Mo	Tu	We	Th	Fr	Sa
						1
2	3	4	5	6	7	8
9	10	11	12	13	14	15
16	17	18	19	20	21	22
23	24	25	26	27	28	29
30	31					

1. Baghdad: Saddam Hussein agrees to US proposals for talks, but he insists that the Arab-Israeli issue is discussed.

1. USSR: Food rationing is imposed in Leningrad.

2. South Africa: Fifty more people are reported to have been killed in a new wave of township violence.

2. Chad: Idriss Deby topples President Hissene Habre in a coup.

2. Sydney: Barry Morse wins the Australian Open golf championship.

3. Argentina: President Carlos Menem foils an attempted military coup.

3. Brussels: Farmers stage angry street protests as the Gatt talks get under way.→

4. UK: The home secretary refers the case of Engin Raghip, sentenced to life imprisonment for the murder of PC Keith Blakelock in 1985, to the court of appeal.

4. Bangladesh: President Hossain Mohammed Ershad resigns after eight years in power, following a series of massive protest rallies.

4. UK: The Aga Khan pulls all his horses out of British racing.

5. London: Salman Rushdie attends a book signing; it is his first public outing since Islamic death threats sent him into hiding in February 1989.

5. UK: John Major appoints Sarah Hogg as head of the Downing Street policy unit.

6. UK: Durham are admitted to first-class cricket; they are the first new county side for 90 years.

7. Ireland: Charles Haughey announces a review of the laws on homosexuality and divorce.

7. UK: Margaret Thatcher is awarded the Order of Merit.

DEATHS

2. Aaron Copland, US composer (*14/11/00).→

6. Tunku Abdul Rahman, Malaysian statesman (*8/2/03).

World trade negotiations break down

Clayton Yeutter, the US representative, tells newsmen of his annoyance.

Dec 7. Fears of an international trade war were heightened today when four years of negotiations collapsed amid recriminations and acrimony in Brussels. A final breakdown was averted by setting a new deadline, but there is no sign of a solution to the deadlock over farm subsidies which caused the impasse, with the United States and the European Community each blaming the failure on the other. Some 107 nations have been involved in the four years of talks under the auspices of the General Agreement on Tariffs and Trade (Gatt), but most were left on the sidelines this week at what were supposed to be the final make-or-break negotiations. The Gatt talks had begun with the aim of reducing trade barriers and thereby boosting the world economy. Now the danger is that protective tariffs and regional trade blocs will be encouraged, thus intensifying the downward spiral of a world economy already heading towards a recession.

Farm subsidies affect only a relatively small part of world trade, but they are seen by the United States as the prime stumbling-block to agreement. European leaders had offered to cut subsidies by 30 per cent, prompting noisy protests by farmers, but the US wanted more. Now it will be up to heads of government to seek a solution if a trade war is to be averted.

Italian students killed by flying accident

Helpers try to improvise first aid for injured and shocked pupils at the school.

Dec 6. An Italian military plane crashed into a secondary school near Bologna today, killing at least 12 people and injuring 65 more. The aircraft went out of control during a training flight, and burst into flames before punching a hole five metres (16 feet) wide in the wall of the school building.

At least three people were crushed to death by the wreckage, but others died in the fire that it set off. One of the pupils survived after being pinned down by one of the plane's wings. A hundred people stranded on the smoke-filled upper floor jumped to safety or had to be rescued by firemen.

An eye-witness said that the plane was in flames as it glided down, before it veered to one side and smashed into the building. The pilot, who baled out, is in hospital with back injuries.

Kohl wins mandate from new Germany

Dec 2. Helmut Kohl tonight reaped the reward for championing the cause – and speed – of German unity when his Christian Democratic Union and coalition allies swept to victory in the first all-Germany election since Hitler came to power in 1933.

Chancellor Kohl's supporters have won an estimated 55 per cent of the votes cast with the Social Democrats (SPD), slumping to just 35 per cent, their worst result since the 1950s. With final results still to be declared, the election looks like being even worse for Germany's Greens; with less than five per cent of the vote in what was West Germany, they will have no members for those areas in the new parliament and only a handful in the former East Germany.

The former Communist rulers of East Germany (now reborn as the Party of Democratic Socialism) polled only two per cent nationally, but with over ten-per-cent support in its former heartland the party will be represented in the new all-German parliament.

Isolation ends with tunnel breakthrough

Philippe Cozette (l) and Graham Fagg shake hands at an historic moment.

Dec 1. Britain's 8,000 years as an island came to an end at 11.15am today when, to a roar of applause from his assembled colleagues, Graham Fagg's jackhammer broke through the last inch of chalk separating England from France. Through a small hole appeared the head of Philippe Cozette, Fagg's opposite number on the French side of the newly-dug service tunnel.

The English soberly sipped mineral water, but the French celebrated with champagne as the two men widened the hole. Then the French and British transport ministers walked through to shake hands. Soon, the chairman of the French tunnel company wandered through to give his British counterpart a green furry frog, setting the seal on this truly historic occasion.

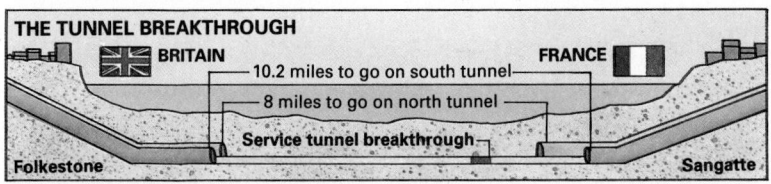

THE TUNNEL BREAKTHROUGH

BRITAIN — 10.2 miles to go on south tunnel — FRANCE

8 miles to go on north tunnel

Service tunnel breakthrough

Folkestone — Sangatte

Alan Bond to face criminal charges

Dec 6. Alan Bond, the Australian business magnate and former chairman of the Bond Corporation, was today arrested on criminal charges relating to his role in an operation he mounted to rescue Rothwells merchant bank in 1987. He was the prime mover in a scheme to persuade businessmen to contribute A$150 million to overcome Rothwells liquidity crisis. The merchant bank has since collapsed.

It is alleged that Mr Bond, who has been released on bail, dishonestly concealed from another Perth businessman that Rothwells had agreed to pay the Bond Corporation A$16 million.

Dec 2. Aaron Copland, the doyen of US music and composer of "Rodeo", has died aged 90.

Iraq to free all hostages

Dec 6. President Saddam Hussein of Iraq has surprised the west by announcing that all 3,400 foreign hostages held since the invasion of Kuwait are now free to leave. If he keeps his promise – and there is every reason for thinking that he will – the hostages could be home by Christmas, and Iraq will have fulfilled one of the central demands of the UN Security Council. President Bush and Mr Major have given the news a cautious welcome. Saddam has evidently concluded that his "human shield" plan was unlikely to deter a foreign attack, and that the chances of peace on his own terms would be greater if he made concessions before opening a dialogue with the US.

Reports that the US is backing a UN plan to hold a Middle East peace conference to resolve the Palestinian question, which were hotly denied by the Americans, may have helped to soften the Iraqi line.

IRA men sentenced to thirty years' jail

Dec 6. Two IRA terrorists, who were caught digging up an arms cache in Pembroke last Christmas, were today sent to jail for 30 years. In passing sentence, the judge described Liam O'Dhuibhir and Damien McComb, both aged 28, as "merciless men intent on carnage". A jury at the Old Bailey found them guilty of conspiracy to cause explosions after hearing how the hidden explosives – 41kg (90lb) of Semtex, plus detonators and other equipment – could have been made into 18 bombs. A hit-list of military and political figures was found in a house where the men stayed. As the men went down to the cells, they shouted "Victory to the IRA" and "Our day will come".

Britain grinds to a halt as snow falls

Dec 8. Winter arrived with a vengeance today as parts of the British Isles faced the worst wintry weather for ten years. An icy Arctic wind brought heavy snowfalls and drifts of up to 3.7 metres which cut off towns and villages, damaged cables and trapped thousands of motorists in their cars. The worst-hit areas were central and northern England and Wales; 650,000 people are estimated to be without electricity and 1.2 million without water, after power cuts closed down treatment plants and pumping stations. The A66 near Barnard Castle was the scene of a major rescue operation after 300 motorists were stranded. British Rail simply cancelled all services to the west and midlands.

Race hatred amazes black Tory candidate

John Taylor with his baby daughter.

Dec 4. An astonishing racist outburst has rattled the normally sedate spa town of Cheltenham, following the selection of a 38-year-old barrister, John Taylor, as the Conservative candidate in the next election. Bill Galbraith, a leading member of the local party and cousin of a government minister, has objected to Mr Taylor on the sole ground of his skin colour. "I do not think we should have a bloody nigger foisted on us," he raged. "We have to repel this boarder. If you lived in this town would you be happy if a bloody nigger from Birmingham came and settled down?" Mr Taylor says he that feels sorry for Mr Galbraith and his like. John Major is reported to be furious.

Su	Mo	Tu	We	Th	Fr	Sa
						1
2	3	4	5	6	7	8
9	10	11	12	13	14	15
16	17	18	19	20	21	22
23	24	25	26	27	28	29
30	31					

9. Poland: Lech Walesa wins a landslide victory in the presidential election.

9. India: Troops move into Hyderabad after 52 people are killed in violence between Hindus and Moslems.

10. UK: The government announces that school teachers are to undergo compulsory appraisal every two years.

10. UK: Robin Cook denies rumours that he will challenge Neil Kinnock for leadership of the Labour party.

10. Kazakhstan: Toyehiro Akiyama, the first journalist and Japanese national to go into space, returns to earth.

10. Yugoslavia: Free elections in the republic of Serbia result in a victory for the Communist party under Slobodan Milosevic.

11. Albania: Following student protests in Tirana, the state authorises the establishment of opposition political parties.→

11. UK: Electricity shares go on the market, with instant premiums of up to 80 per cent.

12. UK: Six fishermen are drowned when their ship capsizes off the Shetlands.

12. Riyadh: An Algerian attempt to find an Arab solution to the Gulf crisis fails, when Saudi Arabia insists the solution lies in Iraqi hands.

13. New York: The UN launches an aid appeal as the threat of a new famine looms in Sudan and Ethiopia.

13. UK: Russell Bishop is jailed for life for the sexual assault and attempted murder of a seven-year-old girl.

13. UK: Following the collapse of his financial services group, businessman Roger Levitt is arrested and charged with theft.

14. Rome: The EC agrees to send food aid to the USSR.

DEATHS

10. Armand Hammer, US industrialist (*21/5/1898).→

12. Sir James Ian Raley Trethowan, British broadcaster (*20/10/22).

Gulf talks founder as Iraq refuses date

Praying for peace? Saudi troops bow to Mecca during a pause in manoeuvres.

Dec 14. President Bush's attempt to open a dialogue with Iraq was on the brink of failure today when he accused the Iraqi president of obstructing the new US peace effort. Saddam Hussein has refused to meet James Baker, the US secretary of state, before 12 January, which date Mr Bush has rejected as being too close to 15 January, the UN deadline for withdrawal from Kuwait. This disagreement jeopardizes Mr Bush's plan to start the talks by meeting Tariq Aziz, the Iraqi foreign minister, first.

With the two sides deadlocked and an Algerian peace initiative killed off this week, the US and its allies have speeded the flow of arms into Saudi Arabia. Yesterday, Iraq announced a major civil defence exercise – starting on 15 January.

Albanians riot for a democratic future

Dec 15. Government forces are reported to have regained control after a week of growing anti-Communist violence in Albania's towns. President Ramiz Alia, who has set in motion a series of reforms to eastern Europe's only old-style Communist regime, appealed for calm in the build up to the country's first multi-party elections, due to be held on 10 February.

The Albanian people, however, are showing little patience. Yesterday, rioters shouting "freedom" and "democracy" went on a vandalism spree in the industrial town of Elbasan, looting shops and destroying a cinema. A state of emergency and a curfew are in force in Shkoder, where troops moved in after protesters stoned Communist Party buildings. Observers fear that the violence will escalate into a bloody revolution, like that which swept Romania last year.

Returning hostages tell of Kuwait rape

Dec 10. Britons held in military installations as part of President Saddam Hussein's "human shield" have started to arrive home. They bring with them new and often horrifying stories of Iraq's determination to extinguish Kuwait.

Nearly everything useful in the country – from industrial machinery to cameras and food – has been loaded onto trucks bound for Iraq. Computers, office furniture, telephones and books have been taken from Kuwait university, while senior doctors arrived from Baghdad to supervise the theft of the Kuwait teaching hospital's library. Paving stones, telephone booths and street lamps have been torn up and carted off. One man reports seeing in a Baghdad shop window goods clearly priced in Kuwaiti dinars.

The hostages tell of how they lived at gunpoint in ramshackle accommodation in munitions dumps, steelworks, power stations and even inside a dam. They survived on cucumbers, rice and tomatoes, and tried to entertain themselves by playing football and card games and telling stories.

ANC leader returns home from long exile

Oliver Tambo (l.) and Nelson Mandela give followers a clenched-fist salute.

Dec 14. After 30 years in exile, Oliver Tambo, the president of the African National Congress (ANC) has returned to South Africa and startled many of his ecstatic supporters by calling for a rethink on the policy of international sanctions against the Pretoria government.

Addressing an ANC conference in Soweto today, 24 hours after his return to South Africa, Mr Tambo said policy changes by the government may require a new attitude to sanctions. Not all the delegates will agree; some already suspect that the ANC leadership is going soft.

HIV haemophiliacs get cash handout

Dec 11. The government today announced that it will give £42 million to the 1,200 British haemophiliacs infected with the Aids virus after being treated with contaminated blood products. The money, which comes on top of £34 million already paid into a trust by the government, will provide lump sums of up to £50,000 for the victims.

The decision, which lawyers representing the haemophiliacs negotiated with the health secretary, William Waldegrave, ends a long and bitter wrangle. The Haemophiliac Society first sought compensation in 1986, but the government maintained that it was a matter to be settled in the courts. Many people were outraged that the haemophiliacs, who are now dying at the rate of one a day, should have to face protracted legal battles to win compensation.

Charming Major sets out views on Europe

Dec 15. John Major unveiled a new style of British diplomacy in Rome this weekend when leaders of the European Community met to discuss the next stages of economic and political union. Only Jacques Delors, the EC president, appeared immune to Mr Major's "charm offensive", warning that he could provoke another political crisis if Britain sought to "derail" the movement to monetary union.

It was the first meeting of European leaders since the summit seven weeks ago which precipitated Mrs Thatcher's downfall. Now a new prime minister was stressing a more positive attitude, even though insisting policies had not changed. "We intend to be wholeheartedly engaged in the task of building, shaping and developing Europe," said Mr Major.

Other leaders welcomed the change of style and gave Mr Major more time to heal his party's Euro-

A positive attitude from the new PM.

pean wounds by avoiding new commitments to greater union. A single currency, a central European bank and political union will now be discussed in detail at ministerial level.

Statistics add up to recession in Britain

Dec 14. Norman Lamont, the new chancellor of the exchequer, is resisting pleas that he play Santa Claus for the benefit of Britons caught in an apparently deepening recession. On Wednesday he appeared to rule out a pre-Christmas cut in interest rates because sterling was too weak within the European exchange rate mechanism. Yet the evidence of recession in Britain has become ever more apparent.

Figures released yesterday revealed the biggest monthly rise in unemployment since 1981, jumping by 57,600 to 1,762,000. Today the government reported a sixth successive month in which manufac-

Australian publishing empire collapses

Dec 10. The Fairfax Group, Australia's oldest newspaper empire, is now in the hands of the receivers faced with A$1,500 million of debts. The 149-year old company, which publishes the prestigious newspapers *The Sydney Morning Herald*, the Melbourne *Age* and the *Australian Financial Review*, has

been brought to its knees just three years after Warwick Fairfax, aged 30, borrowed heavily in order to buy out other shareholders, only to see millions wiped off the value of the company in the 1987 stock market crash. Now Britain's Robert Maxwell is one of several potential buyers.

US to help Soviets conquer food crisis

Dec 12. In an effort to alleviate the growing threat of famine, President Bush today agreed to send a food aid package to the Soviet Union. The measures include emergency medical supplies, long-term help to improve the country's infrastructure and credits to buy $1,000 million (£500 million) worth of grain. Overturning previous policy, which made aid conditional on the Soviets relaxing emigration laws, Mr Bush explained that he wanted to help the Soviets "stay the course of democratization". Eduard Shevardnadze, the Soviet foreign minister, said: "we are in a new phase of our relations."

The announcement comes after Vladimir Kryuchkov, the head of the KGB, said that his forces would step in to prevent the collapse of the Soviet Union. Speaking at the behest of President Gorbachev, he warned that "national chauvinism is being fuelled and mass disorder and violence are being provoked" by "extremist radical groups ... supported morally and politically from abroad," raising the spectre of an old-fashioned KGB clampdown on dissenters.

Dec 10. Armand Hammer, the industrialist turned political fixer, has died. He is pictured here with his friend, Soviet President Brezhnev, in 1978.

Weathering the storm: Mr Lamont.

turing output has declined, with the annual rate of decline, at three per cent, the worst for nine years.

Almost the only good news was a fall in inflation announced today from its peak of 10.9 per cent to 9.7 per cent in November. However, ministers and the Bank of England are resisting calls from industry and retailers for a cut in interest rates. Mr Lamont admits that the recession is much more severe than the Treasury had predicted, but says reducing inflation remains his top priority. "The best way to bring an upturn in activity is to stick to the policy of getting inflation down," he told MPs.

December
1990

Su	Mo	Tu	We	Th	Fr	Sa
						1
2	3	4	5	6	7	8
9	10	11	12	13	14	15
16	17	18	19	20	21	22
23	24	25	26	27	28	29
30	31					

16. Ireland: Cahal Daly is installed as the Roman Catholic Primate of All Ireland; he calls on the IRA to stop its terror campaign.

16. Beverley Hills: Rod Stewart, the 45-year-old Scottish singer, marries Rachel Hunter, a model aged 22.

17. Haiti: Jean-Bertrand Aristide, a radical priest, is elected president.

17. Germany: Allegations that he was a secret police informer force Lothar de Maiziere, the last prime minister of East Germany, to resign from the government.

17. Westminster: MPs vote against reintroducing the death penalty.

17. UK: Friends of the Earth awards Eastern Electricity its "Green Con of the Year" prize for claiming that using more electricity will stop global warming.

19. UK: The footballer Tony Adams, the Arsenal captain and England player, is jailed for four months for drink-driving.

19. Washington: Lieutenant-General Calvin Waller, the deputy commander of US forces in the Gulf, says that his troops will not be ready for war by 15 January.→

20. New York: The UN passes a vote of censure against Israel for October's massacre on Temple Mount, in which Israeli troops killed 21 Arab rioters.

20. UK: Asil Nadir is freed from prison after he finds the required £3.5 million bail.

20. UK: Commuters on the Norwich-London line sue British Rail for providing an unacceptable level of service.

22. Saudi Arabia: The Prince of Wales visits British military units.

22. Israel: Twenty-one US soldiers are drowned when a boat taking them back from leave in Haifa capsizes on heavy seas.

DEATH

18. Paul Tortelier, French cellist (*21/3/14).

Angry politicians turn on Gorbachev

President bloodied in confidence vote

Dec 17. President Gorbachev today won a crucial vote of confidence in the Congress of People's Deputies, and then warned the USSR's break-away republics that they could only win their independence after a referendum of the entire Soviet Union. Asking for more powers, he said that "the crisis has us by the throat". But his words were overshadowed by those of the Caucasian deputy Saji Umulatova, who accused him of deceiving the people: "You brought devastation, hunger, cold, blood, tears," she said.

Umulatova: "You brought hunger".

Shevardnadze: will no longer serve.

Gorbachev: dictator in the making?

Old ally quits with "dictator" warning

Dec 20. Eduard Shevardnadze, the Soviet foreign minister, has badly wounded President Gorbachev and stunned leaders around the world by announcing his resignation. In an emotional speech to the Soviet parliament, the foreign minister said: "Dictatorship is coming. No one knows what kind of dictatorship it will be, what kind of dictator will come ... I am resigning. May it be my personal contribution, or, if you like, my protest against a dictatorship ... But I believe that to resign is my duty as a man, as a citizen, as a communist. I cannot reconcile myself to what is happening in our country and the trials awaiting our people."

Mr Shevardnadze, one of Mikhail Gorbachev's closest allies, made his surprise move after the president threatened to use direct Kremlin rule to impose order on some of the USSR's restless republics. Yesterday Boris Yeltsin, the radical Russian prime minister, accused Mr Gorbachev of amassing more powers than Stalin. Many now fear that *perestroika* will give way to old-style totalitarianism.

Rhondda pit shuts, and noble era ends

Dec 20. For more than a century the Rhondda has been synonymous with Welsh coal-mining. Over 100 men have died hewing coal from as many as 56 pits which once employed 40,000 men. But today, when the afternoon shift ended at Maerdy Colliery, the tradition also ended: the last remaining Rhondda pit had closed.

Three hundred men have lost their jobs; only 17 will move to stay in the industry. Management and union leaders agree that the Maerdy seam is exhausted. Such unanimity is rare. Maerdy in particular has relished its reputation for militancy. No miner crossed the picket lines in 1984-85, and the men marched back to work, beaten but defiant, behind a brass band.

Ripper wife goes a libel action too far

Dec 21. Sonia Sutcliffe, the wife of the "Yorkshire Ripper" murderer, today lost a libel action and could now face financial ruin. Mrs Sutcliffe has been awarded £334,000 from eight previous legal actions against newspapers and magazines. Confident that she would win again, Mrs Sutcliffe rejected an out-of-court settlement for £50,000 before the trial which ended today with the jury's unanimous verdict.

Mrs Sutcliffe had sought damages for an article in the *News of the World* which alleged that she had an affair with a Greek businessman who was the image of her husband. Not only must Mrs Sutcliffe pay costs estimated at at least £300,000; she also faces a possible action for perjury.

Dec 20. A Thai court sentences Karyn Smith from Birmingham, aged 19, to 25 years in jail for trafficking in heroin. Her lawyers plan to ask for a royal pardon.

Failure of jaw, jaw could mean war, war

US tanks and armoured vehicles wait at a Saudi port, ready for the fray.

Dec 21. If the ever-fiercer rhetoric coming from both Washington and Baghdad is to be believed, war in the Gulf is looking more likely every day. It is reported that the White House has given up hope of talks with Saddam Hussein, and today Dick Cheney, the US defense secretary, promised "absolute, total victory" to the American troops stationed in Saudi Arabia.

The Iraqi president, meanwhile, appeared on German television to claim: "Allah is on our side, and we shall beat the aggressor." He said that Iraq had no intention of leaving Kuwait before the UN deadline of 15 January.

Earlier this week both Britain and Iraq called up some of their reserves, and Iraqi citizens practised civil defence exercises in readiness for conflict. Amnesty International published a chilling report of Iraqi torture, repression and summary executions in Kuwait, and the former British prime minister Edward Heath warned that war in the Gulf could bring an apocalyptic disaster (→ 22).

Major's visit reassures curious Americans

Windswept partners: John Major and George Bush address waiting reporters.

Dec 22. John Major returned to Britain tonight after his first visit to the United States as prime minister. It was a visit overshadowed by fears of turmoil in the Soviet Union and war in the Gulf, and Mr Major lost no opportunity of declaring that the change in Downing Street did not mean a change in British foreign policy. His American hosts were pleased, especially as most are still coming to terms with the departure of their staunchest ally.

The man who replaced Maggie was therefore the object of much curiosity, and Mr Major's 48 hours in Washington began with the rounds of the TV breakfast shows, squeezed between weathermen dressed as Santa Claus. He gave a fluent but unexciting performance before making the rounds of the White House, the state department, the treasury and Capitol Hill. The talks with President Bush continued at Camp David, the presidential retreat in the foggy Maryland hills. "Both the president and I understand each other's minds very well," said Mr Major.

Thatcher rewards loyal press and admen

Dec 21. Margaret Thatcher today rewarded her most loyal supporters with awards ranging from life peerages for industrialists to British Empire Medals for Downing Street staff. Bernard Ingham, the former prime minister's combative press secretary, receives a knighthood, as does Tim Bell, an advertising man who played key roles in general election campaigns. Also knighted is Charles Powell, a long-serving foreign policy adviser, while Jane Gow, the widow of the murdered MP Ian Gow, is to become a dame.

Two national newspaper editors and a senior ITN editor were included in Mrs Thatcher's resignation honours list, but there was nothing for Jeffrey Archer, the novelist and former Tory deputy chairman whom leaks had named as a new life peer. Some reports claimed

Ingham, the trusty press secretary.

that his name had been rejected by a scrutiny committee, along with that of Rupert Murdoch, the Australian-born newspaper proprietor who is now a US citizen.

Desperate retailers open up on Sunday

Dec 16. Thousands of English shopkeepers defied the law today to open their stores to try to salvage what they fear may be their worst Christmas for years. Chain stores such as BHS, Curry's and Woolworth's were among those which joined the smaller shops and DIY chains which regularly flout laws against Sunday trading, as was the London toy store of Hamley's.

Last weekend's blizzards were used as the pretext for giving shoppers an extra day, but one lost day is not the problem: trade is down by as much as a fifth in many areas, and the "Sales" signs are prominent in the high streets. Sunday observance groups and shopworkers' unions are pressing councils to enforce the Sunday trading laws.

Nadir fails to come up with record bail

Dec 17. Asil Nadir, the millionaire chairman of the bankrupt Polly Peck trading empire, will spend tonight at Brixton prison after he failed to raise the record £3.5 million bail imposed by Bow Street magistrates. Nadir, who transformed Polly Peck from an East End rag trade company into a multinational success story, is facing fourteen charges relating to the alleged theft of £25 million from his own company and four charges of false accounting. Up to £200 million is said to be missing within Polly Peck, and Nadir is thought to have additional personal debts of about £40 million. The company crashed in October after the fraud squad started to probe an alleged share-rigging operation (→ 20).

December

1990

Su	Mo	Tu	We	Th	Fr	Sa
						1
2	3	4	5	6	7	8
9	10	11	12	13	14	15
16	17	18	19	20	21	22
23	24	25	26	27	28	29
30	31					

23. Britain: The IRA declares a three-day truce (→ 31).

23. Yugoslavia: In a referendum, the republic of Slovenia votes to become an independent state.

24. Surinam: A military coup overthrows the elected government.

24. Australia: A cyclone batters the Queensland coast with winds of up to 150 miles per hour.

25. Moscow: Nikolai Ryzhkov, the Soviet prime minister, suffers a heart attack.→

25. UK: The Queen expresses deep anxiety over events in the Gulf, and the archbishop of Canterbury speaks out against the modern "cult of violence".

26. Kempton: Desert Orchid wins the King George VI Chase for a record fourth time.

26. Saudi Arabia: General Sir Peter de la Billiere, the commander of British forces, says that his men are now ready to fight (→ 29).

27. Reading: Claire, Carla and Craig Vasquez, aged between six and eight, drown when they fall into a canal.

28. London: Eleven-day-old Christie Strachan, the subject of a nationwide appeal for a heart donor, dies when his heart transplant fails.

29. UK: It is revealed that top-secret documents on British military deployments in the Gulf were retrieved from a skip after being stolen from an RAF officer's car recently.→

30. UK: An opinion poll shows Labour slightly ahead of the Conservatives for the first time since John Major became prime minister.

31. Northern Ireland: An inquiry is launched after an incident yesterday in which troops opened fire on a car at a checkpoint, killing an unarmed man.

31. London: The Trafalgar Square Christmas tree is damaged when a man attacks it with a chainsaw.

31. UK: At midnight, the 5p coin – the old shilling – ceases to be legal tender.

Gorbachev wins battle for vice-president

Dec 27. For the climax of his most testing week so far, President Gorbachev staked his career in order to ensure the election of his man to the new post of vice-president. Members of the Congress of People's Deputies today rejected Gennady Yanayev, a trade union official with a reputation as an anti-reformist. But the angry Soviet president warned that Yanayev's appointment was a last chance to keep the USSR functioning. "At this critical time, I want a man near me I can trust," he said, and Yanayev scraped through on a second ballot.

Mr Gorbachev has won a series of struggles to win most of the powers he says he needs to rescue the Soviet Union from collapse. The government will be directly subordinate to the presidency, and a new

Yanayev: approved, after a struggle.

national security council is to try to control violent ethnic and nationalist groups. But plans for an inspectorate to ensure Gorbachev's word is carried out were rejected.

Life of crime gives writer a peerage

Dec 31. P D James, the civil servant turned crime writer, is the only new life peer in today's New Year's Honours list. Barbara Cartland, another authoress, is also honoured; at 89, she becomes a dame. Graham Gooch, England's cricket captain, and Peter Shilton, the long-serving goalkeeper, each receive an OBE while the former England soccer manager, Bobby Robson, goes one better with a CBE. Ian McKellen, the actor and gay rights campaigner, is among 29 new knights, of whom three are Tory MPs. There is one Liberal Democrat knight – former party president Ian Wrigglesworth – but no Labour nominees, because the party opposes "political honours".

Year ends on an uncertain note in the Gulf

Dec 31. As the year ended, the twisty road to war in the Gulf took some unexpected bends, but the chance of its being diverted to the new destination of a peaceful solution in the Middle East receded. Despite a German-led attempt to open a dialogue between European foreign ministers and Iraq, the talk was all of war. Dick Cheney, the US defence secretary, started it all by warning Iraq that the Gulf war clock was ticking away. Then Saddam Hussein said that Tel Aviv

would be his first target if Iraq was attacked. Israel promised to defend itself robustly.

British troops in the Gulf were put on a chemical war alert as Iraq carried out test firings of its modified Scud B missiles; five hundred medical reservists were compulsorily called up; and it was revealed that troops in Saudi Arabia are being vaccinated against biological warfare. Cartoonists captured the gloomy mood by depicting the new year as a baby wearing a gas mask.

Now it's Dame Barbara Cartland.

Exiled monarch's "cheap stunt" angers Romanian authorities

Dec 26. Early this morning, King Michael, Romania's exiled monarch, was deported after an abortive attempt to return to his homeland for Christmas. Michael, aged 69, arrived yesterday evening on a private jet from Switzerland. He set off to visit his family's tombs; but was stopped at a roadblock and turned back. Officials expelled him on the grounds that he had not obtained the correct visas, saying he "came like a thief" for a "cheap stunt". His visit, on the first anniversary of the revolution that toppled Nicolae Ceasescu, came as some Romanians, disillusioned with the new regime headed by Ion Iliescu, want the King to come back to provide a new, more stable focus for the state.

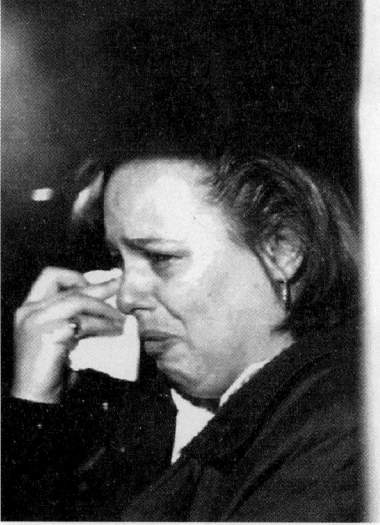

Princess Sophie of Romania cries as a bitter ex-King Michael looks on.

Rushdie bids to end rift with Moslems

Dec 25. Salman Rushdie has proclaimed his belief in Islam and agreed not to publish a paperback version of his book, *The Satanic Verses*. But the author's attempted reconciliation with Moslems, announced yesterday, was brushed aside today by Iranian leaders. A statement from the office of Ayatollah Khamenei, Iran's spiritual leader, said that the *fatwa* [religious edict] calling for Rushdie's death was "irrevocable". Rushdie, who has been living under police protection for nearly two years, yesterday acknowledged Allah as the only god, and he dissociated himself from statements in his book considered to be blasphemous to the Moslem prophet Mohammed. His statement followed lengthy talks with British Moslems.

Kasparov retains the championship

Dec 26. Garry Kasparov (right) today retained the world chess championship by drawing the 22nd game in the 24-match final against Anatoly Karpov in Lyons. Kasparov, aged 27, now leads 12-10 and even if he loses the final two games will, as the defending champion, retain the title which he won from his Soviet rival, Karpov, in 1985.

Australia take 2-0 lead in Ashes series

Dec 30. Australia today won the second test in Melbourne and left England with a mountain to climb: only once before has a team come back from 0-2 down to win the Ashes, and that was Australia in 1936-37 with the help of one Don Bradman. The decisive hour in this test came shortly before tea on the fourth day. England had led on the first innings, but an inspired spell by man-of-the-match Bruce Reid saw England crash from 147-4 to 150 all out. Australia needed only 197 to win and dogged batting by Marsh and Boon brought victory by eight wickets.

Storms put 100,000 homes in the dark

Dec 25. The Princess of Wales lost her hat and thousands lost their Christmas lunch today as storms lashed much of Britain. The royal family were buffeted by strong winds when they left church at Sandringham, causing Diana's hat to fly off. Elsewhere the problems were more severe as gales reached 80mph. Four churchgoers in Wiltshire were injured when part of the roof crashed onto the congregation. The strong winds brought down electricity lines, leaving more than 100,000 homes without power, mostly in southern and western England. Flooding was also a problem in many areas.

Royals are buffeted by the wind.

The things they said – and perhaps wish they rather had not said – during 1990

I am still at the crease, although the bowling has been pretty hostile of late.
Margaret Thatcher, November 12.

I want to drink all the drink in the world, eat all the food in the world and make love, hopefully, to all the women in the world.
Brian Keenan, former hostage.

If they don't come down by midnight, we are going to play Des O'Connor records.
A prison officer during the Strangeways riots.

Something has gone quite badly wrong.
Robin Leigh-Pemberton, governor of the Bank of England.

This is all a German racket designed to take over the whole of Europe.
Nicholas Ridley.

Diana only married me so that she could go through red lights.
Prince of Wales.

Gimme the Plaza, the jet and 150 million dollars!
Ivana Trump.

We shouldn't have had all these campaigns to get the Birmingham Six released if they'd been hanged.
Lord Denning.

It's rather like sending your opening batsmen to the crease only for them to find that ... their bats have been broken before the game by the team captain.
Sir Geoffrey Howe.

I can honestly say that I've written one more book than I've read.
Merv Hughes, the Australian fastbowler, about his autobiography.

He's a very sensitive boy.
Terry Venables on Paul Gascoigne.

She's nice and cuddly.
Paul Gascoigne on Margaret Thatcher.

I think I've got a very good plot for my next novel.
Douglas Hurd.

I have always thought there were only three kinds of women: wives, whores and mistresses.
Mr Justice Harman, on the use of the title "Ms".

I am my own man and on that basis I see no need to beat my chest.
John Major.

It's a funny old world.
Margaret Thatcher, November 22.

Well, who'd have thought it!
John Major.

These were the hits of the year that was

TOP FILMS
Ghost; Pretty Woman; Look's Who's Talking.

TOP VIDEO RENTALS
Shirley Valentine; Lethal Weapon II; Back to the Future II.

TOP SINGLES
Unchained Melody (Righteous Brothers); Nothing Compares 2 U (Sinead O'Connor); Sacrifice and Healing Hands (both Elton John).

TOP COMPACT DISCS
But Seriously (Phil Collins); Sleeping with the Past (Elton John); Three Tenors in Concert (Carreras, Domingo and Pavarotti).

TOP HARDBACKS
The Trials of Life (David Attenborough); Delia Smith's Christmas (Delia Smith); Around the World in 80 Days (Michael Palin).

TOP PAPERBACKS
The Negotiator (Frederick Forsyth); Devices and Desires (P D James); A History of the World in 10.5 Chapters (Julian Barnes).

TOP AUSTRALIAN BOOKS
Web of Dreams (Virginia Andrews) Trevayne (Robert Ludlum); Burke's Backyard (Don Burke).

Sources: Screen International, Video Week, Sunday Times, Daily Mail, Bookwatch.

The year the Cold War ended: a global review

The year began in hope and ended in fear. At the end of 1989 the Velvet Revolution in Czechoslovakia, the fall of communist regimes in the rest of Eastern Europe and, perhaps most of all, the quiet in which way Mikhail Gorbachev made it plain that the Soviet Union would not intervene with armed forces to prevent the Soviet empire in Eastern Europe from choosing economic freedom and political democracy, added up to a reasonable possibility of the peaceful resolution of that division of Europe which had been the world's most obviously dangerous problem since 1945.

Elsewhere in the world, too, especially in Africa and Latin America, dictatorship seemed on the retreat as a political system and democracy and market economics seemed to have earned a new popularity. Most dramatic of all, in South Africa, with astonishing suddenness the government of F W de Klerk released the leader of the African National Congress, Nelson Mandela, after 25 years' imprisonment, and engaged in a political dialogue whose avowed goal was the dismantling of apartheid and the creation, on some terms or other, of a multiracial state in South Africa. That opened vistas of new hope for the poorer nations of the earth, most of whom saw South Africa as the surviving emblem of the European peoples' determination to continue to dominate the world.

In the optimistic fervour of that winter and spring, as the Cold War visibly thawed and the Soviet-backed regimes in Eastern Europe trickled away into the gutters of history, many echoed Charles James Fox's excited comment on the French Revolution, just two hundred years earlier: "How much the greatest event in the history of the world, and how much the best." Some even adopted the millennial view of the American historian and publicist Francis Fukuyama and proclaimed "The End of History".

By the end of 1990, hope had given way to disappointment. Everywhere in Eastern Europe political emancipation had revealed the true severity of economic difficulties long concealed by censorship and propaganda. The first free elections in Poland since 1928 discredited the

If 1989 was the intoxicating year of liberty which had toppled the communist regimes of Eastern Europe, then 1990 was the year when men and women woke up to find that they were indeed free of ideologies that had bemused and oppressed them for generations - free, therefore, to renew old quarrels and find new rivalries. And doomed, too, to rediscover that history, the record of the unchanging, irreconcilable strivings of people and nations, does not end but ceaselessly turns into a new cycle, as fertile and dangerous as the last. GODFREY HODGSON, the foreign editor of The Independent, puts the events of 1990 into perspective and finds hope as well as peril in the Gulf.

Solidarity movement. Similar disillusion assailed the peoples of Romania, Bulgaria and Czechoslovakia as their first post-communist governments settled in. The prospects of constitutional progress in South Africa had to be weighted against daily violence, mostly between the African National Congress's young supporters and the Zulus in the *Inkatha* movement, that claimed almost 1,000 deaths.

The economic failures of *perestroika* in the Soviet Union, and the threat of food shortages brought on, in spite of a bumper harvest, by the sheer inefficiency of the system and the near-breakdown of law and Soviet order, saw Mr Gorbachev obliged to turn to the Red Army and even to the KGB simply to deliver the rations and make things work.

China remained apparently dormant under the unrelenting grip of its elderly rulers, who had suppressed dissent and the demand for democracy so ruthlessly in Tiananmen Square in Beijing the previous summer. The Indian subcontinent was racked with tension and violence. Benazir Bhutto's regime in Pakistan was overthrown by the army, and Sri Lanka was torn by civil war. Moslem unrest and Indian repression kept Kashmir on the point of explosion, and the whole periphery of India, from Punjab through Nepal and Assam to Burma, was on edge. In the Indian heartland, V P Singh's ill-advised attempt to improve opportunities for the lower castes added fierce caste rivalry to communal tensions between Hindus and Moslems and Hindus and Sikhs.

Worst of all, no sooner had the Cold War ended in Europe than a new and perilous confrontation threatened in the Middle East. As 1990 ended, American tanks, aircraft and troops were being transferred from bases in Germany, where even the most suspicious and most bellicose could see that they

were no longer needed to defend Western Europe from the Warsaw Pact, to face the formidable power of a new pariah state: Iraq.

Two of the greatest armies ever assembled, with a fire-power dwarfing that of the Second World War, were drawn up in the Arabian desert in the middle of the oilfields that contain almost half of the world's reserves of oil and gas. Any time after 15 January 1991, according to a resolution of the United Nations Security Council, the United States and its allies, which included Britain, France, Saudi Arabia, Egypt and Syria, would be justified in attacking Iraq unless the latter had withdrawn from Kuwait - something which the Iraqi president made it plain that he had no intention of doing unless compelled to.

History, it was plain, was not over, but was spinning into a new act, at least as dangerous as the long confrontation between Bolshevism and its enemies, a phase in which the resurgent civilization of Islam found itself divided in its loyalties as the United States and - with greater or lesser enthusiasm - its allies prepared to intervene militarily in the very heart of the Islamic world. Such a war, from the western point of view, might be wholly justified. Iraq's invasion of Kuwait might threaten the world's collective security in an unacceptable way. Yet few contemplated with equanimity a new cycle of history in which such momentous geo-political stakes as the control of vast oil reserves and the leadership of Islam were contended for by powers armed with chemical, biological and nuclear weapons.

The Iraqi invasion of Kuwait and the threat of conflagration in the Gulf exacerbated the already flagging state of the world economy. In the United States, the Bush administration proved no more successful than its predecessor in controlling public finance, with the result that the United States found itself more dependent than ever on finance from a Japan increasingly preoccupied with its own needs and a Germany committed to something like a Marshall Aid plan of its own for its newly-acquired eastern lands in particular and for Eastern Europe in general. As the economic →

US troops of the First Cavalry division snake across the desert sands.

heroes of the free market were toppled one by one, socialism remained as widely discredited as ever; but unregulated capitalism was no longer seen as quite the panacea which it had seemed to many in the mid-1980s.

Elsewhere the familiar demons of inflation, unemployment and sluggish growth returned to haunt many economies as they had done in the earlier 1980s, and the gap between the wealthier industrial countries and those dependent on selling raw materials, especially if they had no oil to trade, grew ever more dauntingly wide. In the Sudan, in the Horn of Africa, even in parts of the Soviet Union, the black horseman of famine rode again.

Yet it would be quite wrong to portray 1990 only in tones of gathering darkness. Only the most naive, after all, could seriously have expected the travail of Eastern and Central Europe, let alone the liberation of the captive nations of the Soviet Union, to be painless. What for a generation many had dreaded as the tightest knot of all, the re-unification of Germany, was accomplished with remarkable smoothness. If the removal of the deposits of fifty years of Nazi, then Soviet, rule revealed all the ancient rivalries, the ethnic and religious hatreds of centuries, still the East Europeans seemed determined to master their fate. Nor was Europe

the only continent where people displayed the courage to rise up and overthrow dictatorships.

In the first free elections for decades, the Nicaraguans overthrew the far left Sandinista regime. In Brazil, Fernando Collor de Mello attacked inflation with almost unprecedented zeal. And all over both Africa and Latin America the tide seemed, however fitfully, to be flowing away from dark authoritarian regimes in the direction of greater freedom and democracy.

Above all the crisis in the Gulf itself, for all its perilous potential, demonstrated the strength of the new yearning for peace and unity that had emerged from the ending of the Cold War. For the first time since 1950, the United Nations seemed willing to act promptly, effectively and in something nearing unison to resist aggression and defend the world order. For the first time ever the five permanent members of the Security Council, albeit with nuances of difference and even mental reservations, agreed to work together. As the year came towards an end*, the prospects for savage, large-scale warfare were greater than for many years, but so too were the chances of building a world order that might come closer to outlawing such conflicts.

*This article, and those on the pages which follow, does not cover events occurring after 13 December 1990.

The pain and the deaths continue in the strife-torn townships of South Africa.

Some were winners, others not so lucky

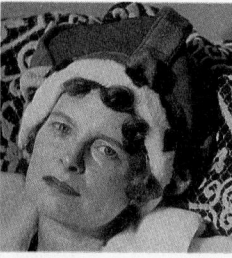

Champions all: Australian swimmer Lisa Curry-Kenny, Designer of the Year Vivienne Westwood, and still going strong at 50, Cliff Richard.

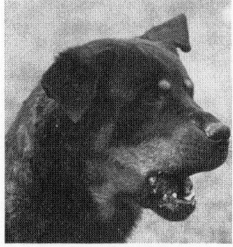

Love 'em or hate 'em: a Rottweiler shows his teeth, Sir Ralph Halpern leaves Burtons with a handsome payoff, but things look bad for Bond.

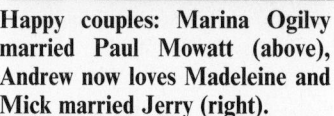

Happy couples: Marina Ogilvy married Paul Mowatt (above), Andrew now loves Madeleine and Mick married Jerry (right).

Nigel Benn, boxing champion.   **Desert Orchid: favourite racer.**

A year haunted by recession: five national views

Money worries hit "sunrise" economy

The most tedious thing about a recession (apart from going broke) is the way it lowers both national and personal perspectives. Money is uninteresting unless you've got loads of it, but Australia in 1990 has been fixated by it – by the inability to hold the right balance in the business of getting and spending.

If we are wage-earners, we have our heads down trying to keep our jobs; if we are farmers, we are staring into the middle distance and contemplating the great stockpiles of wheat and wool, the low prices and debt spirals that are driving us off the land; if we are miners, we are wondering at the global lack of interest in our iron ore, coal, bauxite, gold or any other mineral; if we are one of the high-tech "sunrise" industries, we are watching the sun go down on our best efforts to find overseas markets; if we are tourist operators, we are wondering why the government allowed the airline strike to strangle us in the midst a tourist boom from overseas.

The politicians are getting testy. The opposition leader, John Hewson, said that the treasurer, Paul Keating, should wind down the windows of his Commonwealth car to see what was happening in the real world. Mr Keating called Mr

L. to r.: Australia's Hawke, Canada's Mulroney and Ireland's Robinson.

Hewson "a shiver looking for a spine to run up". Some of the more lurid pigments on the big picture have been the spectacular falls of the high-flyers who rode the boom until 1987.

The erstwhile media mogul Christopher Skase, the property tycoon George Herscu, the mer-

AUSTRALIA

chant banker Laurie Connell and many others are having the fragments of their empires swept into tidy piles in various court rooms about the land. Mr Herscu has been given five years in jail for offering a bribe to Russ Hinze, a former Queensland minister; others are selling assets at bargain prices. Even the Fairfax Group, the jewel of the Australian media, has lapsed into receivership.

In a gloomy nation the gloomiest state was undoubtedly Victoria, where the government has turned financial bungling into an art form. The other news has occurred around the black headlines of the financial malaise: three former Queensland ministers jailed for corruption; the ex-premier Sir Johannes Bjelke-Petersen facing trial; Robert Holmes a Court dead aged 53; Carmen Lawrence in Western Australia the first woman state premier; Adelaide wins the multi-function polis (a Japanese-backed high-tech city); Collingwood overcomes 32 years of "collywobbles" to win the Australian Football League Flag; Canberra wins the NSW Rugby League Flag.

Whether Australia is crumbling or merely waiting for its next boom, television and radio current affairs packed up as summer began, leaving the airwaves free for the things that we *do* understand – test cricket and a seemingly endless supply of tennis and golf tournaments.

JOHN ROSS

The lady bows out, the Majors move in

The Thatcher era is over, and the manner of the lady's departure sent historians scurrying into the past. Here was a prime minister, unbeaten at the polls and unafflicted by failing health or willpower, summarily ousted by her party. Wartime premiers had been ousted, but Mrs Thatcher's forced resignation was unprecedented.

In the short term at least, the Tories galloped into a lead over a Labour Party which had lost its prime asset – the "not-the-Mrs-Thatcher" party. Worse was to come for Mr Kinnock as the Tories

BRITAIN

moved to ditch the poll tax which ministers had dutifully defended through riots and local election reverses. John Major, the fifth successive prime minister from a state school, lost little time in signalling a new spirit within the government and Europe, despite the lip-service paid to his "towering" predecessor.

Mrs Thatcher departed with dignity, but with her record more blemished than she would have wished. Inflation was higher than when she came to power, a balance of payments surplus had become a deficit, and a recession was pushing up unemployment totals. Internationally, Mrs Thatcher had given Britain a distinctive voice in world affairs – too distinctive, some would say; it was her terse reaction to a European summit in Rome which ignited the fuse which led to her downfall.

Mr Major takes a softer style into Europe, along with his hard ecu, but the dilemma about Britain's role remains as the movement for monetary and political union gathers momentum. It would be ironic if Margaret Thatcher is ultimately remembered not for curbing the unions or privatization but for taking Britain further into Europe than any previous leader.

DERRIK MERCER

Here's to you, Mrs Robinson, but Mr Haughey is not smiling

No one gave her a chance when she embarked on a non-party independent campaign for the presidency. A woman had never held the job. It had always been won by the largest party, *Fianna Fail*. And though she was backed by the tiny Labour Party, and the even smaller Workers' Party, she was the voice of the dispossessed, crying from the wilderness about the rights of women, travelling people, the unemployed, emigrant communities and the people of Northern Ireland.

Mary Robinson's victory altered the balance of power, and gave to the office of head of state a previously unacknowledged mandate for change. Her campaign em-

IRELAND

braced a major political crisis in which her principal rival, Brian Lenihan, was dismissed from the government. This in turn led to a revolt against the ten-year leader of his party, Charles Haughey, whose growing uncertainty abut direction became apparent in speeches at the end of the year in which he blamed preoccupations over the European Community presidency for what had gone wrong.

"The great survivor", Charles Haughey is now under permanent threat as Mary Robinson epito-

mizes a different style for tackling people's problems. And these are many: high unemployment, high emigration, serious city crime, agriculture in crisis and the shadow of Northern Ireland over tourism (the second biggest industry) make life in Ireland precarious.

Yet the stimulations are unbounded. When Ireland reached the quarter-finals of the World Cup in June, it was treated as victory. The propensity for triumph turns modest events into historic occasions, and the sense of the country winning, in 1990, was the paramount conviction at the end.

BRUCE ARNOLD

Nation trembles on questions of status

For Canada, 1990 was a year in which the meaning and validity of our national existence were called into question. The crucial issues were the status of the primarily francophone province of Quebec, and of Canada's native peoples.

In 1987, all the premiers concluded the Meech Lake Accord, a deal in which they agreed that Quebec is a "distinct society". Final ratification was set for 23 June 1990 and required unanimous approval. But the political climate had changed as the deadline approached, and debate raged on the meaning of Meech Lake.

Would Meech Lake, in recognizing Quebec's "distinctness", grant it greater powers than the other provinces? Would the Accord undermine the federal government? Would Meech Lake's failure, and Quebec's threatened secession, destroy the nation, or would Canada be better off without its discontented French province? Would the "distinct society" clause supercede the Canadian Charter of Rights and Freedoms, leaving women, native

CANADA

people and others vulnerable? Meech Lake died when Newfoundland failed to endorse the deal in time, but shockwaves also reverberated when Elijah Harper, an Indian member of Manitoba's Legislative Assembly, invoked a technicality to block the Accord. He jolted Canadians into asking themselves: if Quebec is distinct, what about the native peoples?

Shortly after the failure of the Meech Lake Accord, the Mohawks of the Quebec community of Oka and of the Kahnawake reserve near Montreal took up arms in a land dispute. The Mohawk crisis underscored the failure to define and guarantee Canada's native people's status, rights and obligations in the national state. And as the nation slipped into recession, there was a growing disillusionment with traditional parties.

ELIZABETH ABBOTT

George plays tough, Millie strikes it rich

Americans had a geography lesson in 1990. The vast majority of citizens now know that Kuwait is right next to Iraq, which is right next to Saudi Arabia. Also better known are all those men named Hussein. But 1990 also taught Americans that nothing is forever, especially not foes. Picture a meeting in the Saudi desert in October of the chairman of the US Joint Chiefs of Staff and the Soviet defence minister. They shook hands, then threw their arms around one another as their aides cheered.

George Bush was in the desert for a time, too – for Thanksgiving with his troops. Barbara Bush was there as well. But not Millie, the dog. She stayed home, probably to write a second book. Honestly. Her first book (written with Barbara's help) was on the bestseller lists for weeks. Other doings of the year:
* Billionaires and millionaires actually went to jail for such things as insider trading.
* A top music award went to a group called Milli Vanilli which later acknowledged it didn't sing

UNITED STATES

one word but did, without a doubt, perform its very own lip-synching.
* The United States government shut down for a day. No one could get into Yellowstone National Park or tour the White House.
* After elections in which the cry "Throw the Bums Out!" could be heard across the land, less than half of the electorate voted – and sent most of the bums back to power.

George Bush had a topsy-turvy year. Those who criticized him for being on the sidelines while the Germans united and Mikhail Gorbachev charmed the multitudes were the same ones who criticized him later for being too aggressive and vocal about the Middle East. Change is upsetting. What's next? No Castro to berate? A balanced budget? Saddam's withdrawal from Kuwait? What would happen if all this change resulted in stability?

CURTISS PIERSON

The rise and fall of Britain's Iron Lady

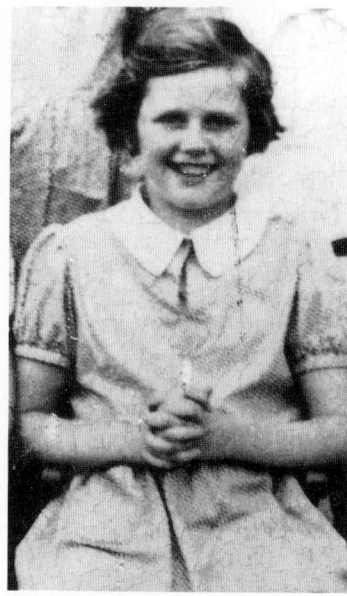
Schoolgirl: Margaret Roberts.

The new MP for Finchley, 1959.

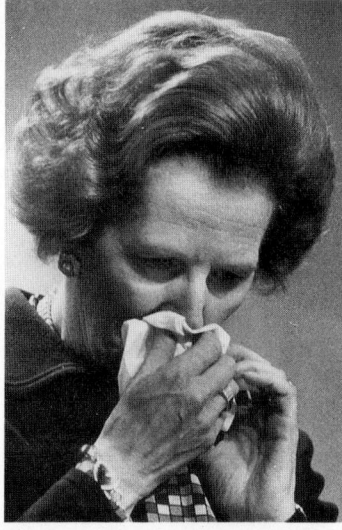
Survivor: after surviving an IRA bomb attack at Brighton in 1984.

Special relationship: with ally and friend President Reagan.

The final act: tears in her eyes as she leaves Downing Street forever.

The year in the arts: from Rushdie to Pavarotti

BIOGRAPHY replaced the novel as the most newsworthy genre in 1990. Few novels in English made headlines. The Booker prize list (it was won by A S Byatt's *Possession*) was called unusually dull. Even Salman Rushdie, from his hiding-place, produced an uncontroversial parable about a story-teller who loses the gift for telling stories. *Haroun and the Sea of Stories* proved that he himself had not.

Its Arabian Nights style caused many to call it the children's book of the year, dedicated to the son from whom he is separated. This made the violent attacks of the Pakistani film-makers of *International Guerrillas* – in which a character called "Rushdie" is struck by lightning and bursts into flames – look silly and irrelevant.

Meanwhile, scarcely a month went by without a biography being hotly discussed, whether it was the insights into the Churchills' un-expectedly stormy marriage in Richard Hough's *Winston and Clementine* or the chilling glimpse into the cold heart of A A Milne, the creator of Winnie-the-Pooh, in Ann Thwaite's much-admired bio-graphy.

The sexual obssession with mother-figures of the unmothered King Edward VIII provided the fas-cination of Philip Ziegler's biog-raphy of him, but it was Charles Dickens who provided enough material for a blockbusting biog-raphy on 19th-century scale by Peter Ackroyd – 1,000 pages which often read as much like a novel as a biography. Ackroyd, also a novelist, claims that biography is an extension of novel-writing, and threw in imaginary conversations with Dickens to demonstrate it. His fat volume was complemented by a far slimmer piece of detection on *The Invisible Woman* in Dickens's life, Ellen Ternan. Claire Tomalin reached a different conclusion from Ackroyd as to the presumed chas-tity of their relationship.

C S Lewis, the Christian apolo-gist and creator of Narnia, was the subject of a biography by A N Wil-son and of the play *Shadowlands* which reduced audiences to tears. The wayward novelists Paul Scott and Jean Rhys were admirably biographized by Hilary Spurling

It was a year when an opera singer soared to the top of pop music charts, when a world-renowned British theatre company closed its London stages for lack of money, and when Glasgow revelled in the title of Europe's City of Culture. PETER LEWIS looks back on the arts in 1990 and finds parallels in the cinema for the burgeoning growth of Europe's ability to challenge the hegemony of the United States. Politics also provided an undercurrent to much of the year's literature, whether as the inspiration for biographies or as source material for novelists. The arts in Australia and New Zealand are also reflected in this survey which otherwise concentrates on the year in Britain.

and Carole Angier, while Anthony Burgess weighed in with a typically irascible but revelatory confession (part two), *You've Had Your Time*. In a year that wiped from the liter-ary slate such names as Rosamund Lehmann, Lawrence Durrell, Pat-rick White, Roald Dahl and Alberto Moravia (and the historian A J P Taylor and the essayist Malcolm Muggeridge), it was reas-suring that literary lives are so often perpetuated memorably in books.

Politically the leaves fell thickly. From the USSR came the memoirs of Andrei Sakharov, and Boris Yeltsin's *Against the Grain*. From the US Ronald Reagan, in 726 pages of *An American Life*, did not once find cause to question whether all that he did or knew was not for the best. And politics even got into fiction.

Frederick Forsyth's new story of international skulduggery, *The Ne-gotiator*, featured Mrs Thatcher as a minor character, as other books

had done before. But without any overt reference to the contem-porary political situation, a former Conservative Party official, Michael Dobbs, showed the un-canniest timing of the year with his novel *House of Cards*. Its uninhibit-ed exploration of the sort of back-stage deals and manoeuvres that accompany the forced changeover from one prime minister to another was soon being dramatized on TV screens, both in fictional form and in reality.

IN CINEMA there were signs that the hegemony of Hollywood was waning. The *Palme d'Or* at Cannes, it is true, was won by an American film, the dark, surreal *Wild at Heart*, an American odyssey direct-ed by David Lynch, and there was violent competition from Martin Scorsese with *GoodFellas*. America produced the biggest money-spinners – *Pretty Woman* and *Ghost* – but it was Europe that

came up with the unpredictable films – *Trop Belle Pour Toi*, *Monsieur Hire* and *Cyrano de Bergerac* from France, *Cinema Paradiso* from Italy's Guiseppe Tornatore, and Bertolucci's *The Sheltering Sky* (British made).

In their third year the European Film Awards, called Felixes, began to look like serious rivals to the Oscars at a ceremony hosted by Glasgow in its role as Europe's City of Culture, 1990. Gianni Amelio's *Open Doors*, set in fascist Palermo, was European film of the year. Britain scored in the form of Kenneth Branagh whose perform-ance as Henry V in his own film beat the Cannes winner, Gerard Depardieu as Cyrano, as actor of the year; The Spanish actress Carmen Maura won best actress for the second time.

From the southern hemisphere there came the New Zealand direc-tor Jane Campion's *An Angel at my Table*, a three-hour tour of the quietly desperate life of the author Janet Frame. Kerry Fox is fascina-ting as she portrays Frame moving from adolescence to 40 and from shyness to apparent schizophrenia. The beauty of her words, her spirit and her homeland are stirring. In Australia, David Parker and Nadia Tass followed up their gentle com-edy *Malcolm* with *The Big Steal*, another funny in which get-the-girl equals lift-the-car.

Meanwhile the old screen god-desses faded into history in remark-able numbers with the deaths of Ava Gardner, Barbara Stanwyck, Paulette Goddard, Irene Dunne, Margaret Lockwood, Joan Bennett, Delphine Seyrig and Greta Garbo. Probably the greatest critical suc-cess of the year was *L'Atalante*, made in 1934, the last film of Jean Vigo, set on a barge on the Seine and now rediscovered and shown in its entirety for the first time.

IN THEATRE the year in Britain was one of deepening financial cri-sis, brought about by declining grants and sponsors made nervous by recession. The Arts Council's theatre clients had a total deficit of £17 million, £10 million of it at-tributed to the two London opera houses and the two "national" theatres. No rescue arrived to →

Richard Gere and Julia Roberts in the blockbusting "Pretty Woman".

Three tenors and a conductor: Domingo, Mehta, Carreras and Pavarotti.

A detail of Constable's "The Lock", which Sotheby's sold for £10,780,000.

prevent the Royal Shakespeare Company (RSC) from closing the doors of its Barbican theatres with a query over their reopening date and a debt of £4.4 million. Overall arts funding from the government rose by a welcome 13 per cent, but it was not immediately clear how it would be divided between the major national companies and the equally impoverished regional theatres.

The RSC had put its trust in musicals, with mixed success. It found a winner in Jerome Kern's *Show Boat*, which it revived with Opera North, but got a flea in its ear with *A Clockwork Orange*. The Royal National Theatre, as the National has become, failed to make a popular hit out of Stephen Sondheim's *Sunday in the Park with George*, with its stageful of pointillist painting by Seurat.

Of the commercial West End musicals, Sondheim's fairytale *Into the Woods* was the only new success. *King* and *Bernadette* were costly failures, while the usually reliable Michael Frayn had a flop with his comedy *Look, Look*. The most produced playwright of the year was Arthur Miller, whose 75th birthday was marked with productions of five of his plays, two of them at the National.

Richard Harris had a triumphant come-back as a stage actor after 27 years away in Pirandello's *Henry IV*. Theatrical dynasties competed *en famille* – the Cusacks followed by the Redgraves in Chekhov's *Three Sisters*, and the Oliviers (Joan Plowright and her daughters directed by her son Richard Olivier) in J B Priestley's *Time and the*

Conways. Peter Brook's flying visit with his multi-national production of *The Tempest* in French was yet another feather in Glasgow's cap during its year as Europe's City of Culture before passing on the cultural baton to Dublin for 1991.

In Australia, the actor John Bell has introduced his National Shakespeare Company, with a full season

"Yet another feather in Glasgow's cap"

planned for 1991. Highlights of the Adelaide Festival were the State Theatre's *Marat/Sade* and the Georgian Actors' Studio presentation of *Don Juan* – a sort of underwater Moliere with Mozartian overtures.

OPERA saw the Royal Opera House £3 million in deficit and also strapped for the money to finance new productions; it cancelled its seasonal opener, yet made a virtue out of not having done *William Tell* for 100 years – till now. The new opera that most took

the critics' fancy was a Scottish Opera commission – Judith Weir's *The Vanishing Bridegroom*, a folk-tale of the Highlands and Celtic twilight which proved that original music can still be written with traditional harmony.

Sir Michael Tippett's space-age, near-Rock latest opera, *New Year*, proved a crowd-puller at Glyndebourne. The perversity of setting *The Magic Flute* in Los Angeles, partly on skateboards and without any dialogue, earned the Glyndebourne equivalent of the bird for Peter Sellars, the director.

The retirement of Dame Joan Sutherland was the sad culmination of an excellent year for opera in Australia. She said she would not "do a Melba", but then agreed to sing with Pavarotti at Covent Garden on New Year's Eve. Dame Kiri te Kanawa braved the tempest at a country concert at Mitchelton winery, while the Australian Opera

went the whole hog with *Tristan and Isolde*. The Melbourne Arts Festival, growing in stature under the directorship of John Truscott, had *Faust* as its thrilling climax.

The operatic highlight of the year for an uncountable audience around the world, however, was the *Three Tenors' World Cup Concert* from Rome – Pavarotti, Carreras and Domingo outsinging each other on worldwide TV, much repeated and videoed.

BALLET moved to the Midlands when what used to be Sadler's Wells became the Birmingham Royal Ballet, with new £4m studios annexed to its theatre. The parent company received the addition of the Bolshoi star Irek Mukhamedov, who came to Britain, he said, attracted by its medical care. The Australian Ballet swept through the US to critical acclaim.

THE ART exhibition of the year in Britain was that of Monet's "series paintings" of the 1890s – haystacks, poplars, Rouen cathedral seen in varying lights and times of day – assembled for the first and only time at the Royal Academy and visited by over 500,000 people in its three-month stay.

Other major events were the complete rehanging of the Tate Gallery collection and the move of the small but brilliant Courtauld collection to Somerset House, once the home of the Royal Academy but now housing the Inland Revenue in neo-classical splendour.

Additional reporting by John Ross in Melbourne.

Left: much-performed playwright Arthur Miller. Centre and right: author Roald Dahl and broadcaster Malcolm Muggeridge, who both died this year.

The sporting year: a digest of the top events

AMERICAN FOOTBALL

National Football League Super Bowl

San Francisco 49ers	55
Denver Broncos	10

ASSOCIATION FOOTBALL

Barclay's League 1989-90
Division 1:
Champion: Liverpool
Runners-up: Aston Villa
Relegated: Sheffield Wednesday, Charlton Athletic, Millwall

Division 2:
Promoted: Leeds United (champions), Sheffield United, Sunderland*
Relegated: Bournemouth, Bradford City, Stoke City

Division 3:
Promoted: Bristol Rovers (champions), Bristol City, Notts County *
Relegated: Cardiff City, Northampton Town, Blackpool, Walsall

Division 4:
Promoted: Exeter City (champions), Grimsby Town, Southend United, Cambridge United *

GM Vauxhall Conference:
Champions (promoted to Division 4): Darlington

* promoted after play-offs; Sunderland, runners-up in the Division 2 play-offs, were subsequently promoted after Swindon Town had been relegated on disciplinary grounds.

FA Cup final:
Manchester United 3; Crystal Palace 3
Replay: Manchester United 1; Crystal Palace 0

Littlewoods Cup final:
Nottingham Forest 1; Oldham Athletic 0

B & Q Scottish League:
Premier Division:
Champions: Rangers
Runners-up: Aberdeen
Relegated: Dundee

Division 1:
Promoted: St Johnstone
Relegated: Albion Rovers, Alloa

Division 2:
Promoted: Brechin City, Kilmarnock

Scottish Cup final:
Aberdeen 0; Celtic 0
(after extra time, Aberdeen won 9-8 on penalties)

Skol Cup final (1990-91):
Rangers 2; Celtic 1

Welsh Cup final:
Hereford United 2; Wrexham 1

Irish Cup final:
Glentoran 3; Portadown 0

ATHLETICS

European Championships, Men

100 Metres
Linford Christie GB 10.0s

200 Metres
John Regis GB 20.11s

400 Metres
Roger Black GB 45.08s

800 Metres
Tom McKean GB 1m 44.76s

1500 Metres
Jens-Peter Herold GDR 3m 38.25s

5000 Metres
Salvatore Antibo ITA 13m 22.00s

10,000 Metres
Salvatore Antibo ITA 27m 41.27s

Marathon
Gelindo Bordin ITA 2h 14m 02s

110 Metres Hurdles
Colin Jackson GB 13.18s

400 Metres Hurdles
Kriss Akabusi GB 47.92s

3000 Metres Steeplechase
Francesco Panetta ITA 8m 12.66s

20km Walk
Pavol Blazek CZE 1h 22m 05s

50km Walk
Andrey Perlov USSR 3h 54m 36s

4 x 100 Metres Relay FRA 37.79s

4 x 400 Metres Relay GB 2m 58.22s

High Jump
Dragutin Topic YUG 2.34m

Long Jump
Dietmar Haaf FRG 8.25m

Triple Jump
Leonid Voloshin USSR 17.74m

Pole Vault
Rodion Gataulin USSR 5.85m

Shot
Ulf Timmermann GDR 21.32m

Discus
Jürgen Schult GDR 64.58m

Javelin
Steve Backley GB 87.30m

Hammer
Igor Astapkovitch USSR 84.14m

Decathlon
Christian Plaziat FRA 8.574pts

European Championships, Women

100 Metres
Katrin Krabbe GDR 10.89s

200 Metres
Katrin Krabbe GDR 21.95s

400 Metres
Grit Breuer GDR 49.50s

800 Metres
Sigrun Wodars GDR 1m 55.87s

1500 Metres
Snezana Pajkic YUG 4m 08.13s

3000 Metres
Yvonne Murray GB 8m 43.06s

10,000 Metres
Elena Romanova USSR 31m 46.83s

Marathon
Rosa Mota POR 2h 31m 27s

100 Metres Hurdles
Monique Ewanje-Epée FRA 12.79s

400 Metres Hurdles
Tatyana Ledovskaya USSR 53.62s

10km Walk
Anna-Rita Sidotti ITA 44m 00s

4 x 100 Metres Relay FRG 41.68s

4 x 400 Metres Relay FRG 3m 21.02s

High Jump
Heike Heinkel GDR 1.99m

Long Jump
Heike Drechsler GDR 7.30m

Shot
Astrid Kumbermuss GDR 20.38m

Discus
Ilke Wyludda GDR 68.46m

Javelin
Paivoi Alafrantti FIN 67.68m

Heptathlon
Sabine Braun FRG 6.688pts

European Championships, Medal Table

Country	Gold	Silver	Bronze
East Germany	12	12	10
Britain	9	5	4
Soviet Union	6	9	7
Italy	5	2	5
France	3	2	5
West Germany	3	2	2
Yugoslavia	2	1	1
Portugal	1	0	1
Czechoslovakia	1	0	0
Finland	1	0	0
Spain	0	2	0
Hungary	0	2	0
Sweden	0	1	3
Switzerland	0	1	1
Bulgaria	0	1	1
Romania	0	1	0
Norway	0	1	0
Holland	0	1	0
Poland	0	0	2
Austria	0	0	1

World Records set in 1990

4 x 100 Metres Relay 37.79 sec
France, Split, Yugoslavia Sept 1

Shot 23.12m
Randy Barnes (US) – Los Angeles May 20

Javelin
89.10m Patrick Bodin (SWE) – Austin, Texas Mar 24
89.58m Steve Backley (GB) – Stockholm July 2
89.66m Jan Zelezny (Czech) – Oslo July 14
90.98m Steve Backley (GB) –London July 20

World Best:
Half-marathon (13 miles 193 yards): 1:00:34
Steve Moneghetti (Australia). The Great North Run (Newcastle-South Shields), Sept 16

BADMINTON

World Team Championships
Men (Thomas Cup). Final: China 4, Malaysia 1
Women (Uber Cup). Final: China 3, S Korea 2

All-England Championships
Men's singles: Zhao Jianhua (China)
Women's singles: Susi Susanti (Indonesia)
Men's doubles:
Kim Moon-Soo/Park Joo-Bong (S Korea)
Women's doubles:
Chung Myung-Hee/Hwang Hye-Young (S Korea)
Mixed doubles:
Park Joo-Bong/Chung Myung-Hee (S Korea)

BASEBALL

World Series
Cincinnati Reds 4; Oakland A's 0

BASKETBALL

Men's World Championship (final)
Yugoslavia 92; USSR 75

Women's World Championship (final)
USA 88; Yugoslavia 78

National Basketball Association (USA)
Championship play-off:

Detroit Pistons	4
Portland Trail Blazers	1

English Basketball Association
Premier League. Champions: Kingston

BOWLS

World Indoor Championships
Singles John Price (Wales)
Pairs final David Bryant/Tony Allcock (England)

EBA National Championships
Finals:
Singles Tony Allcock (Cheltenham)
Pairs John Otway/Roger Guy (Wymondham)

Middleton Cup
Yorkshire 136; Dorset 113

Crown Green
Waterloo Handicap Final John Hancock (Hyde)

BOXING

New World Champions, 1990

Heavyweight
Undisputed: James 'Buster' Douglas (US) Feb 10
Evander Holyfield (US), Oct. 25

Cruiserweight
IBF: Jeff Lampkin (US)
WBC: Massprgilio Duran (ITA)
WBO: Magne Havnaa (NOR)

Light-heavyweight
WBC: Dennis Andries (GB)

Super-middleweight
IBF: Lindell Holmes (US)
WBA: Christophe Tiozzo (FRA)

Middleweight
WBO: Nigel Benn (GB), April 29
Chris Eubank (GB), Nov 11

Junior middleweight
WBC: Terry Norris (US)

Welterweight
WBA: Aaron Davies (US)
WBC: Maurice Blocker (US)

Junior welterweight
WBA: Loreto Garza (US)

Lightweight
WBA: Juan Nazario (P Rico), April 6
WBC/WBA/IBF: Pernell Whitaker (US), Aug. 11

Super-featherweight
IBF: Tony Lopez (US)

Featherweight
WBC: Marcos Villasana (Mex)

Super-bantamweight
IBF: Welcome Ncita (S Africa)
WBC: Paul Banke (US)
WBO: Orlando Fernandez (P Rico)
WBA: Luis Mendoza (Col)

Super-flyweight
WBC: Moon Sung-kil (S Korea)
IBF: Roberto Quiroga (US)
WBO: Jose Ruiz (P Rico)

Flyweight
WBA: Lee Yul-woo (S Korea), March 10
Leopard Tamakuma (JPN), July 28
WBO: Isidoro Perez (MEX)

Light flyweight
IBF: Michael Garbajal (US)

Straw-weight
IBF: Falan Lookmingkwan (Thai)
WBC: Hideyuki Ohashi (JPN), Feb. 7
Ricardo Lopez (MEX) Oct. 25

Commonwealth Games, Medal Table

Country	Gold	Silver	Bronze
Australia	52	54	56
England	47	40	42
Canada	35	41	36
New Zealand	17	14	27
India	13	8	11
Wales	10	3	12
Nigeria	5	13	7
Scotland	5	7	10
Kenya	6	9	3
Northern Ireland	1	3	5
Hong Kong	1	1	3
Malaysia	2	2	0
Jamaica	2	0	2
Uganda	2	0	2
Nauru	1	2	0
Zimbabwe	0	2	1
Tanzania	0	1	2
Zambia	0	0	3
Cyprus	1	1	0
Bangladesh	1	0	1
Jersey	1	0	1
Ghana	0	2	0
Bahamas	0	0	2
West Samoa	0	0	2
Bermuda	1	0	0
Guernsey	1	0	0
Papua New Guinea	1	0	0
Guyana	0	0	1
Malta	0	0	1

Athletics, Men

100 Metres
Linford Christie ENG 9.93s

200 Metres
Marcus Adam ENG 20.10s

400 Metres
Darren Clark AUS 44.60s

800 Metres
Sammy Tirop KEN 1m 45.98s

1500 Metres
Peter Elliott ENG 3m 33.39s

5000 Metres
Andrew Lloyd AUS 13m 24.86s

10,000 Metres
Eamonn Martin ENG 28m 08.57s

110 Metres Hurdles
Colin Jackson WAL 13.08s

400 Metres Hurdles
Kriss Akabusi ENG 48.89s

3000 Metres Steeplechase
Julius Kariuki KEN 8m 20.64s

Marathon
Douglas Wakiihuri KEN 2h 10m 27s

30km Walk
Guillaume Leblanc CAN 2h 8m 28s

4 x 100 Metres Relay ENG 38.67s

4 x 400 Metres Relay KEN 3m 02.48s

High Jump
Nick Sanders BER 2.36m

Long Jump
Yusuf Alli NIG 8.39m

Triple Jump
Marios Hadjiandreou CYP 16.95m

Pole Vault
Simon Arkell AUS 5.35m

Javelin
Steve Backley ENG 86.02m

Shot
Simon Williams ENG 18.54m

Hammer
Sean Carlin AUS 75.66m

Discus
Adewale Olukoju NIG 62.62m

Decathlon
Mike Smith CAN 8.525pts

Athletics, Women

100 Metres
Merlene Ottey JAM 11.02s

200 Metres
Merlene Ottey JAM 22.76s

400 Metres
Fatima Jusuf JAM 51.08s

800 Metres
Diane Edwards ENG 2m 00.25s

1500 Metres
Angela Chalmers CAN 4m 08.41s

3000 Metres
Angela Chalmers CAN 8m 38.38s

10,000 Metres
Liz McColgan SCO 32m 23.56s

100 Metres Hurdles
Kay Morley WAL 12.91s

400 Metres Hurdles
Sally Gunnell ENG 55.38s

Marathon
Lisa Martin AUS 2h 25m 28s

10km Walk
Kerry Saxby AUS 45m 03s

4 x 100 Metres Relay AUS 43.87s

4 x 400 Metres Relay ENG 3m 28.08s

High Jump
Tania Murray NZ 1.88m

Long Jump
Jane Flemming AUS 6.78m

Javelin
Tessa Sanderson ENG 65.72m

Shot
Myrtle Augee ENG 18.48m

Discus
Lisa Vizaniari AUS 56.38m

Heptathlon
Jane Flemming AUS 6.695pts

Swimming, Men

50m freestyle	Andrew Baildon	AUS
100m freestyle	Andrew Baildon	AUS
200m freestyle	Martin Roberts	AUS
400m freestyle	Ian Brown	AUS
1500m freestyle	Glen Housman	AUS
100m butterfly	Andrew Baildon	AUS
200m butterfly	Anthony Mosse	NZ
100m breaststroke	Adrian Moorhouse	ENG
200m breaststroke	John Cleveland	CAN
100m backstroke	Mark Tewksbury	CAN
200m backstroke	Gary Anderson	CAN
200m individual medley	Garry Anderson	CAN
400m individual medley	Rob Bruce	AUS
4 x 100m freestyle relay		AUS
4 x 200m freestyle relay		AUS
4 x 100m medley relay		CAN
1m springboard diving	Russel Butler	AUS
3m springboard diving	Craig Rogerson	AUS
Platform diving	Bobby Morgan	WAL

Swimming, Women

50m freestyle	Lisa Curry-Kenny	AUS
100m freestyle	Karen van Wirdum	AUS
200m freestyle	Hayley Lewis	AUS
400m freestyle	Hayley Lewis	AUS
800m freestyle	Julie McDonald	AUS
100m butterfly	Lisa Curry-Kenny	AUS
200m butterfly	Hayley Lewis	AUS
100m breaststroke	Keltie Duggan	CAN
200m breaststroke	Nathalia Giguere	CAN
100m backstroke	Nicole Livingstone	CAN
200m backstroke	Anna Simcic	NZ
200m ind. medley	Nancy Sweetnam	CAN
400m ind. medley	Hayley Lewis	AUS
4 x 100m freestyle relay		AUS
4 x 200m freestyle relay		AUS
4 x 100m medley relay		AUS
1m springboard diving	Mary de Piero	CAN
3m springboard diving	Jenny Donnet	AUS
Platform diving	Anna Dacyshyn	CAN
Synchron. solo	Sylvie Frechette	CAN
Synchron. duet	C. Larsen/K. Glen	CAN

CRICKET

West Indies v England – Feb-April
First Test: England won by 9 wickets
Second Test: abandoned without a ball being bowled
Third Test: Match drawn
Fourth Test: West Indies won by 164 runs
Fifth Test: West Indies won by an innings and 32 runs
West Indies won the series 2-1

England v New Zealand – June-July
First Test: Match drawn
Second Test: Match drawn
Third Test: England won by 114 runs
England won the series 1-0

England v India – July-August
First Test: England won by 247 runs
Second Test: Match drawn
Third Test: Match drawn
England won the series 1-0

Australia v Pakistan – Jan-Feb.
First Test: Australia won by 92 runs
Second Test: Match drawn
Third Test: Match drawn
Australia won the series 1-0

New Zealand v Australia – March 15-19
Test Match: New Zealand won by 9 wickets

Britannic Assurance County Championship
Final Table

	P	W	L	D	Bt	Bl	Pts
Middx (3)	22	10	1	11	73	55	288
Essex (2)	22	8	2	12	73	56	257
Hants (7)	22	8	4	10	67	48	243
Worcs (1)	22	7	1	14	70	58	240
Warks (8)	22	7	7	8	55	64	231
Lancs (4)	22	6	3	13	65	56	217
Leics (13)	22	6	7	9	62	53	211
Glam (17)	22	5	6	11	64	48	192
Surray (12)	22	4	3	15	54	64	190
Yorks (16)	22	5	9	8	52	55	187
Nortnts (5)	22	4	9	9	61	60	185
Derbys (6)	22	6	7	9	58	52	181
Gloucs (9)	22	4	7	11	51	58	173
Notts (11)	22	4	8	10	51	58	173
Som (14)	22	3	4	15	73	45	166
Kent (15)	22	3	6	13	69	35	152
Sussex (10)	22	3	9	10	51	44	143

1989 positions in parentheses

Benson and Hedges Cup final
Lancashire 241-8; Worcestershire 172

NatWest Bank Trophy final
Northamtonshire 171; Lancashire 173-3

Refuge Assurance Sunday League
Champions: Derbyshire (50 pts)

Refuge Assurance Cup final
Derbyshire 197-7; Middlesex 201-5

Sheffield Sheild – final table

	Played	Won	Lost	Drawn	Points
New South Wales	10	3	3	4	26
Queensland	10	2	2	6	26
South Australia	10	3	3	4	20
Tasmania	10	2	3	5	16
Western Australia	10	2	2	6	14
Victoria	10	1	0	9	14

Sheffield Sheild final:
New South Wales 360 and 396-9 dec (Taylor 100); Queensland 103 and 308. New South Wales won by 345 runs

CYCLING

Tour de France
1. Greg LeMond US
2. Claudio Chiapucci ITA
3. Eric Breukink NETH

World Road Race Championship
1. Rudi Dhaenans BEL
2. Dirk de Wolf BEL
3. Gianni Bugno ITA

Milk Race – Britain
1. Shane Sutton AUS
2. Rob Holden GB
3. Miloslav Vasicek CZE

Kellogg's Professional Tour of Britain
1. Michel Dernies BEL
2. Robert Millar GB
3. Maurizio Fondriest ITA

Nissan Tour of Ireland
1. Eric Breukink BEL
2. Jan Museeuw BEL
3. Sean Yates GB

DARTS

World Professional Championship
Phil Taylor (England)

EQUESTRIANISM

World Equestrian Games
Show Jumping
Individual: Eric Navet (France) on Malesan Quito de Baussy. Team: France

Three-Day Event
Individual: Blyth Tait (New Zealand) on Messiah
Team: New Zealand

Dressage
Individual: Nicole Uphoff (W Germany) on Rembrandt. Team: W Germany

Carriage Driving
Individual: Ard Aarts (Netherlands)
Team: Netherlands

Endurance
Individual: Becky Hart (US) on Grand Sultan
Team: Great Britain

Vaulting
Men: Micheal Lehner (W Germany)
Women: Silke Berhard (W Germany)
Team: Switzerland

How West Germany won the World Cup in Rome

THE FIRST ROUND

Each team played three matches; the top two in each of the six leagues went through, plus the best four losers.

Group A	Pts
Italy	6
Czechoslavquia	4
Austria	2
United States	0

Group B	
Cameroon	4
Romania	3
Argentina	3
USSR	2

Group C	
Brazil	6
Costa Rica	4
Scotland	2
Sweden	0

Group D	
West Germany	5
Yugoslavia	4
Columbia	3
U. Arab Emirates	0

Group E	
Spain	5
Belgium	4
Uruguay	3
South Korea	0

Group F	
England	4
Ireland	3
Holland	3
Egypt	2

SECOND ROUND

IRELAND*	0
ROMANIA	0
(* 5–4 on penalties)	
ITALY	2
URUGUAY	0
SPAIN	1
YUGOSLAVIA	2
ARGENTINA	1
BRAZIL	0
COSTA RICA	1
CZECHOSLOVAKIA	4
HOLLAND	1
WEST GERMANY	2
BELGIUM	0
ENGLAND	1
CAMEROON	2
COLUMBIA	1

* winner on penalties

QUARTER FINALS

IRELAND	0
ITALY	1
YUGOSLAVIA	0
ARGENTINA*	0
(* 3–2 on penalties)	
CZECHOSLOVAKIA	0
WEST GERMANY	1
ENGLAND	3
CAMEROON	2

SEMIFINALS

ITALY	1
ARGENTINA*	1
(* 4–3 on penalties)	
WEST GERMANY*	1
ENGLAND	1
(* 4–3 on penalties)	

FINAL

ARGENTINA	0
WEST GERMANY	1

(Scorer: Brehme, 85, penalty)

TOP SCORERS

SCHILLACI	(ITALY)	6
SKUHRAVY	(CZECHOSLOVAKIA)	5
LINEKER	(ENGLAND)	4
MATTHAUS	(WEST GERMANY)	4
MICHEL	(SPAIN)	4
MILLA	(CAMEROON)	4

THIRD PLACE MATCH

ITALY	2
ENGLAND	1

Show Jumping

World Cup Final
John Whitaker (GB) on Henderson Milton

GAELIC GAMES

Gaelic Football (All-Ireland Final):
Cork (0-11) 11, Meath (0-9) 9

Hurling (All-Ireland Final):
Cork (5-15) 30, Galway (2-21) 27

GOLF

The major championships

US Masters
Nick Faldo   GB   278 °

US Open
Hale Irwin   US   280 °

* after playoff

The Open Championship
Nick Faldo   GB   270

USPGA Championship
Wayne Grady   AUS   282

European Order of Merit
1. Ian Woosnam (Wales)   £ 574,166
2. Mark McNulty (Zimbabwe)   £ 507,540
3. Jose-Maria Olazabal (Spain) £ 434,765

Suntory World Matchplay Championship
Ian Woosnam (Wales)

Dunhill Cup   IRE

Women

Solheim Cup   USA

Curtis Cup   USA

GYMNASTICS

European Championships
Men. Overall: Valentin Mogilny (USSR)
Women. Overall: Svetlana Boginskaya (USSR)

HOCKEY

World Cup
Men's Final: Holland 3, Pakistan 1
Women's Final Holland 3, Australia 1

European Cupwinners' Cup final
Hounslow 3, Amsterdam 2

Nationwide Anglia HA Cup final
Havant 3, Stourport O

Poundstretcher National League
Division One, Champions: Hounslow

HORSE RACING

The Flat

The Classics
General Accident 1000 Guineas
Salsabil (Willie Carson, 6-4f)

General Accident 2000 Guineas
Tirol (Micheal Kinanc, 9-1)

The Ever Ready Derby
Quest for Fame (Pat Eddery 7-1)

The Gold Seal Oaks
Salsabil (Willie Carson, 2-1f)

St Leger
Snurge (Richard Quinn, 7-2)

Prix de l'Arc de Triomphe
Saumarez (Gerald Mosse)

US Triple Crown
Kentucky Derby: Unbridled (Craig Perct)
Preakness Stakes: Summer Squall (Pat Day)
Belmont Stakes: Go and Go (Michel Kinanc)

Leading Jockeys (GB):
1. Pat Eddery (209 winners)
2. Willie Carson (187)
3. Steve Cauthen (142)

Leading Trainer: Henry Cecil (£ 1,927,735)

National Hunt

Waterford Crystal Champion Hurdle:
Kribensis (Richard Dunwoody, 95-40)
Tote Cheltenham Gold Cup:
Norton's Coin (Graham McCourt, 100-1)
Seagram Grand National:
Mr Frisk (Marcus Armytage, 16-1)

Leading Jockeys
1. Peter Scudamore (170 wins)
2. Richard Dunwoody (102)
3. Graham McCourt (100)

Leading Trainer: Martin Pipe (£ 792,544)

ICE HOCKEY

World Championship: Final pool stadings
1. USSR
2. Sweden
3. Czechoslovakia

National Hockey League
Wales Conference final:
Boston Bruins 4, Montreal Canadiens 1
Campbell Conference final:
Edmonton Oilers 4, Chicago Blackhawks 2
Stanley Cup (best of seven series):
Edmonton Oilers beat Boston Bruins 4-1

Heineken British Championship
Final: Cardiff Devils 6, Murrayfield Racers 6
(Cardiff won 6-5 on penalty shots)

LACROSSE

World Championship
Final: USA 19, Canada 15

MOTOR CYCLING

World Riders' Championship (500cc):
Wayne Rainey (US, Yamaha)

MOTOR RACING

World Drivers' Championship
Ayrton Senna (Brazil, McLaren)

Constructers' Championship
McLaren (121 pts)

ROWING

World Championships, Men
Single sculls	Yuri Janson (USSR)
Double sculls	Austria
Coxless pairs	East Germany
Coxed pairs	West Germany
Coxless fours	Australia
Coxed fours	East Germany
Quadruple sculls	USSR
Eights	West Germany

World Championships, Women
Single sculls	Birgit Peter (GDR)
Double sculls	East Germany
Coxless pairs	West Germany
Coxless fours	Romania
Quadruple sculls	East Germany
Eights	Romania

136th University Boat Race
Oxford beat Cambridge by 2 1/4 lengths

RUGBY LEAGUE

Regal Trophy final
Wigan 24, Halifax 12

Silk Cut Challenge Cup final
Wigan 36, Warrington 14

Great Britain in New Zealand
First Test: NZ 10, GB 11
Second Test: NZ 14, GB 16
Third Test: NZ 21, GB 18

Australia in Great Britain
First Test: GB 19, AUS 12
Second Test: GB 10, AUS 14
Third Test: GB 0, AUS 14

Stones Bitter Championship:
Division One final table

	P	W	D	L	F	A	A
Wigon	26	20	0	6	699	349	40
Leeds	26	18	0	8	704	383	36
Widnes	26	16	2	8	651	423	34
Bradford	26	17	0	9	614	413	34
St Helens	26	17	0	9	714	536	34
Hull	26	16	1	9	577	400	33
Castleford	26	13	1	12	424	451	27
Warrington	26	13	1	12	424	451	27
Wakefield	26	12	1	13	502	528	25
Featherstne	26	10	0	16	479	652	20
Sheffield	26	9	1	16	517	588	19
Leigh	26	9	1	16	442	642	19
Salford	26	4	1	21	421	699	9
Barrow	26	1	0	25	198	1133	2

RUGBY UNION

Five Nations' Championship
Jan 20	WAL 19, FRA 29	ENG 23, IRE 0
Feb 3	FRA 7, ENG 26	IRE 10, SCO 13
Feb 17	ENG 34, WAL 6	SCO 21, FRA 0
March 3	WAL 9, SCO 13	FRA 31, IRE 12
March 17	IRE 14, WAL 8	SCO 13, ENG 7

Final Table:
1. Scotland
2. England
3. France
4. Ireland
5. Wales

England in Argentina
First Test: ARG 12, ENG 25
Second Test: ARG 15, ENG 13

Australia in New Zealand
First Test: NZ 21, AUS 6
Second Test: NZ 27, AUS 17
Third Test: NZ 9, AUS 21

Argentina in the British Isles
IRE 20, ARG 18   ENG 51, ARG 0
SCO 49, ARG 3

New Zealand in France
First Test: France 3, NZ 24
Second Test: France 12, NZ 30

Pilkington Cup final
Bath 48, Gloucester 6

Schweppes Welsh Cup final
Neath 16, Bridgnd 10

Courage Cup Championship
Champions: Wasps

SKATING

World Figure and Dance Championships
Men: Kurt Browning (CAN)
Women: Jill Trenary (US)
Pairs: Yekaterina Gordeyeva and Sergey Grinkov (USSR)
Ice Dance: Marina Klimova and Sergey Ponomarenko (USSR)

SKIING

World Cup (Alpine)
Men's overall:
Pirmin Zurbriggen (SWI)
Women's overall:
Petra Kronberger (Austria)

SNOOKER

Embassy World Professional Championship
Stephen Hendry (SCO)

SQUASH

British Open championships
Men's champion: Jahangir Khan (PAK)
Women's champion: Susan Devoy (NZ)

TENNIS

All England Championships, Wimbledon
Men's singles:
Stefan Edberg (SWE)
Women's singles:
Martina Navratilova (US)
Men's doubles:
Rick Leach and Jim Pugh (US)
Women's doubles:
Jana Novotna and Helena Sukova (CZE)
Mixed doubles:
Rick Leach and Zina Garrison (US)

Australian Open
Men's singles: Ivan Lendl (CZE)
Women's singles: Steffi Graf (FRG)

French Open
Men's singles:
Andres Gomez (ECU)
Women's singles:
Monica Seles (YUG)

United States Open
Men's final:
Pete Sampras (US)
Women's final:
Gabriela Sabatini (ARG)

Davis Cup final
United States 3, Australia 2

General Index

117

119